BAR EXAM SUCCESS

A Comprehensive Guide

Third Edition

Sara J. Berman

Professor of Lawyering Skills and Director of the Academic Success Program
University of Southern California Gould School of Law

WEST ACADEMIC

860 Blue Gentian Road, Suite 350
Eagan, MN 55121
1-877-888-1330

Published in the United States of America

ISBN: 979-8-89545-607-1

PRAISE FOR BAR EXAM SUCCESS

"Professor Berman has written an illuminating and helpful book, drawing on cutting edge social science, that teaches students how to master the bar exam and flourish in law school. Her insights are shaped by years of experience and advances in psychological and learning sciences. If law students read this excellent book, perhaps as early as when arriving to law school, they will develop skills they can exercise and master to achieve success."

—**Victor D. Quintanilla**, Indiana University Bicentennial Professor; Professor, Indiana University Maurer School of Law; Adjunct Professor, Indiana University Department of Psychological and Brain Sciences

"From helpful study tips to suggestions for minimizing distractions, this book is an excellent resource to guide students through the challenges of bar study. Professor Berman is a seasoned professional, who condenses years of experience into easy to read and follow advice, perfect for anyone serious about passing the bar exam."

—**Paula Manning**, Professor of Law and Director of the S.T.E.L.L.A.R. Academic Support Program, Western State College of Law

"Wanting to shape your destiny, this book is a must-read coaching manual with action plans to boot. Professor Berman takes the mystery out of bar prep, providing hosts of inspirational tips, courageous learning strategies, and concrete wisdom for overcoming the oft-expressed intimidation that so easily immobilizes many from achieving bar exam success—success that is well within the grasp of all law school graduates aspiring to serve as professional attorneys—none be barred. This book is not meant to be read but lived. Navigate your path through this book and you will be well on your way to passing your bar exam."

—**Scott Johns**, Professor of the Practice of Law and Director of the DU Bar Success Program, Denver University Sturm College of Law

"This is a must-read book for law students and law professors. It provides practical suggestions so that students can be successful in law school, law practice, and the bar exam. It is fun to read and can be used by students on their own or in a class. The self-assessment tools are particularly valuable. As a law professor, I look forward to using this valuable resource with my students."

—**Jane Bloom Grise**, Director of Academic Enhancement and Assistant Professor of Legal Writing, University of Kentucky College of Law

"This book is a fantastic resource. It offers an approach, starting in 1L, that can help varied types of students develop critical skills needed for success on the bar exam with a mix of skill-building and metacognitive strategies that also help students succeed in law school. I am excited to incorporate these strategies in my 1L and 2L classes."

—**Nicole R. Lefton**, Assistant Professor of Academic Support and Bar Preparation, Director of Academic Support and Bar Preparation, Maurice A. Deane School of Law at Hofstra University

"I love the book and use it as a personal reference to coach my students, especially those who are first generation. It captures high expectations for success and normalizes the sense of inadequacy that they all feel and fear. It helps them to acknowledge it and push past it in both substance and tone. The underlying expectation is that the reader will pass the bar exam. When they read it, it keeps them tethered to their goals and their practical strategies amidst the panic, because it builds in intentional recursiveness."

—**Kimberly Williams D'Haene**, Director of Law Academic Success, Georgia State University College of Law

"If I could give only one resource to someone who wants to increase the likelihood of passing the bar exam, it would be this book. Author Sara Berman tells the truth about the challenge of bar preparation while showing the taker how—through preparation, planning, and practice—success is achievable. Rather than scaring them, the book encourages bar takers. That, itself, is why I will refer all my students to it."

—**Benjamin V. Madison III**, Professor and Director of the Bar Passage Initiatives, Regent University School of Law

"This book is like having a personal trainer help you prepare for the bar exam. It is a doubt-busting, confidence-boosting, interactive tour guide on the road to success. Sara Berman gives practical advice on motivation, time management, financial planning, and more. This book both explains and motivates—students will be wise to take Berman's advice, encouragement, and support."

—**Catherine (Cassie) Christopher**, Professor of Law, Associate Dean for Bar Success, Texas Tech University School of Law "Along with the excellent strategies on studying and test taking, Professor Berman illuminates the unspoken barrier to success, namely the student's mindset. This guide aptly describes the various barriers encountered by students and suggests interventions to maintain a positive and healthy outlook for success."

—**Rodney Fong**, Associate Dean for Academic Achievement, Institutional Assessment & Bar Preparation, and Clinical Professor of Law, The University of Illinois at Chicago John Marshall Law School

This book is dedicated to Grandma, who taught me to read, write, and love words; to Mom, who showed me the value of hard work and who loves me unconditionally; and to my children, who make everything worthwhile.

ACKNOWLEDGMENTS

Many people have helped shape my theories about academic and bar exam success, first and foremost my students. Thanks to all of you. It truly is all about you.

Next, I am filled with gratitude for my colleagues and dear friends who are among the finest law professors in the world. How lucky I have been to do great work that I love with people I admire.

Finally, my deepest appreciation to everyone at West who made this book possible, including Pamela Siege Chandler, Louis Higgins, John Moen, Megan Putler, Megan Hoffman, Megan Grove, Laura Holle, Rebecca Schneider, and Michele Bassett and to my original publishers at the ABA, Bryan Kay and Donna Gollmer.

INTRODUCTION

LAW STUDENTS AND LAW GRADUATES STUDYING FOR THE BAR EXAM: THIS BOOK IS FOR YOU

If you are in law school or studying for the bar, this book is *written for you and to you.* Please think of me (the author) as your personal trainer at the academic and bar success gym.

I will guide and share strategies and planning tools. Like any good trainer, I will push you hard to do your very best and get stronger with every workout. And we will work together on skills, knowledge, strategy, and mindset. (A huge part of bar success is a mental game, and this book gives you tools to win.)

What we discuss here covers professional and life skills that help with bar prep and beyond. What you do *and how you think* about today's challenges can pave the way for success dividends for decades to come. I hope this book inspires and propels you toward a lifelong **cycle of success**!

Before we even begin, I will give away the three keys to bar success: mindset, logistics, and preparation. A lot of this book is dedicated to the first two. I would recommend reading in order if you are preparing for your first bar exam but if you wish to zip ahead to preparation and learn what is on the tested exam and how to train for it, you can read Chapter 8 first and then return to the beginning.

This book is for law students **and**:

- **Families, friends, spouses, and partners of law students:** Law students and bar takers may seem so stressed out that you hardly recognize them. You may be offended at their "disappearing" into their studies. "How hard can it be?" you wonder. "Isn't the bar exam just another test?"

  The bar is *not* just another test. This book will help you understand why it is so different and difficult; the book will help you learn how to lend a hand or back off, as needed. As a key player in the life of someone taking the bar exam, your support is critical. So, thank you for helping the law student in your life to succeed.

- **Law students:** please share this book with people whose support you want, people you want to understand what you are going through.
- **Practicing lawyers taking the bar exam in another jurisdiction:** With bar exam score portability, not as many people must take multiple bar exams, but some still do. (For example, at the time of this writing, anyone licensed outside of California, for example, must take the California bar exam to be licensed in California.) If this is your situation, you may think because you passed one bar exam and have been practicing law that passing another bar should be easy. You may believe you do not need to prepare as thoroughly as other applicants. Wrong. You need to set aside your practical knowledge, forget for a moment that you are a lawyer, get back into the mindset of a student, and follow the exam advice and strategies in this book.
- **Law professors:** This book will help you to assist your students and improve your school's bar pass rates. (Law deans and faculty, feel free to contact the author for consulting.)
- **Prospective law students:** This book will help balance any negatives you may hear about legal education and see that despite great challenges, enormous rewards await. I loved law school, and I hope this book helps you decide to go to law school!
- **Experienced attorneys who work with new lawyers:** This book will help you understand concerns facing law students today and help you become stronger mentors.
- **Students working to achieve any academic goal, from high school to graduate school:** Many of the challenges described in this book apply to other situations. As you read, feel free to replace

the words *"pass the bar exam"* with ***"do well on finals or midterms"*** or ***"get a high score on the SAT, LSAT, MCAT or other standardized test."*** You will find success strategies to help you achieve your goals and celebrate your accomplishments.

MINDSET MATTERS: LAW STUDENTS, START BY BELIEVING YOU **CAN** PASS! YOUR FATE IS NOT SEALED BY THE LSAT, GRADES, OR ANY OTHER SINGLE INDICATOR

The LSAT *alone* does not accurately predict whether you will pass the bar exam. The LSAT is not designed to predict bar passage, and it can be destructive to think it does. Law school grades are a better predictor of bar success, but even the person with the lowest graduating GPA (grade point average) in your law school class *can* pass the bar exam. This is especially true if your grades improve from where they started in 1L. Bottom line: it is not your grades but what you learn from *and what you do with* the information that grades provide that matter most.

Too many students fear that bar passage is predetermined by performance in one or another law school course. Not true. The only door that is likely to close because of low first-year grades is a summer clerkship with an elite law firm. No matter what your 1L grades, unless you were academically dismissed after 1L, you *can* improve enough to pass the bar exam after graduation—*if you do the work and are committed to success.*

Again, no matter your law school GPA, if you graduate law school, you *can* almost certainly pass the bar exam. Do not ever resign yourself to bar failure.

Calvin, a third-year (3L) student whose GPA put him in the bottom of his class, came into my office the first week in March, and said, *"Professor Berman, I know that based on my background and my numbers (LSAT and GPA), my chances of passing the bar are not high. Don't sugar coat it. Can I pass this July or not? I want to know now."* I looked at Calvin (not his real name), and stated without hesitation, *"Yes, you can. I know that because you are here in my office now, in March, not June, and because you are here asking this question. That means you can pass, if you do exactly what I say."* I went on to tell him to read this book cover to cover, follow the strategies, get a head start with early bar prep, meet with me regularly until graduation, and then complete his bar review work as thoroughly as humanly possible. I told him he had to throw himself in, full force, from that day forward, continuing in high gear until the last "time" was called. **Calvin passed his first bar exam that same July. So can you.**

Whatever your admissions test scores and undergrad or law school grades, don't get discouraged. Rather than throwing in the towel, throw yourself into a growth mindset.

What do I mean by *growth mindset* and how does it compare to the opposite, a *fixed mindset*? With a growth mindset, you believe (you know beyond a reasonable doubt) that your abilities *can* develop and improve. Let's look at some examples.

A fixed mindset would say, "I did poorly in law school so I'm not going to pass the bar exam first time around." Or "I got a bad grade in property, so I'm never going to understand easements and covenants." By contrast, a growth mindset says, "I'm going to figure out what I didn't understand and focus on improvement." A growth mindset says, "I will have another opportunity to be tested in property on the bar exam, so I'm going to use bar review to learn what I didn't understand the first time."

Empirical studies prove that adopting a growth mindset helps you stay strong, own your power, and pass the bar exam.

If your grades place you below where you would like to be (as a loose guide, if your grades place you in the bottom half of your law school class), or if you find yourself struggling with academic, financial, psychological, or physical challenges in law school, be brave and confront the situation. Know that you are not alone. Find a mentor and reliable assistance, such as from your ASP faculty or a favorite professor. Diagnose why you received certain grades (or what is behind other struggles), learn how to improve, and put an action plan into place to make concrete changes to ensure first-time bar passage.

I know that many students don't want to appear "stupid" or "weak," or somehow "other" by telling someone about their struggles. Many hope that challenges will just go away. I get it.

But you are better served by action than wishful thinking. Know and tell yourself loudly that there is nothing wrong with *you.* The key is realizing what you need to *do* differently. Getting quality, reliable help to guide you is key. Sometimes, we know how to improve, but most often we need guidance to see how to make effective changes.

And, often, including in bar prep, small changes can make big differences. You might need to sleep more, listen differently, or read more slowly and carefully. You might need to exercise more to relieve stress. You might need glasses or contact lenses. You might need to talk with a counselor. You might need some financial advice to get a handle on how you will repay your student loans so that money worries don't keep you from studying. You might need to learn how to take notes that are helpful to you. You might need to take more practice exams, study sample answers, and update your outlines with what you learn from the practice exams.

I often tell students, "You are like a square peg trying to fit into a square hole. You are just tilted slightly diagonally. Make a few changes and you'll slide right in to where you need to be."

So, get help—either from a reliable book or a helpful person—so you can accurately see where you need to improve. Don't just hope it won't matter. Law school grades *do* correlate with bar passage, so you want to use your law school experience to learn how to make any necessary adjustments *before the bar exam.*

WHY *THIS* BOOK?

Most lawyers will vividly recall and happily tell you their bar exam horror stories. Many describe the exam as a "hazing ritual" or worse. Some still have bar-related nightmares.

But studying for the bar exam does not have to be "torture." You can choose to view it that way and be miserable for months. You can even let it get to you so much that you never figure out how to pass and pay the price for years. Or you can view this as an *opportunity* to learn many legal rules, master certain critical lawyering skills, and embrace strategies that will help you achieve professional success. You can find ways to laugh and smile, and celebrate mistakes. (Seeing where you erred in practice exams is the best way to learn!) At the end of the day, you might just look back on the whole thing as *a positive experience*!

Don't believe me? I get it. But know this: I have helped thousands of people pass bar exams nationwide, and I am certain that with the right mindset, strategies, and commitment, training for this exam *can be* an empowering experience.

Bottom line: passing the bar exam is something you must do in nearly every jurisdiction to become a licensed attorney, so let's look at its bright sides and at least let in the possibility that the process may teach indispensable life lessons—including the benefits of struggle and the power of finding ways to thrive in the face of challenge.

LOOK AT FACT PATTERNS AS PUZZLES!

The teaching moment I most look forward to is about ten days before the bar exam when students sheepishly inquire, "Is it *weird* that these questions are getting . . . fun?" With a huge smile I reply, "Not weird at all. It means you are on target."

The practice questions are really *not* much fun until you get to a place where your knowledge and skills are strong enough to work through them. Think about how *not fun* it would be to do a crossword puzzle in a language you don't understand. But, by the time of your exam, I want you to have worked hard enough to declare with conviction, "*Bring it on! Throw any fact pattern at me, on any bar subject. I can break it apart and say something intelligent about the issues. I may not remember every detail of every rule, but the examiners are not expecting me to. The exam is a pass/fail, minimal-competency test. I am not writing an amicus brief for the Supreme Court. In the real world, I will almost always be able to look things up. (Most of the time, I will be required to look things up!) On the exam, I will be relying on what I do know because of the dedicated time and effort I've put into studying, and because of the reasoning skills I have developed. I will carefully read the facts they give me, think logically, and explain my reasoning in a straightforward manner—and on multiple-choice question, reason logically to the best answers. I can do this. I am ready.*"

BUT EVERYONE SAYS "BAR EXAMS SUCK." HOW CAN THERE BE ANYTHING POSITIVE ABOUT THEM?

Beyond the "hazing ritual" critique, many view bar exams as useless wastes of time and money. I will not dispute that the process is costly and deeply flawed. But, since nearly all law graduates must do it for licensure, let's focus on how the process can serve you, (beyond the examiners' stated purpose of consumer protection).

- *The bar exam can be empowering.* If you prepare the way you should, you will develop skills and refine knowledge. Picture the powerful athlete who has trained for the Olympic Games and is poised to run or swim when the starting gun sounds. That will be *you* when you are told you may break the seal, open your booklets, and begin the exam. Visualize yourself as strong and smart, ready to logically approach any fact pattern the examiners might throw at you.

- *Bar preparation can bring clarity.* Studying for the bar provides an opportunity to review what was covered during law school, as well as to learn material that wasn't taught. You spent endless hours focusing on minutiae, concentrating on the veins in the leaves on the branches of trees—or on hundreds of disparate legal rules without ever seeing the forest. During intensive bar studies, you are given the opportunity to pull it all together. You will see connections and parallels in different subjects that previously had no link in your mind.

  Imagine a photo that is out of focus finally becoming clear. Law school blurs information, sometimes intentionally, to prepare you to handle the gray areas in people's lives. Bar review simplifies and clarifies. It boils things down to straightforward rules. Once you have completed the training process, you will just read the facts carefully, apply rules you have mastered, and draw upon reason to reach logical conclusions. Bar review lecturers do not "hide the ball" the way law professors do. You can enjoy a short respite from the mystification before things again become real-world murky.

- *The bar exam can sharpen your ability to reason.* Ideally, you will be applying the rules you have learned (and memorized, by exam time) to thousands of different fact patterns. You will not be delving as deeply into the complexities and subtleties of law as you did when studying appellate cases in school, but you will be reasoning through a far greater volume of factual scenarios that extend into many different areas of law. Your brain will become a power tool. Once you know your stuff, you can go into the exam looking forward to analyzing new fact patterns. They will become intriguing puzzles that you have the ability to solve. Train well and your mental muscles will welcome the challenge.
- *The bar exam levels the playing field.* There is a hierarchy of prestige among law schools and class rank within particular schools. One objective of the bar exam is to certify that *every* passer, regardless of race, gender, or alma mater, possesses the requisite minimal competency to practice law. In some ways, this opens access within the legal profession, particularly for graduates of schools that are not highly ranked, where graduates can honestly say, "I passed the same damn bar exam you did." And, despite the criticism of bar exams as being a barrier to the profession, in at least this one aspect they are an equalizer.
- *Bar preparation can help you train your organizational, time-management, and concentration skills.* Some people have these sorts of executive functioning skills down, but most of us are still working on them. These and other so-called "soft skills" are tools that will help you pass the bar exam and excel in the profession. They are among the most important skills for new lawyers to possess. Our complex world has foisted great time-management demands on us all. Use law school and

bar prep to enhance both your law skills and life skills.

- *Bar study gives you a reprieve from and helps combat life's endless pressures to multitask and hop superficially from topic to topic.* Developing a sufficient command of the law, so as to readily analyze numerous new fact patterns, demands significant mental engagement. While perhaps not as deep as the level of reflection required when called on in class or when writing a law review note, your thinking for bar success must be more like analyzing a novel than skimming social media.

  It is important, and it is good, to give yourself time for real reflection and learning. Too many of us are used to reading on and not stopping when something does not make sense, just hoping that "context clues" will help us understand what we really do not. Part of being a professional is having the integrity, curiosity, and persistence to figure things out, to drill down until you truly understand whatever issue you are wrestling with, and to help others do the same.

Again, I am not a blind supporter of bar exams. In fact, I have joined in calls to reform attorney licensing. However, because alternative pathways are very limited and bar exams are still required in nearly all jurisdictions, I find it most productive for those taking the exam to focus on any positives and work to pass the first time around.

And, a note to my educator and professional colleagues: Given the enormous burden our students carry in loan debt, let's work to continue offering extensive and creative resources to help today's students pass today's exams while at the same time working toward thoughtful licensure reform for tomorrow.

Some readers will continue to fight here. You don't see anything positive about the exam. Take its closed-book nature. "No one needs *memory* in the digital age. And lawyers should not rely on memory anyway but should conduct research to confirm even points they think they know." I agree. That is one of many reasons why I love and have advocated for greater emphasis on the performance test (PT) portion of the bar exam for decades. Performance tests and performance tasks (as they are called on the NextGen bar exam) do not force applicants to rely on memory but rather on the skills they will need as beginning lawyers.

I have worked hard and will continue working to improve legal education and bar exams. But, if I were taking today's bar exam, I would not waste one minute being angry that I must memorize some rules. Why? I can only control what is within my control. You too. You *will* walk into that exam with only your brainpower and a laptop or pen, with no access to outside resources. So, stop thinking about it until after you pass; then argue for meaningful bar exam reform.

In the meantime, try to find some benefits in training your memory. Look for the silver linings! Here are some examples. One, despite our smartphone culture, you will *not* always have ready access to needed information or the time to look things up "in the real world." (I hate that expression. There is nothing unreal about school or bar prep. It's all real, if you take it seriously.) If you have ever run out of battery on your phone, you know the value of having memorized phone numbers.

Two, you might find it freeing to step away, for even a short while, from our dependency on machines.

And, three, even when you can readily look something up, the human brain sometimes makes subtler and ultimately more useful connections than machines or the machine may not have all the data it needs. A scene from the James Bond movie *Skyfall* depicts a perhaps unlikely but interesting moment when human thinking trumps a computer's ability to search for information. The much-younger Q is working frantically to find the location of the villain. Although equipped with the most modern, sophisticated software and programming savvy, Q does not obtain the answer from machines because they were not loaded with the requisite historical logistics data. The older Bond finds the answer and comes to the rescue by connecting the dots using his early memories of the now changed city and his reasoning capability.

Again, not arguing here against AI (artificial intelligence); I'm simply saying that when you have to do something (here, memorize a large quantity of material), make the best of it.

A simple yet powerful principle that helps in finding peace and positivity in life sums this up: Make lemonade out of lemons!

HOW THIS BOOK WAS WRITTEN AND HOW TO READ IT

This text is based on decades of experience teaching in law schools, lecturing in bar review, and considering the extensive body of research on learning science and bar success. (All stories are real, although I have changed names and other details to protect privacy.)

Most readers will start with Part I to plan for a successful first bar exam, then read Part II on repeating the exam for a hefty dose of preventive medicine.

If this will be your first bar, do everything in your power to avoid the enormous burdens of having to retake the exam. It is critical that after the exam you are able to honestly look at yourself in the mirror and know you did your very best. You never want to say, "coulda, woulda, shoulda."

And, you *never* want to treat the bar exam as a practice test.

Readers who are repeating the bar exam might start with Part II for specifics on the unique repeater issues, then read all of Part I to guide you to success on your next exam.

TERMINOLOGY NOTES

Traditional and nontraditional students; first-generation and continuing-generation students. The term *traditional law student* in this book refers to those students who enter law school in their twenties, either just out of or soon after college. They may be working part time but generally not full time. Law is typically their first career. The term *nontraditional student* refers to students who are either older or working full time or both. Nontraditional students may also have extensive family responsibilities, caring for young children, aging parents, and sometimes both. Law will likely be a second or even third career for these students.

These terms have limited value and can be both over- and underinclusive. A twenty-five-year-old "traditional" law student may have a parent dying of cancer or other grueling family demands. And a forty-year-old "nontraditional" student may be financially stable, have grown children, and have a spouse or partner who takes care of nearly all of his or her needs. Neither group has it "easier." Everyone struggles with something. And because of the costs associated with law school, most students are oppressed on some level by the weight of financial worry. Acknowledging their limited usefulness, the terms are still helpful to reveal common denominators with certain groups of students. I will highlight those. I will also occasionally provide notes to particular subsets of nontraditional students, such as those with young children. I do encourage all readers to review all passages, even those targeted to people in "different boats." You might be surprised to find that your own challenges are similar, and that the advice helps.

Whether students are traditional or nontraditional, they are also either *first-generation* or *continuing-generation* students. These terms are commonly used to refer to college students; first-generation students are often the first in their family to attend college, and may not have access to the mentorship, advice, and networks (sometimes called *social capital*) that continuing-generation students may have. A similar divide is found in law schools. Most law students are continuing-generation students—in other words, they were not the first in their family to attend college (and in some cases, not the first in their family to attend law school). However, first-generation students now make up a sizeable proportion of law school classes, and that proportion is likely to increase—first-generation students already make up close to half of the undergraduate population in the United States.

The needs and experiences of first- and continuing-generation students are distinct, but they do overlap. When starting their law school careers, first-generation and continuing-generation students may both face "impostor syndrome," and the (mistaken, but natural, understandable, and very common!) feeling that they don't belong. But first-generation students often lack access to role models and support networks that many continuing-generation students can draw upon.

Even with professional role models, many people feel that they don't *belong* in law school, for a host of reasons. If this is you, you are in good company—with almost everyone in your class who is honest. Susie, one of my students who came from a family of doctors, teachers, and other professionals, recounted trembling with fear in the first days of 1L because she felt so out of place. She was the first to go to law school and had never met a lawyer in her life. To her classmates who were first-generation college students, she was savvy; but Susie's imposter syndrome was real to her.

Whether you are a first- or continuing-generation law student, you have successfully tackled many challenges to get to this point. And later chapters will help you with specific strategies to get the help you need from family, friends, and faculty as you prepare for the bar exam.

July and February takers. This book sometimes refers to first-time bar exam takers as *July takers.* If you graduate in December or for another reason are taking a February bar as your first exam, just replace *June* with *January*, and *July* with *February*. Yours will be a winter rather than a summer timeline, but what you do during the months prior to your exam will largely be the same. (The bar exam is offered twice annually, and although there are myths about one exam being harder or easier than the other, they are just that: myths.)

1L, 2L, 3L, and *4L.* The first year of law school is often referred to as *1L*, while *3L* and *4L* refer to the last year of law school: 3L for students in a full-time program and 4L for students in a part-time program. (Credit here to author Scott Turow whose novel, 1L, popularized this nomenclature.)

Intensive bar review, early start, and *bar planning.* I use the phrase *intensive bar review* to refer to the two months prior to the bar exam when law students hibernate, do nothing but study (if at all possible), and, typically, prepare with the assistance of a commercial bar review course.

Early start refers to the last semester of law school, before formal bar review courses begin. Early-start work may be done independently, in law school extracurricular programs or curricular bar support classes, or with a review course. Early start is essential for many students—especially nontraditional students who are working or have significant family obligations while studying for the bar, as well as traditional students who have struggled in law school.

Students with accommodations that grant them additional time often want to start early since it will take longer to complete practice tests under timed conditions.

Bar planning refers to a range of actions, from gaining familiarity with the exam to researching and enrolling in a suitable bar review course. Bar planning ideally begins on day one of law school orientation. (*You are engaging in bar planning by reading this book.*)

STATISTICS AND PERCENTAGES

I occasionally refer to bar data, but *you* are not a statistic. I have taught students who have a 99 percent chance of passing, based on the most reliable indicators of bar passage, LGPA combined with LSAT scores. And, I have taught others whose chances of passing are statistically much lower. Students who are nearly certain to pass often feel just as much anxiety as do those who are statistically much less likely to pass. But there is one critical difference. The nervousness of those more likely to pass is countered by a powerful growth mindset, the belief that they have what it takes to learn what they need to know in order to pass. However, bar applicants from ranks within schools that typically have lower pass rates may harbor deep concerns that they may not pass.

A primary mission of this book is to change attitudes along with study approaches—to give bar applicants, no matter your statistical chance of passing, the tools *and* confidence to help you break free of fixed mindsets that tell you that you can't succeed.

But let me be very clear: this book is *not* about bestowing false confidence or giving hollow pep talks. It is about the determined and grounded belief that if you work hard and sensibly, and remain doggedly motivated, you can trust that you will succeed.

WHERE ARE YOU NOW? AND HOW TO USE THIS BOOK TO YOUR BEST ADVANTAGE

If you are a 3L or 4L approaching law school graduation, success is nearly yours. You can practically taste it. The bar exam felt so far off in 1L. Now it's here. Intensive bar review usually begins the day after graduation, so expect that to be anticlimactic. Prepare family and friends that while you are taking a brief break to attend graduation. You will celebrate for real when bar results come out.

If you are burned out, find a way to recharge your batteries because you will need to be in the highest gear possible during bar prep.

TAKE OFF TIME IF NECESSARY TO GEAR UP FOR BAR REVIEW

A student e-mailed me about a week into intensive bar prep: "I hate bar review. I am fried. I cannot seem to get back any of the energy I had even last year." We talked. I urged her to take a day off, clear her head, and return ready.

"The bar is the last lap in the legal education marathon. Picture Olympic runners—how tired and wiped out they look. Yet their jaws are somehow set, their steely determination far stronger than their fatigue. The sweat drips, and you know they are aching as they move toward the finish line. Then pure elation when they break through that ribbon! This is your last lap. Of course you're tired. You have every right to be. Take a short break. Change your scenery for a day or even a weekend. Or take a mental break to binge-watch mindlessly for a few hours, with lots of popcorn. Do whatever *you* need to get back into high gear with the energy to finish the race. You did not start this three or four years ago in order to give up now. You owe it to yourself to cross that finish line. So, step away from the stress for a moment. Get off the rat wheel. Rest and recharge. Then get back up, ready to run!"

If you are just beginning 3L or 4L, get a head start. Starting early will help you lay the groundwork to get the most out of bar review and significantly increase your chances of passing the bar exam the first time around.

Wherever you are in the process, consider the bar exam not as an afterthought but as the main event. When you get there, you will need to give it your all, just as you would if you were starring in a Broadway show or climbing an enormous mountain peak. (I refer to the bar exam so often as the "law student's Mount Everest" that one former student sent me a copy after he passed the exam of "The Man who Climbed Everest," addressed to his favorite "Sherpa.")

Give bar prep the kind of professional energy and attention to detail that you will want to give your clients when you are practicing—the kind of caring you would want from a lawyer representing you or a family member.

Do not dread this process. But do not underestimate how much it will take. Climbing this mountain will be tough, but exhilarating. Use every last ounce of energy. Don't hold back. Learning to commit 100 percent with total focus, and marshalling all your resources to achieve what you seek, will serve you well for the rest of your life. It will help you achieve most any future goal to which you set your mind.

When you are tempted to express doubts or bitterness about *having* to take yet another test after graduation, remember this: One does not just wake up and decide, "I'm going to take a bar exam." You *earn* the right to sit for the bar.

When you begin the first session of the first day of your bar exam, know that you *worked for* that seat. You sweated and sacrificed. You made an enormous investment. To even be allowed into law school, you toiled—in both high school and college. You went through countless application mazes and entrance exams. If you are getting ready for bar prep then you also survived law school and earned (or very soon will earn) your juris doctor. Thus, you have unequivocally *earned* the right to take *this* test.

When you begin your bar exam, you can feel proud and humble. Know that you are *fortunate* too; you are among the most educated people in the world. You are working for a license that will give you possibilities that many people will never even dream of, let alone attain. I call legal education "a power tool for social change." When you are licensed as an attorney, the world will know that you earned the right to wield that power tool.

#PowerToolForSocialChange, #PassTheBar, #RaisingtheBar, #IEarnedIt, #LegalEducation, #BarExamSuccess

About the Author

Sara J. Berman is a Professor of Lawyering Skills and the Director of Academic Success at the USC Gould School of Law. Professor Berman previously taught in other law schools in New York, Florida, and California, and served as the first national Director of Academic & Bar Success for the nonprofit AccessLex Institute. Prof. Berman has lectured in bar reviews nationwide, helping thousands of students to pass their bar exam.

Prof. Berman's publications include articles, two co-authored Nolo.com publications (*The Criminal Law Handbook: Know Your Rights, Survive the System* and *Represent Yourself in Court: How to Prepare and Try a Winning Case*) and the West Academic publications listed below.

WEST PUBLICATIONS BY SARA J. BERMAN

1L Success: Becoming a Lawyer, a Professional Identity Formation Workbook

- Sara J. Berman
- 1st edition, ©2024
- (2d. ed. forthcoming, 2026)

California Baby Bar Success: A Comprehensive Guide

- Sara J. Berman
- 1st edition, ©2023
- 2d edition, ©2026

2L Success: Lawyering Skills Training & Professional Identity Formation for Upper Division Law Students

- Sara J. Berman
- 1st edition, ©2025

Bar Exam Prep for the Next Generation: Building a Solid Foundation Before Bar Review Begins

- Steven I. Friedland & Sara J. Berman
- 1st edition, ©2026

Bar Exam MPT Preparation & Experiential Learning for Law Students

- Sara J. Berman
- 2d edition, ©2021
- (3d ed. forthcoming, as **Bar Exam PT Success: Strategies & Practice**, 2026)

Office Hours on Academic Success (Audio)

- Sara J. Berman
- Set 1 ©2022
- Set 2 ©2023

Office Hours on Bar Exam Success (Audio)

- Sara J. Berman
- ©2023

Step-by-Step Guide to Torts

- Sara J. Berman & Steven J. Bracci
- 1st edition, ©2022
- (2d ed. forthcoming, 2026)

Step-by-Step Guide to Contracts

- Sara J. Berman & Steven J. Bracci
- 1st edition, ©2022
- (2d ed. forthcoming, 2026)

Step-by-Step Guide to Criminal Law

- Sara J. Berman & Steven J. Bracci
- 1st edition, ©2022
- (2d ed. forthcoming, 2026)

TABLE OF CONTENTS

PART II. REPEATING THE BAR EXAM: THIS WILL BE THE LAST TIME

INTRODUCTION TO PART II

APPENDICES

Bar Exam Success

A Comprehensive Guide

Third Edition

Part I

First-Time Bar Passage: One and Done

INTRODUCTION TO PART I

Part I of this book focuses on first-time passage. Many jurisdictions tested for decades with similar formats, but bar exams are changing significantly. It is critical that you research the format, subjects to be tested, delivery system (in person or online), timing, and other substantive and logical details about the exam you will take. Be certain that you are looking at information about how the exam will be when you sit for it. (It may be one format this year and another when you are taking the exam.) Depending on what jurisdiction you are in, your exam may be one created by your state or by the National Conference of Bar Examiners. So, in addition to reviewing information on the website of your jurisdiction, study relevant information on the NCBE's website, NCBEX.org.

All bar exams have common denominators. They are all *tough, high stakes exams*. A lot rides on passing them. They are a big deal.

Many students fail the bar exam. Sadly, many *expect* to fail. Too many believe that statistics will dictate their fates. You are not a statistic. Demystify the bar exam. Learn to set and achieve goals. And, start working now to replace any trace of self-doubt with what will become a well-worn path of hard work and strategic training.

Ban thoughts such as, "Sure, I'll try" or "I can take it again if need be." No! From now on, doggedly pursue passing the bar. Do what it takes to succeed.

Equally dangerous is the overconfidence trap of expecting to *pass*. Maybe your school's grades are inflated, and you have a false sense of readiness. Maybe you figure that since the bar exam is a pass/fail test, it can't be that hard. Or perhaps you just know you often get by without working that hard. The bar exam *is* different. You don't "get by." There is a good chance if you pass 1L and graduate from law school that you *can* pass this exam, but *only* if you work really hard, understand what it takes, and plan ahead.

Others want to figure out how to do just enough work to pass, but no more. Why? I suspect that many of you feel insecure about the job market and put pressure on yourselves throughout law school to rack up experiences and bolster your resumes with moot court, journals, student bar associations, competitions, externships, and the like. But in trying to do so much, you may have unknowingly sacrificed the depth of your legal education and bar success training.

How many of you are thinking, "*I will start preparing for the bar after my last set of finals. I just don't have any spare time now. I'm exhausted. I am maxed out. And any energy I do have, I need to throw into resume building. It will look good, and I'll be just a bit more competitive if I serve on the board of one more student organization, compete in one more advocacy round, or take on one more part-time law job. I can focus on the bar exam later. I'll be fine.*"

If you can handle the extras *and* still keep your grades up, OK. But an additional line or two on your resume will *not* make up for failing the bar exam.

So, please, give yourself the time during law school to read this book cover to cover, and plan ahead so you're not taken by surprise and find you just don't have enough time to do it all in intensive bar review.

And, take your current classes seriously so you don't have to *learn* in bar review what you could have mastered during school.

Bottom line: Do whatever it takes. Make it your *business* to pass. And, consider doing the work that is necessary slowly and steadily. (Remind me again, who won *that* race—the tortoise or the hare?)

"Always bear in mind that your own resolution to succeed is more important than any other thing."

—ABRAHAM LINCOLN—

TRAPS TO AVOID

Some students are too busy with work or family to devote the time necessary for bar studies. Some don't pass because they don't enroll in a reputable bar review, or they don't do the work in the courses for which they sign up. Bar reviews keep statistics. Students who complete a significant portion of the work (including *and especially* completing the active work of taking practice tests), pass in far greater numbers than those who do not. Seems obvious. But how many of us have ever paid for a gym membership and not gone to work out?

Others find themselves after graduation doing too much "bar *learning*," leaving insufficient time for *review*. Students may be told that they can easily pick up subjects in bar review and so they take an impressive array of electives but do not take criminal procedure, remedies, or business organizations. When they realize how much they must catch up on, they panic. Time spent learning brand new material in bar review may set in motion a negative cycle: students are reluctant to take practice tests when they don't know the law, so they postpone skills practice, and then end up even further behind.

Two full-time months may be sufficient for bar *review*. It may not be enough to learn several new subjects, review every other subject, and develop the skills needed to pass.

"It's a funny thing about life: if you refuse to accept anything but the best you very often get it."

—W. SOMERSET MAUGHAM—

CHAPTER 1

SET YOUR GOAL AND COMMIT TO SUCCESS

- Do You Really Want the Esq.?
- Why Do You Want to Pass the Bar Exam?
- Believe You Will Pass, and Mirror That Belief with "I Will" Language
- Rephrase Self-Talk in Law School, in Bar Prep, and in Life
- Bust the Sources of Self-Doubt
- Fight Stereotype Threat
- Sometimes It Helps to Let Things Roll Off
- Celebrate Your Mistakes
- Know and Exemplify These Ten Common Characteristics of Bar Passers
- Return to Your Goal, in Print

Declare your commitment to success. **"I will PASS the bar exam in [jurisdiction] on [date]."** Say it out loud. Then handwrite or type it. Post this on your fridge or somewhere you look every day.

"A goal is created three times. First as a mental picture. Second, when written down to add clarity and dimension. And third, when you take action towards its achievement."

—GARY RYAN BLAIR—

Sitting for the Bar Exam

"Sitting for the bar." What an expression! It's from Old English and just means "taking" the exam. But it sounds ridiculous. "*What am I gonna do, stand?*" Sounds more like a tapas bar than a bar exam.

But isn't it fitting that we still insist on using an expression that is so formal, or, some might say, arrogant? Own it. Think of it not as pretentious, but as elevating the process. You're not going in just to *take* a test. This *is* special. Your future rides on it. You are preparing to *be* the lawyer, the person in charge, someone responsible for other people's lives and livelihoods. On test day, you will be on an "interview" before your jurisdiction's bar examiners. So, prepare now to "sit for" *and pass* the bar exam!

The first step toward success is what I call "finding your why." Make certain you know why you *really* want this: to be a licensed member of the bar.

Are you thinking: "What the heck does she mean? *Why do I want it?*" I mean this: too many people fail bar exams because they don't really want to *be* lawyers or aren't ready to assume such a significant responsibility.

I graduated law school at age twenty-five. One of my first clients was an engineer in his sixties who had been forced to file for bankruptcy. His wife, children, and grandchildren depended on him, and he was looking to *me* for advice. That was intimidating and humbling; it taught me real-world "professional responsibility" and what it means to *be* a lawyer. It shaped my professional identity.

And so I ask, with the utmost respect, *are you ready* to be *responsible* for other people's lives and livelihoods?

Now please know, you will not be alone when you graduate. You will likely work for and with other lawyers who can and will guide you. Even those who start solo practices will find plenty of mentoring resources, if you seek them out. But serious responsibilities will fall on you.

Some people went to law school to fulfill a parent's dream. Others opted for law by default. Many are put off by how difficult it is to find good law jobs. Some dread the life of a lawyer, perceiving all attorneys as drowning in billable hours. These are reasonable concerns, and therefore it is not crazy, even after having invested and succeeded in law school, to have continued doubts. My message to you is this:

Do not let career concerns lead to failing the bar exam. Deal with doubts either before graduation or after the exam.

"The desire of reward is one of the strongest incentives of human conduct; . . . the best security for the fidelity of mankind is to make their interest coincide with their duty."

—ALEXANDER HAMILTON—

Do You Really Want the Esq.?

For certain graduates, the J.D. (juris doctor degree or law school diploma) *is* the end goal. They have no need or desire to become licensed to practice law. Many second- and third-career students begin law school as successful professionals in their fields. They desire the legal education and degree to enhance their earning capacity and expand their employment opportunities. All good.

But, *if* you think you *might* want a law license at some point in your life, take the bar exam as soon as possible.

Again, you may have good reasons for never wanting or needing the license and happily decide not to take the exam. If so, fine. What is *not* fine is taking the exam without being fully invested in passing. If you are on the fence, commit **now** to either take *and* pass it, or not take it at all.

A similar thought process occurs with students deciding whether to take the July or February bar. Some do not feel ready so they ask, "Why shouldn't I just take this one for the heck of it and see if I pass? If not, I'll study for real next time." No, no, no!

I cannot say it enough: do *not* go into the bar exam and wing it! Here is why:

- Even if you think you aren't invested in the process, your ego will be. You will get caught up (at least to some extent) in the bar exam frenzy. You cannot avoid it. Sitting for the exam—just being in those testing facilities with other bar takers—will set in motion a host of expectations.
- You will be disappointed in yourself if you don't pass. Even if you know you didn't work for it, your confidence will take a hit.
- Others may think less of your capability. People will learn that you took and did not pass, the exam. They won't know that you weren't really trying. All they will know are the results.
- It "sounds" better for you to have not ever taken the exam than to have taken it and failed.
- It reflects very poorly on your law school. Law schools are judged by bar passage rates. Even if you desire just the J.D., you still want your law school diploma to be as prestigious as possible, right?
- You owe it to yourself and your classmates, and to anyone who ever has or will put your school's diploma on the wall, to try your hardest to pass. You may not have ever thought of it this way, but "winging it" on the bar exam is truly an affront to your law school colleagues.
- It is a colossal waste of time and money.
- Lastly, it's just good practice to do your best at everything you undertake. Success will follow.

There are some tests you can use as practice, such as the PSAT. Do *not* treat the bar exam as a "practice test."

Why Do You Want to Pass the Bar Exam?

So *why* do you want this license? Again, I ask because it will help you commit the time and energy to sufficiently prepare for it. (If you don't *really* want it, you are more apt to be lured away from studying and/or discouraged by setbacks.)

Years ago, a student approached me during the lunch break of a daylong bar review seminar and told me this would be the tenth year (and the twentieth time) he was taking the bar exam. We talked at length. (His story was riveting; I couldn't even think about eating.) It was readily apparent that he knew the law and was very bright. He was also an incredible overachiever. He had come to the United States with nothing and built a life for his parents and his children. He had a thriving practice as an interpreter and volunteered in an adult English as a second language (ESL) program. "What was the hindrance?" I wondered. "Why wasn't this person passing the exam?" I finally thought to ask him how he envisioned life once he passed the bar. He immediately launched into a tirade about how passing the exam would change his life drastically—and *not* for the better. Every lawyer he knew was overworked and bitterly unhappy. Becoming a lawyer had been his parents' dream, not his own. He was happiest teaching English to people from his native country and helping them become Americans. He didn't want to give that up. But none of the lawyers he knew had any time for volunteer work.

Suddenly everything clicked. I made him promise that he would make no changes whatsoever to his life for at least six months after the next bar results were out, regardless of whether he passed or failed. We even talked about waiting for a while to check his results. I saw a weight visibly lift from his shoulders. It turned out that he *did* pass that next exam. Was it because some self-imposed pressure to change who he was as a person had finally been lifted? When we talked again, he told me that he still wasn't sure whether he would ever practice law, but he was proud of himself for finally passing the bar.

I will never know for certain what made the difference, but I have since talked with many students who failed two or three times because they weren't ready for whatever they thought they would *have to* do or become after passing.

What will passing the bar exam mean for you? The goal is that it will *open* doors and create opportunity, rather than saddling you with obligations you don't want.

Reflection: Finding Your "Why"

Take a moment and answer the following questions:

What will passing the bar exam mean for you?

____

____

____

Why do you want the license (or "Esq." title) after your name?

____

____

____

What do you see changing in your life once you have a law license?

____

____

____

Believe You Will Pass, and Mirror That Belief with "I Will" Language

Earlier, I asked you to put your commitment to success in writing. Did you do it? If not, write this now:

> **"I will PASS the bar exam in [jurisdiction] on [date]."**

The wording is not conditional. You are not saying "I *might* pass." You are not promising to go in and give it a shot, thinking that you can always take it again. No! You are saying that you *will* pass this exam.

Note: *This is not:* "I will because I always succeed" or "I will because I deserve to." *This is:* "I will because I am determined to do the work it takes to pass, no matter how difficult and time consuming."

Think about great trial lawyers who have won dozens of cases. Most will *not* tell you that the more they win, the more they wing it. On the contrary, they are apt to prepare more and more carefully as time goes on—perhaps more efficiently and effectively, but no less carefully. Watch really successful people. Most work very hard at what they do.

True story: I was having dinner with someone considered to be one of the greatest legal scholars of our time. He was set to moderate a panel the next day on a topic he could easily have talked about for days (if not weeks) off the top of his head. But instead of winging it, he left the dinner and spent the time necessary prepared thoroughly, almost as if the subject were a brand new one. Successful people rarely take success for granted; they work at it.

You would not have gone to law school in the first place if you weren't a person who thrived on challenge. So, I will tell you what I tell students: *Don't you dare* go into that bar exam and merely give it a shot. Invest in success, train for success, and pass. To quote Yoda, "**Do or do not . . . *there is no try.***"

Rephrase Self-Talk in Law School, in Bar Prep, and in Life

The great basketball player Michael Jordan once said, "You have to expect things of yourself before you can do them."

How Do You Think of Yourself? How Do You Talk to Yourself?

I am asking you from this moment forward to think of yourself *and speak to yourself* as someone who can *and will* succeed.

If you doubt that you'll succeed, read on below to "bust the sources of self-doubt" and crush the demons. Then return to this section on rephrasing self-talk. Change the tone and content of your own inner dialogue (something totally within your control) to empower you in the quest to achieve your goals and propel you toward success. Consider the following examples:

- *Thought*: Why can't I get a higher score on these practice tests?

  ***Rephrase*:** How can I do better on these practice exams next time?

- *Thought*: This easements and covenants stuff [or whatever subject you find challenging] is so difficult. I'll *never* understand it.

Rephrase: Maybe I need to reread the explanations for these questions a couple of times in order to get this. Or, I need to find a different explanation of the concept, one that makes more sense to me. But I will get it eventually.

- *Thought*: I'll never be able to focus for the full length of the exam. I can't go ten minutes without checking my phone before I get antsy.

  Rephrase: It will be challenging to build the endurance needed for full focus while I complete the exam. I will have to wean myself from all distractions, including this phone, a little bit each day. In two weeks, I should be able to focus for a bit longer and in four weeks even longer. I will train so that I'm ready to perform when I must be *on* and focused.

- *Thought*: There is no way I can write answers that are as thorough as the model answers. I can barely retype these in the time allotted.

  Rephrase: I am reading sample and model answers to learn from them, not to judge or criticize myself. I am not taking the bar exam tomorrow. I have time to absorb this way of thinking and writing. The more I practice the stronger I will get. My writing will grow more thoughtful, my analysis sharper and more precise. Whether I feel it or not, I know that I improve with each practice test I take. I just have to keep going. I can do this.

Imagine You Are Midway Through Bar Review

How will you describe your feelings about the bar exam when you are midway through bar review, in about late June (or January for February takers)? Choose one of the following:

A. I'm dying here!

B. I am taking the bar this July and hoping I pass.

C. This is the worst summer ever; knowing my luck, I'll probably be taking it again in February.

D. I'm training for success on this July's bar exam. The experience is giving me an opportunity to review and solidify all the learning I have done for years. I'm becoming a stronger and more skilled reader, thinker, and writer. I will do this. I will pass this bar exam.

The right answer is D! Your self-talk might not be this corny. You may use different words, but you get the point. Beware of slipping into negative language and self-defeating thoughts.

Reflection: Rephrase Self-Doubt

Your turn. Replace your own doubts with language evidencing a positive growth mindset approach, as in the examples above.

- *Thought*: ________________________________

  Rephrase: ________________________________
- *Thought*: ________________________________

  Rephrase: ________________________________

Stay vigilant. It will be hard to maintain a positive attitude. You will get tired. You will get frustrated. You will get sick of it. But this book will talk you through those places where people tend to get stuck. Keep it handy. Reread passages when you start to feel burned out, doubtful, or simply need extra "juice."

Remind yourself constantly that you CAN do this, and you WILL. Keep these thoughts in your psyche every minute of every day until the proctors call "Time" at the end of your exam. Say them out loud and frequently. Post them where you will see and read them several times each day.

Bust the Sources of Self-Doubt

Why *write* your goals? We are biased to believe what we see published online and in print. And you can talk a good talk. You can *say* you want anything. You may well have chosen law because you are a persuasive speaker! But there is a difference between merely wishing or hoping and *doing*.

This book is about achieving; it's about winning. So, if you haven't already committed in writing, get out your pen, laptop, tablet, or phone. Print and post your statement:

> **"I will PASS the bar exam in [jurisdiction] on [date]."**

Are you still thinking, "How can I possibly write that I *will* pass when so many people fail? I *don't* believe for certain that I will pass."

Fair. Look with me at common doubts. Let's expose them to daylight. Let's crush the demons. Let's break down the walls and barriers so you can let go of what is holding you back and focus on success going forward.

- *Doubt:* "My school's bar pass rate is only 60 percent. What if I'm in the 40 percent that doesn't make it? Isn't it presumptuous to say, 'I will' when statistically 40 percent of my classmates won't?"
    - *Doubt-busting*: No, it is not presumptuous at all. *You* are not a statistic. And the reason you are reading this book is because you want to make certain YOU are in the pool that passes. And if your entire law school class adopts this attitude, all the better! Unlike in law school where only one person can be number one in the class, all of you *can* pass the bar.

If your school generally has lower pass rates, you need to work harder and more efficiently than you ever have before. Step up your game. Throw everything you've got behind this. Use statistics if they provide positive peer pressure, but don't let them dictate your fate.

If *you* had a low GPA or ranking within your class (and your chance of passing the first time is therefore statistically lower), ask yourself why you earned the grades you did. Problem-solve now. Did you understand the material? If not, talk with your ASP faculty and professors, or consider getting a tutor for and/or spending extra time on those subjects. Were you thrown by the final? Take additional practice tests in this area. Remember, subjects you struggled with in law school may be easier when seeing them again in bar review.

I am reminded of Jerry, a student who approached me in bar review confessing he had not understood anything in evidence during school, but that it had all come together during bar prep. Had Jerry let his low grade dictate his *ability* to master the material for the bar, he would have failed the exam. Instead, he threw himself in, engaged fully in bar review, found that the rules made much more sense than they had in law school, and passed the bar the first time around. The key to his success was admitting and facing his weakness.

In a way, Jerry was fortunate that his professor gave him a low grade; it was his wake-up call. Law schools do students no favors by inflating grades.

You Are Not a Statistic Unless You Let Yourself Be One

The buzz may be that anyone with a GPA below X has only an Y percent chance of passing. If that Y is anything less than 100, you are rightfully concerned. But, really, since when do important things in life come with 100 percent guarantees? One of my favorite professors used to say, "Toasters come with guarantees; lawyers do not." Stop focusing on numbers; concentrate on learning and improving your knowledge and skills. My motto is simple: "Worry less; work more."

- *Doubt*: "I don't think I can pass. I've kept this a pretty good secret and managed to pass all my classes, but there is a ton of law I just do **not** understand. I took real property, but never really got easements and covenants. I took contracts, but I don't understand consideration or promissory estoppel. And don't get me started on civil procedure! I couldn't explain *res judicata* if my life depended on it."
    - *Doubt-busting*: No worries. While I urge you to do as much early work as possible so that bar review is mostly "review" and not new learning, some intensive bar prep will involve learning. Even if you took every subject in law school, the bar exam tends covers more material than did most law classes. You will continue to learn and memorize new rules, often even up until the day before the exam. This is fine. Remember, there is more material but tested in less depth. (One of my colleagues used to say law school is scuba diving; the bar exam is snorkeling.)

You can never "learn it all," and you don't have to for the bar exam. You just have to learn enough to pass.

Master the major concepts and heavily tested areas as soon as you can. If you can do this in early start, it will help a lot. If you cannot, as long as you are intensely focused and enrolled in a reliable bar review (in which you participate fully and actively), you should be able to learn what you need to know during two months of full-time study.

How can I be so confident? Several reasons:

- First, bar review will likely present rules and concepts in a more straightforward manner than you experienced in law school. In class, law professors try to hide the ball, training students to think like lawyers. But bar review conveys the material straight up.
- Second, hearing concepts again will allow them to sink in. They will be easier to understand this time around because they will sound familiar, and you already have a greater basis for understanding. You are not starting from "square one."
- Third, much of the "new" material you will learn involves refining what you already know, as well as adding an array of narrow exceptions or subparts to your basic understanding of certain concepts. For instance, it is easier to understand when double jeopardy attaches than to comprehend what this right fundamentally protects and why.
- Fourth, you have a greater incentive to really learn it all now! You will work as hard as you need to in order to "get" everything you didn't understand before. If for some reason your bar review doesn't explain a critical concept in a way that makes sense to you, you will find another resource and make sure you get it. You will go into the bar exam feeling more confident and knowledgeable than you ever imagined. And it will feel great.

CAN YOU EXPLAIN THE RULES TO A NON-LAWYER?

Aim to understand every main concept and rule in each bar subject outline well enough that you could explain it to someone who has no legal training (but is intelligent and eager to learn).

Test Your Plain English Translation Skills

Explain negligence to a non-lawyer:

____

____

____

Now, explain consideration to a non-lawyer:

____

____

____

(I told you this book was about doing the work!)

- *Doubt*: "Where exactly do you expect me to get this confidence from? No one in my family ever graduated from college. I'm supposed to pass the bar exam the first time around? Yeah, right. It takes students like me two or three attempts to pass."
  - *Doubt-busting*: You might fear that first time bar passage is simply too ambitious of a goal. It isn't. Few people who really *think* embark on anything big without at least some fear. The key is not to let the fear stop you. Use it. Turn it into adrenaline **(Adopt my 3Ps: "Turn *panic* into *power* not *paralysis*.)** Let fear make you more motivated. You are not your family. You went to law school. You got in. You finished 1L and possibly graduated by the time you are reading this. You have resources. You have support. People in your school and in the greater legal community will help you if you reach out. They want you to pass.

If your family does not know how to or cannot help you, or does not believe in you, find others who do. You would be surprised how many lawyers would want to talk with and help you. I am constantly amazed by the outpouring of generosity from alumni who want to give back.

Let's also look a bit more closely at this particular doubt: *It takes students like me two or three attempts to pass*. What exactly do you mean? Whatever your background, there are those who share your challenges. I am thrilled to be writing this book at a time when current students are not likely to be the first lawyer in any historically underrepresented group. To find support from someone who *gets* you, reach out. Cast a wider net. All you need is one person to believe in you to help you believe in yourself. And do not be too quick to rule out everyone in your law school. Even people with different challenges may empathize with your struggles and be supportive of you.

FIGHT STEREOTYPE THREAT

Studies show that negative stereotypes can be self-fulfilling prophecies. Do not sit for the bar exam feeling inferior because of your race, age, ethnicity, gender, sexual orientation, disability, or any other stereotype-based reason. Know that many others in the room feel exactly the way you do, for their own reasons. Focus on all the positives and on doing your best.

I am not minimizing. I know it is not easy to stop internalizing negatives. But when you are putting yourself on the line as you will be when taking the bar exam, you must compartmentalize that which would tear you down, at least temporarily. I am not suggesting denial. I am advising you to build a mental gate around your doubts to shut them out during bar prep and the bar exam.

Many nontraditional students who are returning to law as second or third careers express how *old* they feel to be taking the bar exam. They doubt that they can compete with the "kids." But once we talk about this and they hear about someone older than they are who passed the bar, they are better able to let go of their concerns.

Many first-gen students battle not only this same sort of self-doubt, but also huge pressures from feeling that they are representing everyone else in their particular sub-group. Those pressures are as real as it gets. Acknowledge them. Realize how awesome you are to be coping as best you can. And, look around for those who struggled with the same or similar pressures who *have* passed. To the extent you can, stop thinking about anything that defeats you or interferes with your confidence until *after you pass. Then* fight prejudice, dismantle stereotypes, and make the world a better place so that others don't have to face the same challenges you did.

The wonderful thing is that *when you pass*, you will be able to use that positive experience of shattering a stereotype to help you believe that you can do so again and again in the future. I keep a picture of a woman punching her fist through a brick wall, shattering the wall, as a reminder of the force it takes to succeed.

What sort of picture might help you?

Remember the "lifelong cycle of success" I wished for you in the beginning of this book? Breaking stereotypes, crushing demons, and busting doubts (self-doubts and those of external doubters) are integral steps in the process of achieving your goals.

I still have doubts, you say, *such as this one*:

- *Doubt:* I have crazy test anxiety. While I'm studying, I basically believe I'll pass; but when test day arrives, I freak out. How can I confidently say I will pass this, the biggest test of all?
    - *Doubt-busting*: Acknowledge legitimate fear without letting it block you. This *is* a tough test. If you weren't at least concerned, there would be something wrong with you. (And if you aren't concerned at all, take a simulated bar exam and give yourself a reality check.) **The key is to turn anxiety into adrenaline, turn *panic* into *power* not *paralysis*.** If you let it, fear can become the most powerful of motivators. It will make you stronger and more prepared for success.

      You can be scared and still pass. You simply may not say you don't believe in your own ability to pass, and you may not let yourself freeze up.

Find tools to help you stay calm and to work through test anxiety including strategies suggested in later chapters such as deep breathing, reading aloud under your breath (subvocalization), and other anchoring and calming techniques. Being prepared and having the right tools will also greatly reduce test anxiety.

"We gain strength, and courage, and confidence by each experience in which we really stop to look fear in the face . . . we must do that which we think we cannot."

—ELEANOR ROOSEVELT—

CELEBRATE YOUR MISTAKES

An interesting professional trait, cultivated from the first days of law school, is a fear of risk-taking and an overabundance of caution.

This fear may begin when one is humiliated in class by an arrogant law professor or put down by classmates in a study group of blowhards. The theory behind some of this "training" is to toughen students up so they will not cave when facing a hostile judge or contentious opposing counsel. Sometimes it strengthens students, but sometimes it makes them all the more fearful.

Identify this as a professional hazard now. Use bar preparation to break the pattern before it becomes ingrained. How? By celebrating when you make mistakes on practice tests. Errors are opportunities to get the concepts right on the actual exam.

Caution may indeed be the mark of a good lawyer; an ounce of prevention can sometimes save your client millions of dollars (and may help ward off malpractice suits). But if you can develop a thick skin and know that *some mistakes are good*, or at least okay, you may ultimately find more solutions and greater success. This is especially true with practice tests in bar review because they can help you learn the root causes of errors and avoid mishaps on the actual exam.

TEN POSITIVE COMMON CHARACTERISTICS OF BAR PASSERS

Make all of these nonnegotiable aspects of your bar preparation experience.

1. You decide you want to pass the bar exam.

You are determined to pass it. Think positively as much as possible: "I *will* pass this bar exam." You have not set yourself up to fail. You NEVER say anything like:

- "I'll just try it out and see what the test is like." (*No!*)
- "I'm too busy to study now, but I'll knock it out at the last minute. I always do." (*No way!*)
- "I can always take it again, right?" (*No. Don't say this, even to yourself. You want to do everything you can to pass the first time around.*)

2. Your priorities are in line with your decision to pass.

You are someone who studies when your schedule says to study. You regard every study appointment with yourself as if it were an appointment with a world-renowned specialist whom you've waited six months to see and who has the cure or treatment you desperately need. Your priorities are studying, sleeping, eating right, and exercising. You have put off everything that can wait until after the bar exam.

3. You have a plan for bar success that includes starting a bar fund and enrolling in a reliable bar review.

You have drafted a bar exam business plan. You made a commitment to invest in yourself by seeking help from experts and enrolling in a reputable full-service bar review. You have set up a bar fund. If need be, you will take out bar loans or work as a "rep" (someone who helps recruit others to take the course) to finance your own bar review course. Your plan also includes time off from work, childcare, household help, and any other assistance you may need.

4. You have a study schedule.

You have calendared exactly how you will *implement* your plan each day, including what, where, and when you will study.

5. You have eliminated or reduced distractions.

Your phone is in the other room when you study. You don't go online to read about everyone else's freak-outs. You don't worry about what people predict will or won't be on your exam. You study everything that the examiners say may be tested and your follow the expertise of your bar review and ASP faculty.

6. You look things up that you don't understand. You learn before you memorize.

You can explain all the relevant rules simply and clearly to someone who has no legal background. If you can't, you look stuff up until you can.

7. You avoid negative people.

You recognize the "negative voices" and avoid them. They may come from people you love or total strangers. They may be blunt and belittling ("Why do you think you are smart enough to be a lawyer?"). They may be passively destructive ("I saw that you took a long break yesterday"—perhaps with a judgmental stare.) They may be bar exam horror stories. You tune them all out.

8. You are routinely taking practice tests in all formats and all subjects, not worrying about scores but working to constantly improve.

Every day, you take practice tests under timed conditions. After completing these tests, you compare and contrast your answers with sample and model answers and determine how to improve after every practice session.

9. You have handled all the details concerning exam days.

You understand test administration details. You have taken care of any advanced planning that will help you prepare for success. You won't be sitting for the bar exam distracted by or worried about how you will upload your answers. You have taken care of every detail—now all you have to do is pass.

10. You have planned a FUN celebration after the exam.

You will be taking yourself and perhaps someone you love to Tahiti, once the exam is over! OK, maybe not Tahiti, but somewhere special for at least a day or two. Or you will be buying something that you, your family, or significant other has very much wanted. If you are on a tight budget, plan a laughter-filled potluck at a beautiful local park. Just make sure that you and those who sacrificed with you have something superb to look forward to, and that you find a concrete way to thank them.

"The test before us as a people is not whether our commitments match our will and our courage; but whether we have the will and courage to match our commitments."

—LYNDON B. JOHNSON—

RETURN TO YOUR GOAL, IN PRINT

Have you written or typed your goal yet?

If you still feel uncomfortable writing, "*I will pass,*" figure out why. A thoughtful person should have a healthy respect for the exam, but courage is pushing through fears, moving forward despite them.

So, try it! Write or type, then print and post:

"I will PASS the bar exam in [jurisdiction] on [date]."

Name: ______________ Date: _______

Signature: ____________ Date: _______

Chapter hashtags: #PasstheBar, #Growthmindset, #IWillPass, #FindYourWhy, #ConquerYourFears, #BarExamSuccess

CHAPTER 2

DEVELOP A PLAN: SET YOUR GPS DESTINATION TO BAR SUCCESS

- Plan Early
- Become a Critical Reader
- Develop a Bar Success Plan and Start a Bar Fund
- Six to Twelve Months Before the Exam
- Learn More About Your Bar Exam
- Embrace the Eight-Week Countdown
- Planning for Bar Exam Success
- Early Start: A Good Idea for Everyone; Essential for Many
- What Should I Work on in Early Start?

Imagine driving across the United States without a GPS. Unless you are taking a route you travel regularly, even short journeys require road maps. Intensive bar preparation is a "long, strange trip" (apologies to the Grateful Dead). You need directions. This chapter gives you a timeline overview and guidance on beginning to draft your plan. (Later chapters will help you complete specific portions of the plan.) Like a business plan, your success plan will include numerous ingredients needed for bar passage include time, funding, and other resources. Bar success plans and study schedules are "living" documents, meant to be adapted, revised and updated when you encounter challenges or find ways to maximize your productivity.

PLAN EARLY

Bar planning begins on day one of law school orientation. The most important skill for bar success is critical reading—the same skill needed for law school and success in the profession. Note: if you are just starting law school, you will find targeted guidance in **1L Success: Becoming a Lawyer, a Professional Identity Formation Workbook** (West Academic).

After critical reading, you need analytical skills, substantive knowledge, and consistent practice with all testing formats.

> DON'T BE BLINDSIDED BY UNEXPECTED COSTS
>
> Many students don't realize they will have to pay for a bar review course *after* law school, and the bill may come due after graduation when there are no more student loans. (Even students who work for firms that will cover the costs of bar review may have to pay first and later seek reimbursement.) Other students budget for bar review but are caught off guard by exam-related fees and the cost of living while studying. Plan so that you have sufficient funds for two months of full-time studying after graduation, without working if at all possible. Consult your law school's financial aid office and other financial information resources for assistance. And, start a bar fund as early as possible.

Bar success also is significantly affected by:

Physical health. Get in the best shape possible before the bar exam. If you have an exercise routine, continue it. If not, start one. It helps relieve stress, increases your energy and acuity, and often makes you sleep better. Get your eyes tested regularly and schedule a general physical exam if you have not had one recently. Tell your doctor if you have any concerns so that they can be addressed right away.

A student came to office hours toward the end of 3L describing back pain she feared might prevent her from sitting for the required time blocks during the bar exam. She had been tough and suffered through the pain all through law school. I urged her to seek treatment immediately. Hopefully, that would help relieve the pain, but, if not, she needed to begin documenting the condition as soon as possible in case she needed special disabilities accommodations during the exam.

Mental health or substance use. These are common issues that can not only affect your health, relationships, and academic success, but your character and fitness applications. Get help if you need help. You are not alone. Talk with someone in Student Affairs, ASP, or your law school's or university's counseling center. Or consult your local lawyer assistance program (LAP). Lawyer Assistance Programs provide confidential services and support to judges, lawyers and law students who are facing substance use disorders or mental health issues. Help from LAPs is confidential and can assist you in planning ahead to work through any potential character and fitness issues. (Use ABA resources such as the ABA's comprehensive state-by-state directory of LAPs at https://www.americanbar.org/groups/lawyer_assistance/resources/lap_programs_by_state/ and the ABA's online pamphlet, *Substance Abuse & Mental Health Toolkit, for Law School Students and Those Who Care About Them.*)

Other Parts of Licensing, in Addition to the Bar Exam

Part of your success involves fulfilling licensing requirements in addition to the bar exam such as passing the MPRE and completing your jurisdiction's character and fitness requirements, and any other requirements in your jurisdiction. There will be fees, fingerprinting, and forms. Start early. Applications take time to process. You may need a referral to an attorney, physician, psychologist, LAP (see above), financial counselor, or other professional.

Study your jurisdiction's website carefully. Also, seek assistance from your law school's Dean of Students. Your law school application may need to be amended so that it is consistent with events in your background that might raise concerns, including but not limited to involvement in criminal (and sometimes civil) cases, having filed for bankruptcy, and/or mental health or substance use issues.

TESTING ACCOMMODATIONS

Being granted accommodations for a disability in law school does not mean you will receive accommodations on the bar exam. Research what your jurisdiction requires and how to apply. Seek input from your law school and/or university's disability officer. Do not wait until the last minute. Often the documentation requirements are more stringent for the bar exam than in law school, and the process may take a long time. For more information, see the ABA's Directory, "Bar Information for Applicants with Disabilities."

Also, if you will have testing accommodations that allow for additional time, consider starting bar preparation early so that you have sufficient time to take all of your practice tests under timed conditions.

CHALLENGES IN READING OR WRITING ENGLISH

If you aren't confident that you can produce grammatically correct, well-written answers, work on this in advance of your bar exam. Again, seek help from a reliable resources and answer as many practice questions as possible, studying model answers closely. Retype answers not only to learn the law but become familiar with the proper phrasing of rules.

Note: terminology on bar exams can throw even native English speakers. A criminal law burglary question asked about a defendant breaking into a "gazebo." Some students, unfamiliar with the word *gazebo*, missed the issue of whether it was a "protected structure." Take as many practice tests as possible, and look up every word that you do not know.

Six to Twelve Months Before the Exam

In addition to preparation that you may begin on day one of law school, you will do some planning as the exam gets closer. For example, it can be very helpful to determine who will be supportive of you during intensive bar prep and who won't, and to begin preparing those who will be supportive but only if they understand what your needs will be. (Later chapters will help you do this.) Line up summer housing; care for children, elderly relatives, and pets; and make plans to delegate work responsibilities and hand over leadership reins in any student organizations.

Learn More About Your Bar Exam

Bar examiners, unlike law professors, tend to reveal nearly all their cards. There are few surprises. The questions will cover the material the examiners say they are testing, and typically in the format used on previous tests. But bar exams nationwide are changing so you must study the content and the testing format of the exam you will take.

Know how much each part of the exam is worth. This will likely be in your bar review materials. But why wait? Find out by reading your jurisdiction's bar examiner website, consulting your ASP faculty, and reviewing updated information from the NCBE.

Which subjects are tested, and in how much detail? Your bar review course will help you devise a study plan to learn everything you need to know. But, your memory "disk space" is limited; you will want to know which subjects to emphasize and which to hit more superficially. It may be wise to spend more time on areas that you know either will definitely be tested, or are tested frequently, than on those that are tested less commonly. Strategizing in advance will help you work efficiently, maximize your time, and not burn out.

PREDICTIONS AND BETTING THAT A CERTAIN AREA OF LAW WILL NOT BE TESTED

Giving more attention to frequently tested areas is *not* the same as hoping a subject won't be tested and skipping the area altogether. I have seen students do this largely for two reasons: (1) they feel weak in a particular area and decide to ignore it and hope it won't be on their exam, rather than tackling it until they have gained the requisite competence, or (2) a bar review instructor or law school professor says that area won't be tested on this bar.

I happen to have worked closely for decades with someone whose ability to predict which subjects will appear on the bar exam is legendary. His success rates are extraordinary. If I could get him to predict the stock market with equal accuracy, he and I might well be multimillionaires. I nonetheless advise everyone to regard all predictions with extreme caution. You can certainly take steps to make sure you are extra comfortable handling questions in predicted areas. If they are tested, you can smile with secret delight at your "edge." But, get very comfortable with *every* tested area and do *not* bank on anyone's predictions. Next, do not try to "game" the exam. Prepare for questions on every topic the examiners say may be tested. End of story. (And if you don't believe me, ask lawyers about their bar exam horror stories. Many [including yours truly] remember facing bar questions on topics that instructors promised would not be on the test.) Bottom line: study the content scope outlines. If the examiners say it is within the scope of tested areas, learn it.

Re-cap of advanced planning strategies:

- Gather reliable materials to learn any subjects tested on your bar exam that you didn't or won't take in law school. Study those before bar review, if possible, so that bar review is indeed review and not bar learning.
- Review bar examiners' content scope outlines (or tables of contents of bar review outlines) for *all* testable subjects, and become fluent with terminology so that you will better understand bar review lectures. Start a folder on each subject in which you will place practice exams, plain English explanations of tricky concepts, and definitions of key terms.
- Complete or update your bar success plan.
- Continue work on the moral character and fitness portion of your bar application.
- Enroll if you have not yet done so in a reputable bar review. (More later on choosing a bar review.)
- Become aware of how you spend your time and what distracts you, and consider time management strategies detailed later in this book.
- Begin taking some practice tests, for example those posted as samples on your jurisdiction's or the NCBE's website.
- Review your bar fund and savings strategies. Hopefully, you have been stashing away money since orientation and now have enough to pay for the bar review course, but now is the time to research bar loans and scholarships if your fund is low. Talk with your law school financial aid office. Consult your ASP faculty to learn about other ways to finance bar review if you do not have savings. Figure out a way to obtain the money you need to get the expert help you deserve. Do not opt to skimp

on bar review because you don't have the money. If you fail the bar exam, your costs will multiply, and it will be even longer before you can begin paying back your student loans.

Embrace the Eight-Week Countdown

We will look in detail at, and plan for, intensive bar preparation in later chapters, but, as a preview, think about this sequence: (1) finals, (2) graduation, and (3) a boatload of bar review materials to master!

Your bar review will provide a study schedule, taking you through eight weeks, subject by subject, and covering most everything tested on your exam. The schedule will tell you what to do and in what order. Most bar reviews will prompt you to do work including to:

- listen to lectures reviewing the law tested on your bar exam, noting heavily tested areas and distinctions where your exam requires knowledge of state and federal law;
- actively read and test yourself with outlines that provide summaries of the relevant law you need to know for each subject, along with illustrative examples, charts, and other visuals;
- develop testing skills for different testing formats; and
- answer practice questions, self-assess and improve by studying sample or model answers, and submit your own answers for grading and critique.

Grossly oversimplified, the first month will be slow and overwhelming; the second month will fly by and be filled with adrenaline. Your schedule is vital. Stay on track. You may need to add extra practice tests to your training routine, but, at a minimum, plan to complete your bar review course.

Midway into intensive bar review (June or January), you will want to take a hard look at your skills and substantive knowledge, assessing and adjusting your schedule to target and improve any weaknesses. Make every effort to stick to your bar review, avoid distractions, and cement what is hopefully now your regular practice test routine.

A key point: Don't be overly concerned with practice test scores, especially at the beginning of bar review. Focus on your training by completing the questions under timed conditions, studying answers, and self-assessing to improve. Your goal is simply to learn and improve each and every day.

By the end of June, you may need to fight burnout. You will have come through what essentially amounts to four to five weeks of finals. (How tired were you in school after any single final exam?) But seeing the calendar turn from June to July will bring a boost. You can finally see light at the end of the tunnel and know that you are in the homestretch. On July 1, you will still be nearly a month away from taking the bar, though, so you must pace yourself. You don't want to peak too early and be exhausted by the time the exam comes.

A few weeks before the exam, you will likely be finishing the formal bar review schedule, having at least briefly reviewed all subjects covered on your exam. This is a good time to complete a simulated exam and learn from that experience.

By a week before the exam, draft one-page "cheat sheets" for every subject on your exam. (I will never forget one of my law school professors shoving paper in his back pocket to demonstrate, saying, "*Pretend* that you were going to cheat on the exam, and you could fit only one page of notes on each subject in your pocket. What would you write on those pages? Get that ready at least a week before the exam." It was a graphic demonstration, and very helpful advice!)

The week before the exam, you will also take care of last-minute test day details. Review the rules on what your jurisdiction allows you to have with you during the exam.

You'll want to plan your exam mornings and evenings, as well as your lunch breaks. Later chapters provide tips and strategies for how best to structure bar days and nights.

You will be exhausted after completing the exam, most likely not knowing how you did. Don't worry. People who are "certain" they passed may not have seen all the issues. I am happiest when people say, "Well, I don't know how I did, but I did my best."

You will be enormously relieved when the exam is finally over, but the months of waiting for your results will weigh heavily until the moment of truth arrives; this varies from about September to November. (Tom Petty had it right with his song lyric, "The waiting is the hardest part.") Either you will have passed and can celebrate, or you will need to dust yourself off and prepare to pass the next exam.

Again, this timeline is an overview intended only to give a basic sense of what lies ahead. These stages will be detailed in later chapters. And each person may experience them differently. For now, just a few more pieces of strategic advice for planning ahead.

DO NOT MAKE RADICAL CHANGES DURING BAR REVIEW

It's not the time to experiment with a new diet or to quit smoking or drinking coffee. Do those things, if you want, *after* your bar exam!

A student who did unexpectedly poorly on a simulated exam met with me to discuss the results. When I noticed she looked tired, I asked a few questions and determined that she had begun a diet with no protein or carbohydrates. She hadn't connected her body's lack of nourishment with her exam score. I did. Before we discussed any content issues, we talked about her postponing any diet plans until after the bar exam.

PLANNING FOR BAR EXAM SUCCESS

Business plans start with mission statements. Your mission is the goal you put in writing in Chapter 1: to pass the [*insert date and jurisdiction*] bar exam.

For some people, deciding where to sit for the bar exam is easy. They know where they want to live, work, and pass the bar. Others either do not yet have employment lined up or may look for jurisdiction that will allow them to "port" their score to another jurisdiction. If you need help in determining the best place to sit for the exam, talk with faculty in your school's ASP and career services offices.

After clarifying their mission, successful businesspeople typically research the actions they will need to take before launching their enterprise. Because intensive bar review begins immediately after graduation, your window for this preparation phase is during your last year of law school. Traditionally, students need to plan ahead to dedicate at least two months to full-time study.

Anyone needing or wanting extra time should plan ahead to dedicate six to eight months to part-time study. Bar review courses typically open in March (for July exams). Don't wait until after graduation. Plan to start early!

Planning ahead will prevent problems, reduce stress, and increase the likelihood of your passing the bar the first time around. It will allow you to focus on your studies and get in shape for peak performance in June and July. You may have pulled all-nighters before finals in college or law school, "learning it all" the week before an exam, but you cannot pass the bar exam that way. *You simply cannot cram for the bar exam.* In learning science terms, you must engage in "distributed" rather than "massed" practice, or, as many of us are fond of saying, "The bar exam is a marathon, not a sprint."

Reiterating an earlier point, during your last year of law school, well before graduation:

- *Get a handle on bar subjects you never took or learned in law school.* If there are either subjects you never studied in law school or areas you studied but never really understood, take some time in your last year of law school to at least read through a good supplement or study aid on the subject.

DON'T BLAME YOUR PROFESSORS OR YOUR LAW SCHOOL

Don't fall into the useless trap of blaming your professors for not teaching everything you need to know. For example, it might be great if every torts class covered every possible area tested on the bar. But many torts professors go into such depth regarding intentional torts and negligence that time runs short when considering defamation and economic torts. (A friend of mine skipped intentional torts altogether when he taught torts in order to spend time on more complex damages issues.)

None of this is a problem. The depth of study in the areas you did cover taught you how to learn rules. Would you have wanted a class that rushed through everything so fast that you covered it all, but did not really understand anything? Of course not. You needed the depth to master the analytical skills. It allowed you to focus on metacognition (learning how to learn).

From now on, spend your time doing instead of complaining. Learning and studying will get you to bar passage; complaining will only compound your frustration. For the rest of your life, there will be things you do not know and need to learn. (Before appearing in court, you will study so the judge doesn't ask questions you cannot answer.)

This is your opportunity. Learn what you need to know now, and learn it well. And be thankful that you have learned how to learn.

- *Start exercising.* I mentioned this earlier and will discuss it again because it is very important. You will need this stress release during bar review. If you do not have a daily exercise routine, start one now. I am *not* suggesting you try a new sport or do anything strenuous that you are not used to. You don't want an injury now. But if you are currently not very active, you will be surprised by how much better you will feel and handle stress by adding even a daily walk into your routine.
- *Take care of business.* Whatever details you think you may have to deal with in June and July, handle them now (or put them off until after August). Examples include arranging for childcare or pet care during bar review and the bar exam, buying birthday presents ahead of time, and paying bills in advance if you can. Anything you don't have to concern yourself with during the summer means more time for studying, self-care, and getting yourself primed for success.

WORKING STUDENTS

Especially if you are working full time, consider part-time opportunities, and look into vacation time, unpaid leave, and any other ways to free up as much time as possible to study during the months just prior to your bar exam. Quitting a job may not seem feasible but might make sense if it allows you to pass the bar exam first time around and get a better job after doing so.

- *Research (and, if possible, assemble) the resources you will need.* Using the business plan analogy, if you know you will need administrative assistance to run a company, you will want to secure funding to pay personnel and perhaps even begin interviewing candidates ahead of time to find the best employees. If you have not yet enrolled in a reputable full-service bar review, you will need to sign up for one. If you start early, you can shop around. Look at the materials different companies produce, check out their websites, chat with their representatives, and talk with recent graduates who passed your bar exam and ask them what they liked and disliked about their bar review.

You will also need time and money, as detailed below. A business needs to operate efficiently and productively to make money. This may require start-up capital, equipment, personnel, and a physical space to operate. Think of yourself as a sort of business; to facilitate first-time bar passage, you will need:

- a budget and funding to pay for things like test fees, bar review, and living expenses;
- time dedicated to study (a lot of time!);
- an efficient calendaring system;
- a good place to study (somewhere you can concentrate);
- reliable resources to learn from; and
- "buy-in" or support from your inner circle (or the tools to distance yourself if they are not supportive, as outlined in later chapters).

"Before everything else, getting ready is the secret of success."

—HENRY FORD—

Reflection: Draft Your Bar Success Plan

Start filling in the information below, and you will have the basics of your bar success plan. You will also see what you still need to do to prepare to pass.

Bar Exam Administration

I am sitting for ***and will pass*** the

____

(fill in administration)

bar exam on ______________ in ______________

(fill in dates) *(fill in location).*

Website for bar exam rules and filing requirements in the jurisdiction where I plan to sit:

____

NCBE website for information if my exam is produced by the NCBE:

____

Deadlines for timely filing of my application and payment of fees are:

____

I have completed my bar exam registration requirements:
[ ] Yes [ ] Not yet

I have booked bar exam travel arrangements and lodging—if my exam requires me to travel to a testing site:
[ ] Yes [ ] Not yet, but I will by _____ [date] _____.

I have completed my jurisdiction's moral character and fitness requirements: [ ] Yes [ ] Not yet

Note: character and fitness components may be complicated and take time to complete. Research the requirements and filing fee information. Also, get reliable advice (including legal counsel if you need it) before completing paperwork if you have concerns about anything in your past or present, such as arrests or convictions, mental health or substance use issues, academic dishonesty accusations or issues such as plagiarism or cheating, and/or financial issues such as bankruptcies.

About My Bar Exam

My bar exam will test the following subjects:

____

____

____

____

____

____

My bar exam will test in the following formats:

- Test format_________ percentage of total score _______
- Test format_________ percentage of total score _______
- Test format_________ percentage of total score _______
- Test format_________ percentage of total score _______

Bar Review

I am enrolled in the following bar review course:

Dedicated Time

I have dedicated ___ hours per week to bar exam study beginning ______, 20____.

I will increase that number to ___ hours per week by _________, 20____.

For working students: I have requested time off to focus on my bar studies. [ ] Yes [ ] No

If I cannot take off entirely, I have reduced my work hours from ____ to ____ per week for the months of ______________.

I have cleared my calendar in May, June, and July (December, January, and February for February bar takers) of any commitments (professional, social, or otherwise) that I can put off until after the bar exam, including:

____

____

____

I still must find a way to put off or minimize the time I will spend on the following. (List commitments you are still figuring out how to defer, manage, delegate to others, or eliminate.)

____

____

____

Managing Distractions (More on this in later chapters)

I have identified the following as potentially taking time away from my studies, (for example, friends and family members who text me all the time):

____

____

____

My biggest distractions tend to be (e.g., binge-watching; once I get into a series, I can't stop):

____

____

____

I will eliminate/reduce the following distractions and defer the following obligations from May through July:

Example 1: I will deactivate my social media accounts and reactivate them after the bar exam.)

Example 2: I will put my phone in the other room while I study and look at it only at times when I am ready to take a break.)

____

____

____

Bar Exam Budget

I have already paid for or set aside money in a bar fund for the items below. [ ] Yes [ ] Not yet but I am working now to secure loans, gifts, or other funding for the items below:

Bar review cost $_____

Cost of living for two months of bar study (include rent, food, etc.) $_____

My jurisdiction's bar registration fees: $_____

(Be sure to calendar deadlines so you avoid late fees.)

Moral character and fitness application fees:	$_____
MPRE fees:	$_____
(If you have not yet passed the MPRE, enter the date you are taking or retaking it here.) _______________________________	
[ ] Check this box if you already took and passed the MPRE.	
Any incidental costs, such as fingerprinting or laptop fees	$_____
If applicable, travel to and from the bar exam test site:	$_____
If applicable, hotel and food at the test site:	$_____
Childcare/housekeeping during bar studies:	$_____
Trip or something fun after the bar exam:	$_____
Other costs:	$_____
Estimated total of funds needed:	$_____
Funds I currently have: (Be sure to account for earning less money because of time you must take off from work to study.)	$_____
TOTAL FUNDS I STILL NEED TO OBTAIN:	$_____

BAR COST-SAVING TIPS

- Calendar exam registration deadlines to avoid late fees. These add up.
- If your exam requires travel or lodging, book transportation and hotel reservations early. Comparison shop for the best rates, and look to find a room with a refrigerator so you can bring or buy your own food. Not only will it be cheaper than hotel food, but you will also have control over what you eat.
- If renting a car, flying, or taking a train to an exam site, book early.
- If there is a choice of test site location, you might want to pick a less expensive or less crowded one.

Written Study Schedule (See Chapter 7)

I have a written study schedule [ ] Yes [ ] Not yet or I will create a written study schedule by ___________.

The following are places I can study effectively, without interruption (e.g., office, home, law library) ___________.

People in my inner circle know my study schedule so they know when I cannot be interrupted. [ ] Yes [ ] Not yet

My study schedule includes hours for specific tasks, such as:

- Listening to bar review lectures ____
- Actively reading and studying bar review outlines ____
- Completing all bar review assignments ____
- Creating my own summary outlines (personalized "cheat sheets") ____
- Memorizing the law ____
- Outlining practice questions and reviewing sample answers ____
- Completing practice exams under timed conditions and studying sample and/or explanatory answers ____
- Other ____

Calendaring System

[ ] I calendar all deadlines, commitments, appointments, etc. in my phone laptop, tablet, or planner.

[ ] I have an effective reminder system.

Confidence and Motivation

At this point, my greatest strengths going into bar exam preparation are:

1. ______________________________
2. ______________________________
3. ______________________________

At this point, my biggest challenges going into bar exam preparation are:

1. ______________________________
2. ______________________________
3. ______________________________

Other Bar Planning Issues

Health issues:

I have taken steps to deal with any health issues that might interfere with my ability to do my best on the bar exam. [ ] Yes [ ] No

I received accommodations in law school and expect to receive the same or similar accommodations on the bar exam and have thus completed all the necessary paperwork to apply for such accommodations. [ ] Yes [ ] No

I have had my vision and hearing checked in the past year. [ ] Yes [ ] No

Dependent care:

I have taken steps to arrange for any needed care for children, older or ill relatives, pets, etc. [ ] Yes [ ] No

EARLY START: A GOOD IDEA FOR EVERYONE; ESSENTIAL FOR MANY

If you will be working while studying, start *before* June. If your GPA puts you in the bottom half of your law school class, start early as well.

What to Work on in Early Start?

One of the best places to start is the performance test PT. PT used to stand for performance test; on new exams this will be called a performance task. In this book, we will call both the PT. Nearly all jurisdictions now include a PT, though they differ in length. For example, as of this writing, the NextGen PT will be 60 minutes, the legacy UBE PTs are 90 minutes each, the CA PT is 90 minutes (but used to be 3 hours), and the NV PT is 2 hours. PT preparation strategy is the same regardless of the exam's length. There is more on PTs in Chapter 8 of this book, and I've written a book dedicated to PTs called, Bar Exam PT Success: Strategies and Practice (West Academic), that includes detailed strategies and access to many practice exam opportunities.

A bit more on PTs now, though, as they are a great place to begin early start. PTs test lawyering skills in "real-life" situations. You, the bar applicant, will role-play a lawyer or other legal professional, such as a law clerk or legislator, in a mock situation in which you perform basic tasks within the time allotted. Your written answers must demonstrate proficiency in legal analysis, factual analysis, problem solving, and awareness of professional-responsibility issues. You must also organize information well, manage time efficiently, and communicate with clear, effective writing.

Why start with PTs? PTs are skills-based exams that are essentially "open book." They require little or no memory. The earlier you develop a strong command of PT skills, the more time you will free up for any memory-dependent and/or knowledge-based exam components. Because memory fades, at least some memorization must be done closer to the exam. In contrast, skills that you develop well become part of you. Drafting PT answers is a bit like riding a bike; once you learn how to do it competently, you don't forget. So, invest the time early on to master PT skills, and train extensively by taking at least a dozen practice PTs.

If you think that it feels too time-consuming to take practice PTs before bar review starts, trust me when I say that you will feel much more time pressure in June and July. You alleviate a great deal of summer stress by mastering the PT in early start.

You can also train early by answering practice questions in other testing formats to gain familiarity with and begin getting comfortable with each type of exam question and to begin reviewing and learning rules in context.

Just as important as learning the law is, so too is getting into the *habit* of reading different types of exam questions.

Do not worry in early start about getting a high percentage correct. Just get in a practice test routine. And, always take advantage of learning opportunities by studying explanatory answers after each practice set.

You can obtain practice questions from your jurisdiction's bar exam website, your bar review, or a reliable publisher. Ask your ASP faculty or law librarians if you need suggestions on where to obtain practice tests.

When you take practice tests early on, you can afford to spend more time than what may be allotted on the actual exam. Closer to the exam, you *must* train under timed conditions. At first, though, it often helps to read and reason through them slowly, one at a time, reading each explanatory answer right away to lock in the reasoning and understand why the correct answer is best and the other answers are not.

It will also help to write out any exam formats that require written responses well ahead of June. I know you are thinking, "There's no way I can take exams on subjects I haven't studied in years. I don't remember any law." *Yes, you can.* Just write them open book. Do what you can by issue spotting, organizing, and applying the rules you know closed book; then look up the other rules. Looking up and writing out rules will help you learn and memorize them.

While they are fresh in your mind, be sure to put any rule statements you have looked up and learned into a memorizable form, such as paper or electronic flash cards, outlines, flowcharts, or checklists. Organizing and assembling these sorts of memory tools is another great project for early start; it frees up precious time in June and July.

Get in the habit of drafting written responses in full so that they reflect the length, depth, and organization required for a passing answer. Study sample answers and self-assess your performance. Many jurisdictions' websites list past questions and answers that you can download for free. If you aren't motivated on your own to do early start work, you may want to enroll in an early-start or supplemental program so that you can turn in your answers for review and critique.

Reflection: Early-Start Questionnaire

In addition to practice tests, *thinking and planning* ahead will help prepare you for the two months of intensive review. Below is a list of questions to think about as you look ahead to bar success. Fill them out for yourself, and perhaps share them with a mentor or ASP professor.

If you are working, how much time can you take off before the bar exam, and when?

____

What will your study schedule look like and when will you begin?

____

____

____

What bar review courses are you taking and is it reputable?

Do you have a mentor or supportive person to help you stay on track?

Can you study effectively at your place of work?

Do the people you work with know that you are studying for the bar exam?

Can you study effectively at home?

What are you doing to get rid of distractions so you can focus fully on studying?

Do you have young children? If so, do you have reliable childcare?

What might come up in June and July that you could take care of before intensive bar prep or after the bar exam? (Bar season is not the time to pick fights with a family member or significant other. It is not the time to make major household or family decisions. Ask yourself, what can you do to free up as much time for studying as possible?)

Note: This is a living document. Personalize it to fit your needs and adapt it when you need to so that your onward march to success is as efficient and productive as possible.

Chapter hashtags: #PasstheBar, #EarlyStart, #PlanAhead, #aLatteaDay, #BarExamBusinessPlan, #BarFund, #BarExam Success

CHAPTER 3

THE TRANSITION FROM STUDENT TO PROFESSIONAL

- Hard Work Is Not Glamorous, but It Is the Most Important Part of Success
- Visualize Yourself as a Lawyer
- Find Your Why: Draw upon Your Inspiration
- Ethical Rules and Professionalism
- The Rules
- Fees, Fingerprinting, and Forms
- Professionalism at the Micro Level: Daily Actions Matter
- Communicate Carefully, Respectfully, and in a Timely Manner
- Read Your E-Mails
- Return Calls and E-Mails Promptly
- Be Careful About What You Post on Social Media
- Be Organized
- Meet Deadlines, Be on Time, and Comply with Rules

Some think of the bar exam as a bridge between law school and law practice. I see it more like a mountain. A bridge makes the journey easier. The bar exam is not designed to make your transition easier, but to test whether you have what it takes to survive on the other side. The good news? Once you make the climb successfully, you never have to do it again.

HARD WORK IS NOT GLAMOROUS, BUT IT IS THE MOST IMPORTANT PART OF SUCCESS

Above all, the cornerstone of successful law study, successful law practice, and being a successful professional is and always will be *hard work.* This point is missed by many who fail the bar exam.

Perhaps it is human nature to seek the easy route. Some bar reviews try to make bar studies easier with short lectures, apps, and games. I have nothing against fun in studying or in life. I am all for it. But I remain steadfastly convinced that working slowly, steadily, carefully, and *hard* is essential, especially in law.

Persistence and attention to detail may not be glamorous, but they are required for success. Succeed slowly, and you will go far. Rush, and you will fail or produce slipshod work. There are no shortcuts. On the bar exam, you will have to be "on," and performing at peak levels. This requires slow and steady training.

"The harder I work, the luckier I get."

—SAM GOLDWYN—

In this chapter, we look at how to refocus—how to turn away from the temptations of our instant-gratification society and toward developing the patience necessary to acquire a command of legal knowledge and skills required to pass the bar exam. Patient persistence is a pillar of professional success. (Apparently, I am fond of "P" alliterations.)

I frequently hear complaints from stressed-out students: *"I have to work for* how many *months to get ready for the bar? I should take* how many *practice tests? They really expect me to know all these rules? This is ridiculous. This is so hard!"*

Duh! Of course it's hard. It's law school. You are seeking a license that will enable you to be responsible for people's lives and livelihoods. It should be hard! I suspect that you would not have enrolled in law school if deep down you really wanted things to be easy.

Think about it from another perspective. Let's say you were falsely accused of a crime and needed legal counsel. Would you want a lawyer willing to stay up all night to give you the best defense, or would you want someone looking for shortcuts?

We have come to expect *quick* and easy solutions. We expect to find every answer in a moment's Internet search. We are told that instructional videos should be no more than a few minutes in length. But, the legal analysis you are expected to perform was developed, and many of your professors were trained, in an age when we had to look for hours for the right book and correct passage in that book, not to mention the travel time to and from a law library.

And just because information may be available any time of day or night, at the touch of a finger, does not mean the information is easy to understand. And, even if you read and understand concepts quickly, it takes training to learn to communicate a logical, thorough, reasoned analysis of legal issues to someone else.

Law school and the bar exam, although they require a bank of knowledge, are not about regurgitating facts. They are about *reasoning*. They are about seeing how rules and principles apply to new facts, and *why* a particular outcome should result in each new situation. There is no way you can "learn it all." But you can and must learn a lot, and also take the time and effort necessary to develop your ability to skillfully apply law to facts and reason to logical conclusions.

In the "real world," you will wish that *all* you had to deal with were facts, rules, and logic! People's lives and legal problems are riddled with emotion and passion. You may work with opposing counsel, colleagues, or even decision makers whose concerns are not about following the rules, fairness, or justice, but about revenge, self-promotion, and climbing the ladder. They may exhibit displaced anger. (Picture the person who is angry at the boss but kicks the dog.) Such issues pose far more difficult challenges than law school or the bar exam because they are irrational.

Do not expect the hard work to get faster, to get easier, or to end. Toss aside the microwave mentality and welcome the slow cooker. Your days will be filled with challenge, so make peace with hard work; learn to embrace challenge and delight in victories that come after the sweat and tears.

When in doubt, in bar review and in life, always and at every turn, get back to work. Hard work is not punishment. Seasoned with a bit of luck, hard work is the key ingredient to success. (And, if you believe people stop working hard when they have "made it," listen to Beyonce's words on how many hours she put into the two-hour 2019 film, *Homecoming*.)

And you will be happier if you see it all as worthwhile and rewarding in the end, and realize how fortunate you are to be able to pursue an academic or professional goal.

We will return to working hard at every phase of bar prep and sitting for the exam: creating a bar plan, actively listening to lectures and taking notes, taking many practice tests under timed conditions, studying sample answers, and looking up rules you don't understand.

If you are expecting to find some magic formula, some incantation you can recite to pass the exam, there isn't one. And if someone is trying to sell you a bar review or study course so foolproof that the exam will write itself, don't waste your money.

Do not waste one moment feeling bitter or angry or annoyed that you *have to* study. You *get* to study! It truly is a privilege. Change any perspective you may have to the contrary. Consider the daily work struggles of manual laborers or the far too many people fighting to survive war, hunger, and homelessness. Recognize the gift that it is to be able to spend time studying.

VISUALIZE YOURSELF AS A LAWYER

Practice introducing yourself as a lawyer. I know that may sound silly, but somehow just saying the words underscores how close you are to achieving this goal. Go ahead. Stand in front of a mirror and privately say the following: *"Hello, my name is _________. I am an attorney licensed here in [your jurisdiction]. I'm pleased to meet you."* Repeat it a few times. Get comfortable saying it. Being a lawyer is not just what you are doing, but who you are becoming.

There are many ways to connect with your identity as a future lawyer while in law school including to take clinical courses, join a local bar association as a student member, or even just take an hour out of a morning or afternoon during law school to stop by a local courthouse and walk the corridors. Imagine yourself as one of the "suits" rushing around with your briefcase.

Now, look into your immediate future. Imagine yourself taking another high stakes exam. You may take it in a large room, with clacking keyboards, where the air seems to be equal parts oxygen and nervousness. In-person, proctors will pace the aisles. You will sit next to others who seem slightly crazed. (Or you may be taking it online, all alone except for the remote proctors beaming in to watch your every move.)

When you are told you may begin, you will find fact patterns similar to those you have practiced with. Picture yourself with no anxiety, reading with curiosity! These are puzzles, and you have the knowledge to solve them.

You know what to do. You proceed methodically. You have a plan. You employ the skills you have developed. And you proceed with confidence to reading carefully, writing thorough, logical responses to written questions, and reasoning to the selection of best answers on multiple-choice questions.

Now picture yourself standing before a robed judge raising your right hand and being sworn in as the newest member of the bar in your state.

Now try introducing yourself again as a lawyer. Does it feel more real?

Reflection: See Yourself as a Lawyer

How would you describe yourself as a lawyer? How would you want others to describe you?

____

____

____

If you or a close family member had a legal problem, what qualities would you want in the lawyer you hire to represent you or your family?

____

____

I know if I needed a lawyer, I would want someone thoughtful, who listens and reasons well, and reads carefully-someone who is detail oriented, keeps her or his word, and has earned the respect of colleagues and clients alike. Anything you want to add about how you see yourself as a professional and how you want to be seen by others?

FIND YOUR WHY: DRAW UPON YOUR INSPIRATION

We talked a little about this in an earlier chapter. Have you thought any more about why you chose law school? It may feel like a lifetime ago when you sat down to draft law school admissions essays. What did you write? What were you thinking about? If you entered law school with a passion or dream, what was it?

It will help to keep front and center the reasons that drew you in and propelled you to invest the time and energy, money, and effort to get your J.D., especially on long study days when you are tired and don't feel like working. Remembering the dreams will keep that fire lit!

Take a moment and write out why *you* chose law school? What power will this license give you? Will it enable you to earn a living and support yourself and your family? Will it serve as a tool to effect positive change, help people, and make the world a better place?

I am reminded of another speech, a graduation speech from an alum who passionately described several superheroes and what she admired about them. Some, such as Superman and Spiderman, had impressive magical powers. But she was most inspired by Batman, a guy who achieved amazing things *without* supernatural powers, a distinctly human individual. What makes Batman so strong? His knowledge and his power tools! She spoke of the power of her legal education. She said she wore her law license like a "tool belt," and felt an awesome force each time she rose in court to speak on behalf of clients.

Some go to law school to fulfill a parent or grandparent's dream. If that is you, think about how proud you are making that person. You will forge your own path because you are earning a degree that brings opportunity and flexibility, but your accomplishments will also bring joy to someone you love.

What if you really had no good reasons to go to law school? Let's say it was purely a default choice—you weren't interested in business or medicine, so it seemed like the best option for grad school. Great. You are in good company. But, you still need your *why*. Look around now and find at least one lawyer or legal organization you admire. Consider people who were trained as lawyers and are not practicing lawyers, for example, entrepreneurs, politicians, or people who serve on boards of directors of corporations or nonprofits. Look at lawyers who speak for people who cannot; look at lawyers who solve problems or give advice. Look at a political or historical figure you identify with who is or was a lawyer. Find at least one lawyer with qualities you respect or who has professional opportunities you seek.

Whatever your unique motivation, identifying your purpose for pursuing a law degree will help you get through law school and succeed on the bar exam.

You may scoff at this discussion of dreams. You came to law school to find a job that would pay the bills and repay your student loans. You don't just want to pass the bar exam; you *need* to. Good! Needs are much stronger motivators than "wants." (Look for silver linings in everything.) Needing to pass the bar exam will keep that fire lit. In fact, not *needing* to pass poses a significant challenge to many students, especially those who already have jobs. If you are in the "don't *need* to pass" boat, find a way to *want* to pass so badly that you will do whatever it takes.

YOU MAY NEED THE LICENSE LATER

One of my nontraditional students didn't think he needed to pass the bar exam. He had a steady, well-paying job for years, was getting his J.D. for promotion within the company, and decided to just take the bar exam because all of his classmates were taking it. Midway through bar review, however, he was unexpectedly laid off. Suddenly, he *needed* to pass the bar exam.

He has since gone from working in a small practice to being a partner in a large firm and is licensed in multiple jurisdictions.

Hard work is easier when you hold onto your dreams. It's a bit like tennis; your eyes must focus first on where the ball is coming from and then on where you want it to go with your stroke and follow-through. Here, too, you need to first look briefly back to when you began your studies and why you pursued a legal education, so you can then look confidently toward where you are heading.

ETHICAL RULES AND PROFESSIONALISM

In practice, you will have to follow certain rules. Learning these rules during law school will help in your professional responsibility course, on the MPRE, and then on the bar exam.

In addition to following required rules, you will be well served by developing habits of acting as a conscientious professional and sharpening your organizational skills; these will make bar passage easier and lay the groundwork for a lifetime of success.

The following is an excerpt from the ABA's Comprehensive Guide to Bar Admission Requirements

> *Standard of Character and Fitness. A lawyer should be one whose record of conduct justifies the trust of clients, adversaries, courts, and others with respect to the professional duties owed to them. A record manifesting a significant deficiency in the honesty, trustworthiness, diligence, or reliability of an applicant may constitute a basis for denial of admission.*

As you prepare for the MPRE and to pass professional responsibility portions of bar exam questions, your primary focus will be on rules. This chapter is about seeing yourself as a lawyer. As a lawyer, you must not only protect your character and fitness but build your reputation. Strive to become known not only as smart, but as reliable and hardworking. If you were the hiring partner in a law firm, would you hire someone like you?

In addition to identity, image, and reputation, there are rules—what you must do and what you may not do. And, in terms of ethics, it is no defense to say, "Well, the senior partner told me to do it." If you are signing a document or appearing in court and stating words on the record, or taking actions with respect to client funds, confidentiality, or other matters, you'd better be ready to stand by what you write, say, and do or fail to do.

If your boss asks you to do something you are not comfortable with, refuse. Better to lose a job than to lose your license!

Reflection: MPRE Test Yourself Quiz

Skip this if you have taken and passed the MPRE. If not, this quiz will help get you thinking generally about the MPRE. Note: this is based on information from the NCBE at the time of writing; please verify the most current details on the NCBE's website.

Check which of the following are tested on the MPRE:

___ Admission to the profession

___ Regulation after admission—lawyer discipline

___ Mandatory and permissive reporting of professional misconduct

___ Unauthorized practice of law—by lawyers and nonlawyers

___ Multijurisdictional practice

___ Fee division with a nonlawyer

___ Historical incidents of lawyers committing crimes

___ Law firm and other forms of practice

___ Formation of the client-lawyer relationship

___ Scope, objective, and means of the representation

___ Termination of the client-lawyer relationship

___ Client-lawyer contracts

___ Communications with the client

___ Fees

___ Client confidentiality

___ Conflicts of interest

___ Acquiring an interest in litigation

___ Business transactions with clients

___ Competence necessary to undertake representation

___ Candor to the tribunal

___ Fairness to opposing party and counsel

___ Communications with represented persons

___ Communications with unrepresented persons

___ Establishing and maintaining client trust accounts

___ Advertising and other public communications about legal services

___ Judicial conduct and assisting judicial misconduct

ANSWER: All of the above (and more), with the exception of historical incidents of lawyers committing crimes, will be tested.

Chapter hashtags: #PasstheBar, #FeesFormsFingerprints, #AlmostThere, #PatientPersistence, #HardWork, #DailyActions Matter, #YouMatter, #ProtectYourReputation, #BarExam Success

CHAPTER 4

GET READY FOR SUCCESS: REDUCE DISTRACTIONS, INCREASE YOUR FOCUS, AND MANAGE YOUR TIME

- Time Management for Bar Applicants
- Some Basics of Time Management During Bar Prep
- Align Your Schedule and Body Clock with "Bar Standard Time"
- Engage in Active Learning
- Set up a Calendaring System
- Protect Your Time
- Keep Commitments to Yourself, but Maintain Flexibility Within Your Schedule
- Track Your Time
- Combat E-Distractions
- Time-Management Tips for Law Students Who Are Parents
- Multitasking, Building Endurance, and Increasing Focus
- Strive for Consistency
- Stay Healthy: Reduce Stress, Eat Right, Exercise, and Sleep

During the months of intensive bar review, your primary focus should be on passing the bar. This does not mean you will do nothing but study. It means that everything you do must *move you toward* achieving your goal. For example, you will want to make time to sleep well, exercise regularly, and eat healthy foods as these will prepare your body and mind to perform most effectively. And, you will need some social outlet, some time for family and/or friends.

But time for anything but the bar exam is strictly limited if you are doing what is needed to pass. For two months, your world will essential be "bar exam boot camp." You must be "on"—in mind, body, and spirit. To do this, you will need to ruthlessly protect your time. You must learn to manage distractions and demands that steal your study time.

This chapter will help you assess where your time goes so you can cut back on and eventually eliminate whatever distracts you or does not move you forward. Self-assessment charts and worksheets will help you track your time and maximize efficiency. You will develop strategies to resist what pulls you away from study, and you will learn language to help you say "No" when offers tempt you.

Some of you are working full time or raising families while studying. You need strategies to juggle your competing responsibilities. Many nontraditional law students are also physicians, pilots, accountants, engineers, architects, nurses, or businesspeople who cannot simply set aside the many demands they face. These "distractions" are obligations. One cannot tell a young child who needs to eat, "Not now—I'm studying." One cannot delay a critical medical procedure for an aging parent. You may not be able to put off a transatlantic flight, especially if you are the pilot! But you are still taking the same intensely challenging exam as are other students. You may need to employ different strategies. But much of your battle will be the same and to prepare for that battle, you must carve out and protect as much of your time as possible. (Remember that phrasing and say it out loud, "*I must protect my time.*")

Each student is also unique. You learn and process information in different ways. You may be "on" at different times of the day; what helps you focus may differ greatly from what works for others. To be at your best and most productive, find what works for you. Pave your own path to success.

TIME MANAGEMENT FOR BAR APPLICANTS

Passing the bar exam requires focus and self-discipline. Distractions must be reduced and eventually eliminated. Ease into the high-gear months by tackling time management early.

"In reading the lives of great men, I found that the first victory they won was over themselves . . . self-discipline with all of them came first."

—HARRY S. TRUMAN—

SOME BASICS OF TIME MANAGEMENT DURING BAR PREP

Effectively managing your time during bar prep is similar to time management generally, but the need for efficiency is greater. You don't have a moment to waste. Intensive bar prep is like two months of finals. To fit everything into the most efficient schedule, you must first know how you currently spend your time, then prioritize.

The charts and tips below will help you consider how much time things take and determine the best order in which to accomplish tasks. Pay attention to whether something is better done before or after another task. For example, it may be more productive to listen to the lecture or review the outline before doing a certain practice test. You should also get into the habit of noting the times of day you are most productive so you can schedule things earlier or later accordingly.

Align Your Schedule and Body Clock with "Bar Standard Time"

By the time you sit for the exam, your internal body clock should be on "Bar Standard Time" (BST). In other words, your peak concentration periods should mirror the times you will have to be on for your bar exam. (Those differ in different jurisdictions so study up on the timing of the exam you will sit for.) There are two ways to get into that routine: either make the bar schedule your schedule from the outset, or study when you are most alert (even if that's 2:00 a.m.) and gradually switch to BST by the month before your exam.

Efficiency is greatly assisted when you are honest with yourself about your productivity. Knowing when you are most and least productive will help you schedule tasks effectively. Try to complete active work at times when you are most alert and passive work when you are less revved up. For example, you need to be "on" to do independent tasks such as taking practice tests and analyzing model answers. Doing those when you are dragging is counterproductive. But you may be able to listen to bar review lectures even when you are not quite as alert; they may help keep you awake and engaged. (You can also try things like standing up and stretching while listening to a lecture to wake yourself up when you are fading.)

Engage in Active Learning

I think of active learning as "full engagement in a quest to understand information and master skills." Passive learning, by contrast, is a sponge-like process of letting yourself absorb information. Studies show that the more you interact with material, the more you will retain.

Active learning also saves time because you tend to "get" concepts more readily when you are fully engaged, reducing the time necessary to review. (Ever zone out and find yourself "reading" the same passage several times but not understanding a word? You know what I am talking about. I call this "glazing over." And, it wastes time. You must fight to zone in, not out!)

Bar preparation requires both active and passive learning. Why? You just cannot be "on," in high gear, all day every day, for two months. You need breaks. You also need to make the most of both high- and low-energy cycles by balancing active and passive learning. You may be too tired to effectively continue high-gear work but can push yourself to continue studying for another few hours if you switch to a less-active task. For instance, let's say you have been taking practice tests and studying sample answers, consulting a bar review outline to look up concepts you don't understand, and you are tired. You could take a break or call it a day and go to sleep. You could also switch to lower energy learning and re-type a sample answer from a practice test, close your eyes and listen to (or re-play) a bar review lecture or recording of yourself reading rule statements. All of these more passive tasks can help not only with learning but to "seal in" the phrasings of rules.

To help calendar both active and passive learning, you need to determine what sorts of tasks require full engagement and what you can learn more easily by simply letting in information. Start by completing the exercise below. As you read about different aspects of bar preparation in this book and on your bar review course website, think about which tasks require more energy than others, and use that information to help make your study schedule as effective and efficient as possible.

Self-Assessment: Active/Passive Learning

Categorize the tasks in the list below as "A" Active or "P" Passive in the first column, then rank them in order from 1 to 12, 1 being the least active and 12 being the most active.

Task/Activity	Active/Passive	Rank
Read outlines.	______	____
Study outlines.	______	____
Attend/listen to bar review lectures.	______	____
Complete practice tests and analyze answers.	______	____
Copy model answers to practice tests.	______	____
Make flash cards/charts/ checklists.	______	____
Look up rules you don't understand.	______	____
Make recordings of rule statements.	______	____
Listen to recordings of rule statements.	______	____
Prepare and eat meals.	______	____
Pay bills, do chores, and exercise.	______	____

List at least five additional tasks below and categorize them as active (A) or passive (P).

Task/Activity	Active/Passive
________________	________________
________________	________________
________________	________________
________________	________________
________________	________________
________________	________________

Set up a Calendaring System

The better you are at calendaring, the smoother bar prep (and life!) will likely go.

Protect Your Time

We face endless distractions, from the external onslaught of invasive texts, alerts, e-mails, and phone calls, to the deeply internal distractions of worry and fear. There are worthwhile distractions (those that nourish and recharge your batteries), and distractions that can only be called an extraordinary waste of time.

Become aware of where your time goes. Then, armed with awareness, manage your days and make certain you are on—and stay on—the path to success.

Combat "time thieves" that steal minutes sometimes without us even noticing.

One sneaky time thief is transition time. You may not be aware of how much time gets wasted when you move between tasks. Unconscious spending of time is like unconscious consumption of calories. Minutes like snacks between meals add up.

Another time thief is procrastination. To battle this, return to the lists above of active and passive tasks. When you are too tired to do an active task (take practice tests) or find yourself procrastinating, do something less demanding but that nonetheless needs to be done. (Pay bills. Take walks.) If exercise feels like you are wasting time, listen to recorded lectures or your own voice reading rule statements while you work out and sweat off or the temptation to procrastinate.

Above all, keep commitments to yourself. You are important. And your future is worth every ounce of the time, energy, and money you are investing right now. Don't let anyone tell you otherwise.

Reflection: Time Saving Quiz

You must study and you must do some other chore, for example pay bills. Do you:

A. Start the day paying a bill, then begin worrying about money, look up something on your mobile banking app, start thinking about student loan repayments and job-related issues, only to find you have wasted a full hour?

B. Study first and pay the bill quickly at the end of a productive day, when you are too tired to read or think?

C. Study for a four-hour block; then take a break to have a snack and pay the bill while eating something?

D. Put off paying bills until you incur late fees, then feel down on yourself, and lose time with guilt instead of productive studying?

B or C make sense, and some people are fine doing chores in the morning and moving on to a productive day. But A and D are time traps that you simply cannot afford during bar review. Beware of time traps.

Keep Commitments to Yourself, but Maintain Flexibility

Think of a study commitment to yourself as you would an appointment with an expert physician you have waited months to see. You would not cancel on the doctor unless there were an emergency. Don't cancel on yourself.

But, have a "Plan B" ready to modify your schedule if necessary. Let's say you calendared 7:00 to 8:00 a.m. to work on some practice questions. But you find it's an off day; you are unable to focus. (You catch yourself zoning out, reading the same fact pattern over and over again.) What should you do? First, try forcing yourself to focus. Get up. Stretch. And try again. If that doesn't work, drink some water or splash the water on your face. That may wake you up. But if after these steps you still aren't alert enough to work and learn productively, shift to another less active (but necessary) task and return to the practice questions later.

In other words, stay committed to your schedule, but not rigidly so. Push yourself, but not if it's counterproductive. (If you have put in a good day and are just too tired to focus well, go to sleep.)

If you are working while studying you may be more successful with goals of accomplishing certain tasks over several days, especially if you have an unpredictable work schedule. A Monday one week may be particularly heavy, but later in the week things lighten up. That's fine. Just stay accountable to yourself.

Track Your Time

How do you start reducing distractions and make more time for bar preparation? Begin by identifying what takes up your time. Look at each day for a week. Start when you wake up and end when you go to sleep. Log what you do in fifteen-minute increments if you can, just as you might bill a client. You cannot effectively reduce distractions when you do not know what is distracting you!

Reflection: Daily Time Sheets

Complete the sample chart below to see where your time is going.

Date/Day	Activity	Initiated by	Total time	Necessity/ Distraction	Notes: Eliminate? Defer? Do at a Different Time? Multitask?
Morning					
Afternoon					
Evening					

Reflection: Weekly Time Tracking

Enter the time you spend each week on the following activities/tasks.

Remember, there are only 168 hours in a week!

Hours	**Task**
_____	Work (include the work you do at work and at home for any jobs).
_____	Non-work-related communication (include texting, audio or video calls, and in-person visits with family/friends).
_____	Family/friends commitments, including dinners, parties, celebrations, and helping relatives with errands or tasks for which they depend on you. Only log these once, so if you include these in another category below, leave this one blank.
_____	Commute (to work, to school, and to bar review if attending a live course).
_____	Exercise.
_____	Religious observances, including prayer, services, holidays, weddings, bar mitzvahs, christenings, and the like. Be sure to log time for home observance.
_____	Community, neighborhood, or other volunteer work.
_____	Childcare, care of elderly or other relatives, pet care (including walking the dog).
_____	Sleep.
_____	Meal preparation (include shopping and cooking).
_____	Eating meals (be sure to log the time to actually eat and social time around meals).
_____	Self-care (showering, hair care, dressing) for you and dependents.
_____	Health care (your own, and what you do for young children or others who depend on you).
_____	Personal finance and record keeping (paying the bills, sorting mail, etc.).
_____	Personal recreation and relaxation (TV, movies, social media, and whatever you do to unwind).
_____	Other:
_____	Subtotal:
_____	*Study:*
_____	**Total:**

Reflection: Does your list total more than 168 hours? How much time is allocated for study? Are you actually studying for as much as you think you are? I intentionally listed study last because people tend to inflate the time spent studying, and I want you to see how much time you actually have left for study after everything else on your list. Before intensive bar review begins, re-order this list *with studying first*. Then fit everything else in, after your study time. If you run out of time, borrow it from an area you can better afford to skimp on for two months.

Reflection: Capturing and Saving Time

Above you got a picture of how you spend your time, and a sense of what is productive versus what steals or wastes your time. Here, we'll turn to what specifically you can eliminate, reduce the amount of time spent on, or defer until after the bar exam.

I can eliminate:

____

I can defer until after the bar exam:

____

Of the activities you cannot eliminate or defer, is there anything you can complete in less time or while multitasking? Consider these examples:

- I have to eat, but I can shave off prep time by shopping, cooking, and freezing meals for the week each Sunday evening while listening to bar review lectures.
- I have to walk the dog, but I can use that time to get my own exercise in (and listen to bar review lectures while walking or running).
- I have to pay bills, but that doesn't require the same kind of focus that studying does, so I'll do that *after* I have put in a good day's work, when I'm too tired to study.
- I have to acknowledge the birthdays of family and friends, but I will send them a note that says, "rain check for a birthday celebration in August."

Your turn:

I have to __________, but I can save time by

____

I have to __________, but I can save time by

____

I have to __________, but I can save time by

____

I have to __________, but I can save time by

____

What about things to defer until after July (or February)? Here are some possibilities:

- Take a social media break until after the bar.
- Set up automatic reply messages with "away until August" (or March) on e-mail, voicemail, and so on.
- Stop checking online sites that spread rampant misinformation or panic about the bar exam.
- Stop your own posting, unless it helps you. (One of my former students posted a tip for every practice question she got wrong; these later became her flash cards and thus were helpful.)

Your turn: List at least two things you can spend less time on, two you can eliminate, and two you can defer until after the bar.

I can spend less time on:

____________________ ____________________

____________________ ____________________

____________________ ____________________

I can eliminate:

____________________ ____________________

____________________ ____________________

____________________ ____________________

I can defer until after the bar exam:

____________________ ____________________

____________________ ____________________

____________________ ____________________

Do not interrupt yourself or your study flow for calls, texts, or other messages. It is too easy to say, "It's just one call," or "I would have needed a break anyway sooner or later." No. What will break is your concentration.

Will you be answering texts during the bar exam? No! So don't interrupt yourself now. If you must look at texts and e-mails, create "communication office hours." At those times only, once or twice daily, check your messages. Be vigilant. Do not cut into your study, sleep, or exercise time. Protect your time. Everything other than passing the bar can wait.

IT CAN WAIT

In a movie-theater public-service announcement requesting quiet during the film, actor Billy Crystal asks the audience to silence their cell phones. The theater darkens, the audience munches popcorn, and then everyone turns and stares when Billy Crystal's phone rings. He doesn't realize it is his and complains that the phone's owner should turn it off. When he sees the ringing is actually his own phone, he sheepishly sinks into his chair and panics. Should he answer or not? What if it's his doctor telling him he only has a short while to live? He succumbs to temptation and listens to the message: his dry cleaning is ready! Crystal's expression is priceless as the screen flashes, "It can wait!" When you are studying and you get a call or text, tell yourself, *"It can wait!"*

Combat E-Distractions

Reducing e-distractions is particularly difficult because most of your studying is online. The very same tool you learn from also lures you away. But combat them you must. Unless something provides positive peer pressure or otherwise moves you toward bar success, it is at best a distraction and often blatantly destructive. Why take on other people's anxiety when you have more than enough of your own? Social media is a haven for misinformation. If you must take an online break from bar review (if scrolling has become an addiction), visit reliable sites that you know are helpful. For example, go to the websites of your bar examiners or the NCBE to reread exam logistics rules or see if there are updates, or go to sites recommended by your ASP faculty. Bookmark trustworthy websites.

Self-Assessment: Handy Websites for Reliable Bar-Related Content

Name	Website
1. NCBE	ncbex.org
2. ____________	____________
3. ____________	____________
4. ____________	____________
5. ____________	____________

List five e-distractions. Next to each, think of ways to manage or eliminate the distraction.

E-distraction	Manage or Eliminate By:
1. ____________	____________
2. ____________	____________
3. ____________	____________
4. ____________	____________
5. ____________	____________

Time-Management Tips for Law Students Who Are Parents

If your children are in elementary, middle, or high school, your studying *is* positive role modeling. You are teaching your children discipline and the value of hard work through your actions. (Studies show that role modeling is much more effective than preaching, so don't be surprised if your children do better in school when you are also studying.) So, lose the guilt.

These tips might also help:

- If you have dependent children or aging parents who must be able to reach you in an emergency, give them a special ringtone. Or use the "do not disturb" functions; people you favorite can still reach you in an emergency by phoning twice.
- Keep personal "office hours" (or "study hours") so your family knows when you are studying and not to be interrupted, and when you are available.

- Be sure to include your family (children, significant other, parents) in studying when you can productively do so. For example, at meal breaks you might ask family to test you with flash cards. Just be prepared, your kids may memorize the rules before you do!
- Listen to the audio of bar review lectures while driving, cooking, cleaning, or playing with your kids.
- Bring flash cards (hard copies or on your smartphone) and test yourself if you are at the park or waiting in line at the market.
- If you have young children, read or sing your bar review outlines aloud. Infants and toddlers mostly just want to hear your voice and be close to you. They don't care if you are reading Dr. Seuss, *Goodnight Moon*, or *The Conviser Mini-Review*!
- Plan a fun after-bar trip or activity and let your kids (if age appropriate) decide what that will be.

FIND A QUIET PLACE TO STUDY, EVEN IF IT MEANS A TEMPORARY MOVE

A student recently told me of his significant involvement with a nonprofit organization involved in animal rescues. The work required him to frequently and with no notice drop everything to help homeless and abused animal emergencies. This same student also had family and friends who often stopped by his home unannounced. He decided to move out for June and July so that he could have total focus, without interruptions. Another graduate (recent bar passer) told me that with her family's blessing, she moved out for six weeks prior to the exam, and lived in a summer dorm on a college campus near the location of her bar exam. Another student whose home was too noisy to concentrate "shopped around" in April and May, visiting all local libraries and coffee shops until he found a comfortable place to study. If your home is not quiet and the law library at your law school is not conducive to studying, find a place suitable for you to concentrate. If a university environment will help, check to see if your school or another local university has inexpensive summer housing. Ask if any alumni from your law school might donate space in their office or conference room. Or, see if a local public library, bookstore, or café might provide the atmosphere you need to focus. Find your best "study spots" before intensive bar review begins.

MULTITASKING, BUILDING ENDURANCE, AND INCREASING FOCUS

In order to leverage your time and energy for bar studies, you must know where your time is going. The self-assessments in this chapter help you see where and how you spend your time and learn to strategically manage commitments so that as much as possible, you are in control.

Some people categorically badmouth all multitasking; others praise it blindly as the height of efficiency. I fall in between. Concentrated, singularly focused work is critical, but selected and strategic multitasking can also be productive. For example, you might effectively "capture time" by simultaneously doing things that require your eyes and hands (such as exercising, commuting, or cooking), *while* listening to bar review lectures or audio of yourself reciting your statements. Multitasking is not productive, however, when you are trying to do two or more tasks that require full concentration and not fully focused on any of them. For example, you do *not* want to be checking texts while you are taking practice tests.

We are so used to constant input that we tend not to give intense focus to anything.

Most people try to do so much at once that they don't give themselves an opportunity to ever be truly focused.

To build the physical and mental endurance required for bar success, you must train. The good news? Given the hectic lives of many law students, it may feel like a break to *just* focus on studying. It can be a relief to say "No" to everything else for a few months, to put aside all the stuff you don't want to do or deal with and give total concentration to something you really desire.

Give it a try. Put your phone in the other room when you study. If your mind wanders, force yourself back into the question, into the moment, perhaps by reading aloud.

Practicing meditation and mindfulness can also help improve your focus, calm, and centered concentration skills.

Try to build up to focusing productively in four-hour blocks. If you can be "on" for four-hour stretches, three-hour bar exam testing blocks will seem very doable. (If you are used to lifting ten-pound weights, five-pounders feel easy.)

MULTITASKING AS "CAPTURING TIME"

All or nothing advice with respect to multitasking does not make sense. Be discerning. Multitask where you find that to be productive. For example, (1) Record yourself reading rules from your outlines and listen while you commute, exercise, or meal prep. One of my students purchased waterproof headphones so she could "study" while swimming! (2) Use time with willing family and friends to let them test your rule memorization. (3) Use mealtimes to study with classmates, explaining rules to each other.

"Do a little more each day than you think you possibly can."

—LOWELL THOMAS—

BE SELECTIVE IN THE MATERIALS YOU BUY

Do not buy too many supplemental resources. Too much information will distract you and waste your time. Worse still, some of that material may not be reliable. Studying incorrect law is not only a waste (a neutral), but it will undo progress you have made (a severe negative—a time thief and an underminer.) If you get caught up in contradictory sources, you may find yourself more confused than ever and having to start over. No time for that! Enroll in a reputable bar review and trust their materials. Remember, too, that rule statements are often phrased differently while still conveying the same elements or factors. Learn the underlying concepts and learn buzz words for common phrasing of legal terms.

Strive for Consistency

Whatever time you give each day to study, keep your schedule as consistent as possible.

Bar prep is a temporary but full-time gig, even if you are working while studying. A student e-mailed me two weeks into bar review, saying how shocked she was that the study schedule mapped out activities for seven days a week. She thought it would be a five-days-a-week schedule, with time to "catch up on the weekends." No.

I don't care how smart you are—if you don't put in the time, you will regret it.

Stay Healthy: Reduce Stress, Eat Right, Exercise, and Sleep

These are all interconnected; the more you eat right, exercise, and sleep, the less stressed you will be.

Your brain cannot function at peak performance without sleep to replenish your energy.

You need to exercise. The more fit you are, the better you will be able to concentrate. Physical activity also helps to both relieve stress and improve sleep.

Sleep and exercise help, but it is still normal to feel tired. People often underestimate the physical demands of intellectual work. A judge once told me how surprised she was when first appointed to the bench that she felt so tired after hearings. After all, she was just "sitting" on the bench. She soon realized that it was the focused listening and critical analysis that made her so tired. I recall that wisdom every time I feel tired after writing, or teaching, or attending a conference. So, if you are studying with sufficient intensity, you too should be exhausted.

You may feel like people do not *get* how much work this is and how much pressure you face. They don't. Don't expect them to understand unless they themselves are lawyers.

Another reason for fatigue during bar review is sleeping difficulties. Anxiety may rob you of a good night's sleep, and then create a vicious cycle where you become even more anxious and less productive because you are sleepy. This too is normal. Many bar applicants find it hard to fall asleep because they are so wound up. Others wake frequently in the middle of the night with nightmares about fact patterns. But sleep you must! So, try to find ways to combat insomnia and find ways to relax enough to sleep well before the exam.

Some students find it helpful to read a novel before bed; reading about another world takes them far enough away from the law to relax. (Studies indicate that reading on a screen before bed may deter sleep, so try reading a paperback or hardback book.) Others find that a hot bath, hot milk, or a cup of herbal tea does the trick. Learn what works to get you to fall asleep and stay asleep. (One former student shared that the only way to take his mind off law and fall asleep each night was to read histories of naval battles. He would think about how and where to move the ships and other military strategy issues and would relax enough to forget about his bar studies. Crazy but true!)

If all else fails, just get up and study if you can't sleep. Keep the Wadsworth quote below in mind. You are toiling. And your hard work will pay off.

"The heights by great men reached and kept were not obtained by sudden flight, but they, while their companions slept were toiling upward in the night."

—HENRY WADSWORTH LONGFELLOW—

CHAPTER TAKEAWAYS: TOP TEN TIPS

1. "Believe you can PASS!"

You set your goal and stick with it even if you are tempted to slip into negative thinking. Reframe your thoughts using a growth mindset.

Read Part II of this book if you think you can always take it again. To paraphrase *Apollo 13*, "failure is not an option."

2. Secure "buy-in" from family and significant others.

Help those in your support network to understand what you need while studying. Plan something fun to celebrate and thank them when the exam is done. (Later chapters includes advice on how to deal with people who are not supportive.)

3. Start early!

When you cannot study as many hours in the day as other students can, you must start earlier. Eight weeks might be sufficient for full-time students who average sixty hours per week of studying. But if you are working a demanding job or have extensive family commitments, start early and begin your bar studies during your final year of law school.

4. Identify your most productive hours each day.

Determine when you study most productively and dedicate those hours exclusively to bar prep. Post your study schedule so that anyone who wants some of your time knows when you may not be interrupted. You cannot afford to waste time.

5. Stay organized, disciplined, and committed to success.

Get systems in place to handle whatever must be done while you are studying. Put off everything that can wait until after the exam.

6. Don't skimp on sleep, exercise, or motivating study breaks.

The bar exam is both a physical and mental challenge; and it is a marathon not a sprint.

7. Protect your time. Protect your workspace.

Your study hours are precious. Do you hand over the keys to your home without very good reason to do so? Don't hand away your key to success: your time!

Another thing that boosts their concentration and productivity is a clear workspace. If you have an office or desk that is all yours, keep it that way. Do not share your computer with anyone during bar prep. Don't open any attachments unless you are certain of their origin; keep your spyware and antivirus protections up to date. The last thing you need is a virus on your computer in the weeks before the bar exam.

If you study in a coffee shop or library, don't leave your laptop unattended. I hear stories every administration about students losing or having laptops stolen just before the exam. Control what is in your control.

8. Reduce distractions.

Don't get sucked into anything unless it helps you study, sleep, or recharge your batteries. Don't let your family guilt you into a trip or participating in an event. This is not the time to buy or sell a house, figure out relationship issues, stop smoking, or go on a diet. (Each example above is from actual students who were unnecessarily derailed during bar review.)

It is not productive to worry about anything other than the exam during bar prep. Easier said than done, so here are two options if you cannot get rid of the worry entirely: (1) worry like crazy for one day in May (or December), then put the worries in a box, compartmentalize, and tell yourself you will open that box in August. (2) Designate one hour per week as "worry hour." At the appointed time, you can rant, cry, scream, complain, or write a nasty letter (that you will never send) listing everything that is bugging you, bar-related or otherwise. When your worry hour is over, put your concerns away for the week and get back to work.

Try as hard as possible not to allow any stressing over how much material there is to learn. Working will get you much further than worrying.

9. Set realistic expectations.

Do not rush yourself through outlines, lectures, or practice tests. It is better to learn what you're spending time on than to hastily skim the material and not really absorb it.

10. Use every minute effectively.

Study when you study. Don't fall into the trap of feeling guilty that you are not studying when you are with family, and feeling guilty that you are not with family when you are studying. All that gets you is a lot of guilt. Be in the moment.

Chapter hashtags: #PasstheBar, #ProtectMyTime, #Strategic MultiTasking, #ItCanWait, #BeYourBest, #FindYourStudySpot, #KickOutDoubt, #InTheZone, #BarExamSuccess

CHAPTER 5

GET AND USE QUALITY EXPERT HELP: RELIABLE BAR REVIEW COURSES, ASP FACULTY, AND TRUSTED MENTORS

- Invest in Yourself
- The Need for and Benefits of Bar Review
- Beyond Bar Review
- Get the Most out of Your Bar Review
- Be Present and Engaged
- Concentrate
- Personalize Your Bar Review Materials
- Make Sure You Understand What You Hear and Read
- Book-Ending Bar Review Lectures
- Bar Review Outlines
- Finding a Mentor
- Mentor Credibility

This book is about achieving. It is not about pipe dreams. Nowhere am I saying, "Just be confident, and you will pass."

Bar review is like a gym membership. You must do more than simply sign up and pay the fee. If that is all you do, you will lose time *and* money and not pass the bar (or get fit).

To succeed, you must fully engage. For bar review, that means sticking to the schedule, listening carefully to (and hearing *and making sure you understand*) the lectures, and completing and turning in all assignments. You must take many practice tests and study reliable sample or model answers.

(*Sample answers* are student answers that are passing, but not perfect. *Model answers* are those written by bar reviews or bar support faculty and designed as teaching tools.) And, you must then integrate your learning from lectures *and* practice exams into context in your outline and in your mind. (Remember, you will go into the exam without any notes or outlines.)

Some goals are easier to achieve with the help of experts. Bar passage is one of those. You must learn, memorize, and be able to clearly articulate many rules and concepts. You must master numerous skills, including critical reading, factual and legal analysis, clear and effective writing, and time management. It helps enormously to train with and learn from a team of experts who know what they are talking about. Conversely, it is an act of sabotage to solicit (and often pay dearly for) misinformation. Going it alone or with unreliable tutor or review course versus working with a trustworthy bar review nearly always means the difference between succeeding or not.

Beware. If anyone promises you a foolproof, quick, or easy system to pass the bar exam, walk away. Quality bar review instructors, like personal trainers, do *not* make it easy. They keep you on track. Reliable experts will tell you there are no shortcuts. Studying for the bar just is hard work.

A good teacher can clarify confusion and simplify complex concepts. You may have been lucky enough to have had professors in law school who were able to do that, and if not, you will in bar review. But even with a clear understanding of the rules, bar preparation is still challenging. The sheer volume of material, the simultaneous testing of multiple subjects in different formats, and marathon nature of the exam is what makes it so difficult.

Most of us do not have instant-recall brains; there is no *search* button in our memory that readily delivers every answer. Most of us succeed because we work really hard. And those who fail often do so because they are not engaged fully in disciplined preparation. So, again, do not fall for any course or tutor who sounds too good to be true. There are many scams in bar review; too many prey on the doubts and fears of first-time takers and even more take advantage of the vulnerabilities of repeat takers.

INVEST IN YOURSELF

Keeping the above-noted caveats in mind, a reliable bar review is a must. You might have made it through law school without supplemental materials or tutoring. This is different. Those who take and complete most of the work in reliable bar review courses succeed in much greater numbers than those who study on their own.

If you think you cannot afford a bar review course, think again. You cannot afford *not* to take one.

- Start a bar fund now, as you are reading this book. Save whatever you can put aside.
- Talk with your school's financial aid office to determine what sources you can draw on so that you have sufficient funds to not have to work while studying for the bar.
- If you need one, find out how to obtain a bar loan. Such loans are available but often with high interest rates and strict qualification restrictions, so check them out carefully. You may also reach out to family to lend you money or a local bar association that may also have a bar scholarship.
- Consider earning a free course by serving as a bar review representative.

However much it may appear that you can't add another dime of debt to that mounting pile, you must continue investing in yourself for this last stretch of your legal education. Would you spend time in Chicago in winter without a warm coat, scarf, and boots? Would you go mountain climbing without proper training and sturdy ropes? Of course not. So don't take the bar exam without a reliable bar review. Just don't. Don't sabotage yourself before you start by being pennywise and pound foolish; spare yourself the far-greater costs of repeating the exam.

MONEY HELPS, BUT THE GRASS IS NOT ALWAYS GREENER . . .

It may taste like a bitter pill to watch wealthier classmates have what seems like an easy time financially, especially if you are struggling to budget every dime. But energy spent on resentment generally does not yield productive dividends. Try to focus on these points instead:

(1) you are you, and you are in the position you are in. Resenting someone else will not change your position;

(2) what you must work harder for, you likely will appreciate more; and

(3) you don't know the full "price" someone is really paying for whatever funds that they have been given. There may be strings attached that you would never want.

So, focus all your energy on passing the exam. Let everything else go.

THE BENEFITS OF BAR REVIEW

You need a *reliable* bar review to stay on track and to confidently trust the process. Especially toward the end of June, you may start dragging. You may get some low scores on practice tests and, with the exam a month away, you may question your preparation.

You want to avoid time spent doubting yourself or your course and continue to focus on increasing your knowledge and improving your skills. So, what will a bar review offer? Among other things, a reliable bar review will:

- Provide lectures that review each of the subjects tested on your bar exam.
- Provide outlines that summarize the relevant law for each tested subject.
- Provide skills training for different testing formats.
- Flag heavily tested areas.
- Highlight areas that differ or rules that conflict in those jurisdictions where you are expected to know both state and federal rules.
- Provide practice questions and quality answers to those questions.

- Provide practice test grading. (Note: The most productive time to learn from taking a practice exam is just after completing it, so even if your bar review offers unlimited grading, study the sample answers and complete your own self-assessment right after you finish it. I will give you details on how to self-assess your practice exams in later chapters.)
- Answer your questions if you don't understand a rule or concept after trying to figure it out on your own. (Remember, the bar review instructors are not taking your bar, you are. *You* need to know the rules and be able to apply them. So, try hard to figure things out on your own before jumping to ask questions.)
- Provide a structured study schedule.

Bar review also helps identify what you do and do not need to know. The bar exam tests an enormous amount of material. In an ideal world, we would say to master everything before you go in. But (a) the world is not ideal, and (b) that would be a waste of your time, energy, and brain "disk space." A reputable bar review will flag what is generally heavily tested and what areas have historically never or rarely been tested. That doesn't mean that a never-before-tested area cannot suddenly appear on your exam, but history repeats itself and so do bar examiners. One of the most helpful parts of being enrolled in a reputable bar review is getting sound advice on what should be covered only superficially, and what you should know in depth.

You may want or need to supplement your bar review, but you should not cut corners. Bar review is a floor, not a ceiling. In other words, you can (and often should) do more than your bar review recommends. But, without very good reasons, do not do less.

I must include a metacognition (learning how one learns) caveat here: Bar review is not "one size fits all." Courses are designed to help the majority of students. You may have to add or modify certain tasks so that you become as skilled and knowledgeable as possible.

Note: sometimes you simply cannot do all the work, or you know that certain assignments are just not helpful *to you.* Use your best judgment to tailor some aspects of your bar review to meet your needs. You are the one taking the exam. No one else. If you are not learning from a particular certain assignment, switch it up. And, if you need advice or help doing this, talk with your ASP faculty or bar mentor. All this said, it may not be clear that a task is helping. Bar review is a process. And, the data is clear; those who *thoroughly* complete most of the work in a reputable bar review course pass in much higher numbers than those who do not.

BAR REVIEW IS NOT A MAGIC PILL

Many bar applicants pay for bar review and then expect the knowledge will magically enter their brains, kind of like sleeping with textbooks under your pillow. There are no quick fixes. As we said above, joining a gym will not get you fit. Buying a bar review course will not make you pass the exam. You must do the work, the learning, the thinking, and the heavy lifting of practice tests.

We talked about the importance of selecting a reliable bar review. It is also important to select a bar review that works for you, not just one your friends sign up for. There may be a few trustworthy choices. Be an active consumer. As you learn about your options, list pros and cons, who recommended it, your own impressions, and ask the company any questions you have.

Bar Review Selection Worksheet

Available Full-Service Bar Reviews

Name/ Contact Info	Pros	Cons	Recommended By	My Impression	Questions

Available Supplemental Bar Reviews

Name/ Contact Info	Pros	Cons	Recommended By	My Impression	Questions

Active Study

Most bar prep is done independently. It can be isolating. If you find that it's too much solitude, coordinate with classmates to sit together to watch video lectures. (You all may have your own earbuds in, listening alone but together.) Or, plan to complete practice tests together.

Whether you are working entirely alone or partly with classmates, you cannot just *watch* bar review lecture videos and expect to pass the exam. That's sort of like going to a lecture on tennis and expecting to compete at Wimbledon. You must study actively and complete practice exams, learn and memorize rules (testing yourself to see what you recall and looking up what you do not understand), then retest yourself to make sure all the information has sunk in. Testing yourself in this way also increases your familiarity with each testing format.

Even after listening to the best bar review lecturer, there may still be rules or concepts you do not understand. Do the work to figure them out, especially if they fall within areas identified as heavily tested. Start by reviewing the bar review outline or your lecture notes. Read examples out loud. Find a practice question that tests the concept and study the question and explanatory answer. Try to explain the concept in your own words. If you still don't understand it, perhaps someone at your bar review or law school can clarify your question. Or, you may consult another resource, such as a hornbook. That said, be strategic. You don't need to know every nuance of every rule to pass the bar exam. If it is an obscure rule, let it go. But if it's a critical area that you just don't get, find a way to understand.

A word about what I just said—that you *might,* when you find it necessary, consult another resource. Generally, it is *not* recommended to go back into your law school class notes during bar prep. Law classes often have a different emphasis and different objectives from bar review. However, if you happened to have a professor who explained an area of law in a way that makes more sense to you than the bar review lecturer, it can be helpful. (I was fortunate enough to have had as one of my law professors the late Jesse Dukeminier, one of the nation's foremost property experts and an extraordinary teacher. I consistently turned back to his materials on property because they made more sense to me than other rule explanations.)

Another empowering point: sometimes if you just hear or read a different explanation from a different source, a concept that was previously mystifying suddenly becomes clear. It can help to realize that your confusion may not be exclusively about *you*. But, please, wrestle with material a little harder before going to another resource. There just isn't time to wander during bar review.

CAVEAT: DON'T BE TOO QUICK TO CONSULT ANYTHING BEYOND BAR REVIEW MATERIALS

During intensive bar prep, consult outside sources *only* with respect to major concepts that you don't understand after trying hard to understand the bar review materials. Do not go to outside sources just because the review course phrases a rule differently from how you learned it. *In other words, don't spend precious study time second-guessing your bar review*. Enroll in a reliable course and trust it. Different sources often state rules slightly differently. Bar review may vary from how you learned rules in law school. That does not mean your bar review *or* your professor was wrong. As long as the fundamentals are the same and as long as you understand the concepts, your time is best spent continuing to review additional rules and concepts, and taking additional practice tests. Do not waste time drilling down to catch minor disparities.

Get the Most Out of Your Bar Review

One size does not fit all, not in shoes nor in bar preparation. Your bar review course is the principal component of your schedule. Make your bar review experience as effective as possible:

(a) be present and engaged,

(b) personalize the materials (e.g. type notes or draw pictures in the margins that help you),

(c) make sure you understand what you are doing and learning, and

(d) follow the schedule and do the work.

Be Present and Engaged

You can enroll in bar review, pay the money, log in and sit in front of your laptop—physically present but mentally miles away. But do not tell yourself you are paying attention if you are constantly checking your phone or social media. Fooling yourself makes you the fool. The people whose texts you are reading will not pay the price if you fail the bar. You will.

Think of it this way: "The buck stops here." At the end of the day, you and you alone walk into that exam. You are responsible for and accountable to yourself. When you sit for the exam, you want to know that you have done your best. Similarly, as an attorney, it will be on you if you show up unprepared to represent a client. It is your responsibility. There is no one else to point to or blame.

Concentrate

To develop concentration, start by observing your level of focus. If you find yourself drifting off or zoning out while reading, try to sit up and read the words aloud, in a barely audible mutter (a technique called subvocalization), as you look at and touch the words on the page or the screen. This is reading with multiple senses. If you need to, increase your screen to 200% and touch words on the screen as you read them. This will ensure that you don't miss words. Especially when taking practice tests, you will see that even one missed word can change a question or answer entirely.

If you continue to lose focus, stand and stretch and sit back down. Still not alert enough to concentrate? Go to the bathroom and splash water on your face. Yes, stopping to try to wake yourself up wastes time, but not nearly as much time as will be lost if you are not learning from the time you are putting in.

A bar exam bathroom-related tip now, in case I forget to tell you later: If you need to use the bathroom during the actual bar exam, read a question first so you can work on the analysis in your head on your way to and from the restroom.

Because time is so valuable during intensive bar prep, it is counterproductive to spend even a minute "reading" material from which you do not learn. This is not reading like a lawyer;

it's just *glossing over* the words. One of my former students who later became a supportive alumni bar mentor, calls this "hanging out with the outlines."

If you can't focus on reading switch to an active task, for example, take a practice test (open book if needed, looking up rules you don't know as you write your answers). Learning rules in the context of fact patterns helps you remember them.

Remember on the bar exam you will have to focus for an extended block of time without breaks. Effective bar preparation includes preparing yourself to be ready to perform under these timed test conditions. A trap we sometimes fall in is taking breaks we tell ourselves are *necessary*. When weaning yourself off social media and texting, for example, you may suddenly "need" more bathroom and coffee breaks. Sometimes those are genuine necessities, but other times they are ways of procrastinating. You may be subconsciously avoiding facing up to what you do not understand by passively playing lectures you are not really carefully listening to rather than digging in to practice tests.

It is easy to go through the content superficially. It is far more difficult to really understand and learn the key rules in every subject, and consistently work to improve your test-taking skills. But it is deep learning and hard work that gets you to your goal. And, mastering the ability to be fully and actively engaged will serve you well for the rest of your life.

During bar prep using focused, active learning:

- you will learn a greater quantity of material, more effectively and efficiently;
- you will be attentive to detail, something required on the bar and in law practice, and rather helpful in much of life;
- you will get ready for exam days, including learning to do without your phone and other devices; and
- you will have a much better shot at completing all the questions within the allotted time, something that is hard to do when you haven't built up your endurance and can't concentrate for long, uninterrupted time blocks.

Of course, I know you will not have your phone with you in the exam, but unless you go through phone withdrawals and train to really focus before the exam, you will still find ways to drift off during the test. You'll look at the person next to you, watch the proctors, listen to keyboards clacking, or clean your fingernails. You may find you have read the same paragraph several times before you even realize your mind was wandering. The price is simply too high to "check out." Do everything you can now to train your stamina and ability to concentrate deeply.

Personalize Bar Review Materials

One great way to be present and get the most out of your review course is to take good notes that are personal to you. You can also:

- Type in the margins of e-outlines.
- Draw diagrams and pictures in the margins of print outlines. For example, in learning areas of real property such as easements, visuals can be super useful.
- Create hypotheticals or write down examples that illustrate a rule in a way that makes sense to you.
- Translate formal rule statements into colloquial, short phrases. For example, you might call *inadequacy of the legal remedy*, a required element for certain equitable remedies, as the "money won't cut it" element.
- Talk yourself through concepts. Continuing on the remedies theme, you might say to yourself, "Yeah, well, to get a court to order specific performance of a contract, the court must be persuaded that money just won't cut it for this plaintiff; dollars just aren't going to fly; it just doesn't give the plaintiff what he bargained for." Note: you would *never* write *that* on an exam. You might write something such as, "The legal remedy must be found to be inadequate. Here the plaintiff wanted to buy Blackacre, and because Blackacre is a unique parcel of land, money damages will not suffice to fully compensate the

plaintiff for the loss of Blackacre." But, writing plain-English versions (translations) of legal concepts in the margins or in your notes may make the meaning of rules clearer for you and may help you remember the concepts on exams.

I also suggest making your own flash cards rather than or in addition to buying them. You can also personalize printed or electronic flash cards. When making your own or personalizing commercial cards, write the official legal term on the front. On the back, write *both* a succinct and proper phrasing of the rule (one you might write in an essay or short answer question), and write a plain-English phrasing of the rule *that make sense to you*. If it helps, add a mnemonic or picture (or something you find funny) beneath the simple phrasing.

Reflection: Personalized Flash Cards

The front of the card says, "*The law that governs contract disputes.*" Note what you would write on the back of the card in the space below.

Hopefully you wrote something such as: "Contract disputes may be governed by different bodies of law depending on the nature of the dispute. Where the dispute regards movable goods, the governing law is typically the Uniform Commercial Code (UCC), whereas disputes about land or services are typically governed by the common law."

Now, take a moment to write something in your own words that will help you remember how to *apply* this on a bar exam question.

Perhaps you wrote something like: Start contracts analyses with which law applies: UCC or common law. UCC—transactions in goods—moveable things like refrigerators or "widgets." Common law—basically land (Blackacre) or services (doing something). UCC may be influential even when not controlling.

Next, note any "tips" you want to remember about which law governs in contracts questions:

____

____

____

You might have written something like:

Remember tricky fact pattern where "growing crops" were considered land, but when harvested or severed from the land, they became goods. Also, when you get a mixed UCC and common law contracts, ask (1) can I divide into two contracts? (2) If not, which predominates, goods or services? Remember the practice question with guy building a fence; he supplied wood (goods), and with that wood, built a fence (services) or the photographer where the pictures were goods but taking them was a service.

Personalizing your flash cards (or writing notes in the margins of your outlines) will help you master simple and complex points alike and prepare you to apply your learning to practice tests. Try to personalize cards or notes for every concept your bar review flags as important. Also, create a flashcard every time you get a practice question wrong because you did not know or understand a rule.

Make sure your notes make sense to you. Let's try another contracts example. What is consideration?

Formal definition:

____

____

____

Define in your own words:

____

____

____

ANNOTATING

One of my favorite law professors told our first-year class to write in our casebooks. He suggested we not only take notes in the margins, but also write our own opinions and reactions to the decisions. ("*What was this judge thinking?!*") Why did he advise this? Someday we would find the notes fascinating, he said, and the books would be valuable if we ever became famous. (He mentioned a former US Supreme Court Justice's schoolbooks had just fetched a large sum of money.) Looking back, I suspect his real motive was simply to keep us actively engaged in the material. It worked.

I have looked back on this advice over the years many times and talked with students about it for this reason. On law exams, graders do not care what your opinion is. It's what the facts state that matters, or for bar exams, whether the facts prove or disprove rules of law. But we all care about our own opinions! And, it's hard to be fully engaged in the study of law and not occasionally feel like a rule is or is not just. If you have a burning emotion that rises up as you are studying, create a place in your notes for this. It won't be something you use on exams but it will get the thought out of your system—and may even help you remember the rule. (*Oh yeah, that rule I think is totally unfair and might try to change some day.*)

Make Sure You Understand What You Hear and Read

This is a basic premise. But how often do we stop and look up legal terms or rules? Too often we just move on and hope we will "get it" from context clues. That *may* work for leisure reading, but it does not work for law.

We must know rules well enough to recite them and use them. And to fully understand rules, we must understand the nuance of the terminology used in those rules or used to explain those rules.

You need to know rules when you see them for multiple-choice questions. And, on essays or show answers, you often have to *state* rules, rapidly and accurately. Having a command of relevant legal terms is critical. (This is what I call being fluent in Legalese.)

Bottom line: All the stockpiles of knowledge in your head won't do any good if you cannot deliver and/or apply that information effectively. I have counseled countless graduates who passed the multiple-choice portion and failed the written portion of the bar, or vice versa. Each testing format on your bar exam may require different skills.

So again, by exam time at the latest, be sure you are fully fluent in legalese. Yet another reason to start early!

Bookend Bar Review Lectures

Bar review includes lectures during which professors summarize the most important legal concepts and rules tested on your bar exam. You can improve your understanding by "book-ending" the lectures with your own independent work. What do I mean? Before the lecture, read through the outline's table of contents looking up any terms you can't readily define. Knowing the terminology will help you to follow lectures more easily. This pre-lecture work will "prime" you to get the most out of each lecture.

During bar review lectures, listen as carefully as possible. Don't try to write down every word; this may actually prevent you from *hearing* the professor. Make shorthand notes about points to look up later or to highlight particularly good examples. You may want to star or flag concepts the lecturer says are frequently tested. Remember, you will have an outline to look up what you don't understand. You do not need to be a court reporter and log every word. You need to "lean forward and listen." (See story below.)

After the lecture, while the material is still fresh, annotate your outline with your lecture notes, examples, charts, lists, and tips on what the professor said is or is not frequently tested. This will help seal in what you learned. Make your own or annotate commercial flash cards for every major rule, looking up rules or concepts you didn't understand during the lecture in your outline. (When I studied for the bar exam, I set aside time after each lecture to do just this. Often just an extra half hour of looking up or re-writing certain points, thinking a bit more about some of the most important concepts, made the learning from that lecture much more useful.)

LEAN FORWARD AND LISTEN

I once attended an outdoor theater production of George Bernard Shaw's *Heartbreak House*. There were no microphones to amplify the actors' voices; but even if the voices were louder, there were words and thoughts that required effort to understand. After the performance, I spoke with one of the actors who asked how the sound was in the back row. He then said, "No matter what seat you are in, you have to sort of lean forward and listen to really get what we're saying." I loved the way he put it. You have to lean forward and listen to get this bar stuff.

LEARN HOW YOU LEARN, AND HOW TO TAKE EFFECTIVE NOTES

Throughout this book, we have talked about metacognition—learning about learning. Some people need to take notes to pay attention. For others, the opposite is true: they can't really focus and absorb concepts while taking notes. Most of what was said in a lecture will probably also be in the outline, so you can look up terms and flesh out your notes after the lecture.

Experiment to see whether taking notes by hand or typing them on your laptop or phone helps you learn best. Don't feel peer-pressured into studying or taking notes in ways that are good for others. Get to know yourself and how note-taking during lectures helps or hinders your learning.

A colleague once shared a story about knitting while listening to bar review lectures. She later recalled rules by thinking about the color scarf she was knitting at the time of each different lecture. (I believe at the time she was told, "No serious law student could knit and listen at the same time." She showed them!)

Bar Review Outlines

Bar review outlines are essentially mini-hornbooks or summary treatises. A good outline will not only summarize the area of law but provide clear and easy-to-memorize rule statements, explain the logic and reasoning behind those rules, and provide examples showing how they have been tested in fact patterns. An outline may also indicate the frequency with which certain areas have appeared on previous exams in your jurisdiction. To help make outlines work for you, you will want to do the following:

- Annotate them with examples and phrasings *that make sense* to you. (These can come from a bar review lecturer, a law school professor, or an answer to a practice test.) Write in the margins or type into the text file.
- Chart key areas with flowcharts.
- Create mnemonics or abbreviations to memorize lists of elements. Some people think of the basics of a contract cause of action as FPBD (formation, performance, breach, damages). Some people remember mnemonics with the help of another catchy phrase. For example, DBCD stands for the elements of negligence: duty, breach, causation, damages. You may recall DBCD by remembering the phrase, "delicious brownies, cake, and donuts." (Or, if for sugar opponents, "desserts bring calories and diabetes.")
- Condense outlines to usable size as you get closer to exam time. Most bar review outlines are long—often hundreds of pages. You will want to reduce them to a more user-friendly form. Often it helps to work in stages, first reducing the subject to ten to thirty pages, and then, by the week before your bar exam, to one to three pages. Remember: you can only use what is in your brain on the actual exam! So be sure you are using the outlines as learning tools, and that the most critical information gets *and stays* in your head.

Bottom line: Outlines are only as useful as you make them. So, begin bar review doing the assigned reading in the major outlines. Use them as companions to the lectures, helping you learn the frequently tested rules and concepts. As you get closer to test time, you will likely only consult large outlines when you need to look something up. You will shift your focus to using your own shortened summary outlines or "attack plans" along with continuing to take practice tests.

Eventually, by the week before the bar exam at the latest, condense each subject into one page. On that page, write summary approaches, checklists, a shorthand outline, or whatever would help you answer an essay question on that subject. If you need an idea of what to include, think: *What would help me during the actual exam?*

The most important part of learning is understanding the material. You can create beautiful charts and clever mnemonics, but if you don't *understand* the concepts, you probably won't be able to apply them correctly. Recalling the phrasing of a rule and making sense of it are two different things. Can you explain a concept to someone who is not a lawyer?

If so, you probably understand at least the basics fairly well.

Reflection: Quick Rule Memorization Test

Explain felony murder to a very smart 16-year-old. (I use the fictitious "very smart 16-year-old" standard to determine if you are able to explain heavily tested concepts in terms that non-lawyers can understand.)

UNDERSTAND WHAT YOU MEMORIZE

Students often memorize the elements of injunctive relief as IPFBD (inadequacy of the legal remedy, property right, feasibility, balancing of equities, and defenses). You must know what those terms mean, though, rather than merely memorizing them. Student sometimes mistakenly assume *feasibility* refers to whether it is feasible for the *parties* to carry out the order, rather than the accurate meaning, which is whether it is feasible for the *court* to supervise implementation of the order. Do you recall discussions in remedies about whether it would be easier for a court to supervise the tearing down of a second-story house or the building of a new one-story home? This would have been a discussion regarding the element of feasibility.

FINDING A MENTOR

Dictionary definition of mentor: *a trusted friend, counselor or teacher, usually a more experienced person who advises and serves as by example.*

I suggest mentors for at least two purposes: a bar mentor (some call them *bar coach*) discussed below and a career mentor described later in the book. Mentors are important for everyone, especially first-gen law students. A bar mentor can:

- serve as proof that the exam is passable (you want to look at your mentor, feel encouraged that he or she passed, and believe unequivocally that you can, too!);
- review your study plan or study schedule, remind you of things you may have forgotten, and give you tips (perhaps something simple like reserving your hotel room for an extra night so you don't have to worry about packing up or checking out as you head into your last day of the exam);
- check in with you weekly in June and July (or January and February) to see that you are staying on your study schedule (this is sort of the "mentor as coach or trainer" function);
- give you moral support to stay focused and not be bothered by those who don't understand when you say no to social invitations and hibernate to study;
- help you think through adjusting your study plan or schedule if something is not working for you;
- encourage and reassure you if you feel guilty or irresponsible when you need extra money for bar studies, reminding you that it is smart not to skimp in your preparation if you want to pass the bar the first time; and
- be a friendly face who "gets it," someone who just pats you on the back and says, "Stick with this. You can do it!"

Mentor Credibility

An effective bar mentor must know and appreciate what *you* are going through. They do not have to have had the same experience.

Your family and friends, even if supportive, are *not* great as bar mentors unless they themselves took and passed the bar exam. A supportive professor can be a fine mentor, as can a lawyer in the community, but best may be an alum from your law school who recently passed the bar.

Do not rely on your bar mentor to help you learn the law. Do that work with your bar review and independently, and with your school's ASP faculty or bar support program. Your mentor is a coach not a tutor.

You are training for the "Bar Exam Olympics." Each form of testing is one of your competition events. A mentor can help hold you accountable for completing all your practice sessions, your daily training.

Good mentors help their mentees to believe in themselves. In the words of a former student, "Thank you for everything! Thank you for being there for us, for keeping us in your thoughts, and for having confidence in us even when we did not believe in ourselves. I don't know if you recall, but one time I happened to mention that the PT was going to be my Achilles' heel. You immediately shot back that you would not let me fail the PT. That was the turning point. I knew then that I would blow them away, and I am certain now that of all parts of the exam, I actually did the best on those PTs."

Reflection: Who Are People I Can Turn to as Potential Mentors?

Chapter hashtags: #PasstheBar, #MentorMe, #MyNotesMySuccess, #PersonalizeIt, #LearnMyWay, #Metacognition, #OneSizeDoesNotFitAll, #BarMentorsRock, #BarSuccess, #BarExamSuccess

CHAPTER 6

ENLIST YOUR SUPPORTERS AND LOSE THE NAYSAYERS

- Admitting That Some People in Your World Will Not "Get It" and Will Not Be Helpful as You Prepare for This Exam
- Helping Those Who Are Supportive to Help You
- Think of Analogies to Explain Your Challenges to Family or Friends
- Saying "No" to Supportive People Who Still Want Your Time During Bar Study
- Beware of the Naysayers and Saboteurs
- Competitive Classmates
- Negative People—Friends and Strangers
- Keep Doubters at a Distance: Build a Protective Wall Around Your Confidence
- Relatives and Others Making Destructive Comments
- Special Problem in Law School: Professors Who Doubt You
- The Naysayers Are out of Line

"Do what you feel in your heart to be right, for you'll be criticized anyway. You'll be damned if you do and damned if you don't."

—ELEANOR ROOSEVELT—

Bar success takes a village—of positive people!

We talked in previous chapters about believing in yourself and your ability to pass; we also noted the importance of investing in yourself so you have the resources to succeed. This is easier said than done, especially if you are a first-generation or nontraditional law student, and/or if you do not have a great support system. It is harder still if you must battle people who seek to undermine you.

A host of challenges can undermine:

- Some of you contend with imposter syndrome and/or stereotype threat based on culture, race, religion, ethnicity, gender, etc.
- Some people have a parent, grandparent, or other important person in your life who does not approve of your becoming a lawyer.
- Others battle financial pressures that cause you to doubt the wisdom of a long-term investment in this professional career.
- Some face explicit comments or implicit suggestions that you are not smart enough to pass the bar exam and become a lawyer.
- First-generation students may find it difficult to get support from family members who are unfamiliar with the rigors of the bar exam, and who may believe that the bar exam is "just another test."
- You may find yourself in a relationship with someone who resents the time and energy that bar success requires and either intentionally or inadvertently sabotage your bar-passage goals. (Some students, when they step back, recognize a pattern of getting into fights with a partner, spouse, or significant other before *each* set of final exams. If this is you, be aware and be as careful as possible to protect yourself when you are getting ready for the bar exam.)

Please take time now to take an honest look at your surroundings and determine who and what is helping you.

Recently one of my 3L students e-mailed me, saying how helpful it had been to plan ahead to battle distractions and surround herself with positive influences. She discussed with her significant other the commitment bar studies would entail and realized they had to break up. He was not willing to support her in the way she would need to pass. She was grateful to have realized this before, rather than during, intensive bar preparation. In her words, *"I am glad that you prompted us to take an honest look at how our lives were organized. I feel like I am allowing myself to have a true chance at achieving my goals. I want to truly be able to say I put everything I could into passing the bar."*

You may not realize how helpful it can be to avoid those who are not supportive (at least during bar prep). It may be hard for some readers to imagine that one's family could prove to be more of an obstacle than an asset. But this is all too real an issue for many law students. Facing this now will help you not only to pass the bar exam, but to more confidently reach for and achieve all of your professional goals.

This chapter will help you get rid of or at least dilute negative influences, seek support that is truly useful, avoid "help" that hurts more than it supports, and ask directly and explicitly for what you need during this stressful period.

So, who are the people in your world? Who makes up your "team," your support system, your inner circle? Start by sorting into three categories:

- People who are supportive and "get it" now;
- People who will support you but need help learning how to be supportive; and
- People who are not helpful or will be destructive as you prepare for the bar.

Learn to rely primarily during intensive bar prep on those who are already supportive: your mentor, other recent graduates who passed the bar exam, ASP faculty and other trusted professors, possibly also lawyers or law clerks with whom you work.

Where you can, help people who are not currently supportive to become so. Where you can't, (for example, where people are naysayers or worse), avoid them until after the bar exam.

Urban Dictionary notes: "Naysayers are distinguished by their tendency to consistently view the glass half empty, make frequent one-way trips to negative town, and constantly emphasize the worst of a situation." Negative town is not a place we want to go!

RECOGNIZE THAT SOME PEOPLE WILL NOT "GET IT" AND WILL NOT BE HELPFUL AS YOU PREPARE FOR THIS EXAM

There may be people you cannot enlist for support now. They may come around eventually. They may even end up being huge supporters later in your life and career. But right now, they don't get it, and they will not help you pass your bar exam.

You may have a parent or other relative who really didn't want you to go to law school in the first place and now doesn't support your becoming a lawyer. Even if you're financing this goal yourself, and not asking for a dime from that person, this person may disapprove of your career choice. Below are some of the many situations my former students have shared:

- The dad, who repeatedly told his law student son to be a "real man," get a "real job," and "stop with the schooling already."
- The mom, who often wondered aloud why being a secretary "like Mom" was not "good enough" for her daughter.
- The grandmother who scolded her granddaughter, "Your parents are worried sick that you won't get married. And, you know all lawyers are liars and cheats. This is not what girls in our family do."
- The grandpa who told his grandson, "I heard about those bar pass rates, and people from schools like yours not getting jobs; they said if you weren't at the top of the class you weren't going to make it. Are you at the top of your class? If not, I don't know why you are wasting everyone's money."

- The overachieving lawyer dad who told his slightly laid-back son how much harder he had worked than his son in law school and that all of his "lazy" friends in school didn't pass the bar exam.

When comments or disapproval come from parents, grandparents, or other close relatives, it can be particularly hard to ignore them. But, for self-preservation, you must believe that your legal education and pursuit of a license to practice law are important, worthy goals. When you are studying for the bar exam, get away (literally or figuratively) from the negativity.

While still in law school, you may be able to reason with certain people, perhaps pointing to someone they admire who is a lawyer or explaining that even if jobs right out of school may be harder to find, you will gain a lifetime of earning potential that over the long run will be more than worth it.

But while you are studying for the bar exam, wall off comments and people who erode your confidence and undermine your efforts. Always be ready to change the subject when hit with negative comments.

Family may be the most hurtful, but friends can also be naysayers. I recently led a gathering of students who had just finished taking the bar exam who all shared stories of friends who had "broken up with them" during law school and written them off completely during bar prep. These friends just did not understand or accept that there was no time to hang out in June or July.

Know that you are not alone if friends or family are not supportive. Your best strategy may be to express understanding so as to not feel angry or bitter, but let go of any expectation of support from such persons during the two months of intensive bar prep. Approach them later, after the exam. In the meantime, find at least one person who *is* supportive and reach out to that person now, so you have someone in your corner.

HELPING THOSE WHO *ARE* SUPPORTIVE TO HELP YOU

Some people mean well and want to help but don't know how. It can be beneficial to enlist the support of your immediate circle of family and friends, but sometimes you need to guide them. Unless they are lawyers, they will likely have a hard time understanding the intensity of your studies. Even other professionals, such as doctors or accountants, often don't get it.

Still another level of challenge may arise if you are living with someone who doesn't get it. Let's say it's your parent or partner. If you are not able to help that person understand what you need, your best strategy may be to study at a library, an empty room in your law school, or any place conducive to focus that is outside your home. Find a place that will allow you to stay and comfortably spread out your books from 8:00 a.m. to 10:00 p.m. every day. The less you are around home, the less likely you will be to succumb to distractions, frustration, or defeatism. (I have had some former students who moved out temporarily for total focus on bar studies.)

To help them understand your situation, I drafted some letters to family and friends. You will find two versions of this letter below. Read both and find the language that seems most relevant to you, and either draft your own letter or share one of these. (Some students have asked their family members to read this entire book in order to get the support they need.)

If it's easier to talk with someone instead of writing, or if your friend or family member does not speak English, borrow whatever language or ideas are useful. Non-law analogies may help in talking with and explaining the kind of pressure you are under to those who have little familiarity with law.

Remember, these letters are intended for people you expect to be supportive. Do not bother sending such a letter to naysayers or doubters. Stay away from those people if at all possible until August (or March if you're taking the February exam). It is not worth the energy and time it will take to try to bring them on board before the exam, and you risk their toxic influence permeating your confidence should you try.

In talking with someone who is generally supportive, though, it may help to say something such as, "I know it's hard to understand. It may seem to you like I'm just taking another test. But to pass this bar exam, I cannot spend any time with you in June or July." And every time you are asked, simply say, "Let's plan something in August." Remind yourself that you are totally justified because preparing for the bar will take all your time for two months.

FAMILY/FRIENDS LETTER VERSION 1

Dear ____________,

As you know, I am taking the bar exam this July [February]. I would very much like your support, and I want to let you know how you can help.

Studying for this exam will be a huge challenge. My professor calls it "the law student's Mount Everest." I don't know yet how hard the actual test will be, but I know that to walk in the door prepared, I must totally focus in June and July [January and February]. Total commitment. 100 percent. There is no way I can allow myself to go in knowing I have not done my best, and I know you would not want that for me either.

So, here's what I'm thinking:

- Expect me to be gone for at least two months. Even when you see me, *if you see me,* I may not really be present. (If you ask me something, I may not hear you. Even if I respond, I may not know or remember what I said.)
- I've been told that people become consumed with thinking about exam questions while eating, showering, and even dreaming. The person you have known these past few years as a slightly crazed law student will come down with a disease: bar examitis. The good news is that it's temporary!
- I'm preparing for a fierce, exhausting competition. Some compare the exam to a war. Pre-battle preparation is key. If you want to help me win, first and foremost understand that is why I'm gone—not because I don't care about or want to spend time with you, but because this is what it takes to pass. I have to be "all in" for at least two full months.
- If you want to see me just to say hello, you can drop off meals so I don't have to cook or get takeout. But unless you don't mind bringing food over and testing me with flash cards while we eat a quick

meal, we'll have to put off spending time together until August [March].

- I will return after the exam, physically and mentally, and we'll plan something fun.
- I'm officially RSVP'ing "No" in advance to all social commitments during bar prep. You can feel free to tell me when you are planning get-togethers, but don't expect me to come. If at the last minute I feel I've put in a productive enough study day and can get away, great. I know that I will miss things. I realize this may sound flaky, but it just has to be this way. It's only two months.
- If there is anything you need me to help you with—even an important decision—please wait to ask me about it until after the bar, unless it is truly a life-or-death matter.
- FYI, I likely won't even look at, let alone respond to, any messages. Apologies in advance if you think I'm ignoring you. I'm not. And I am not trying to be rude. If I can, I may check in once a week for messages labeled "urgent," but consider me offline until August [March].
- If I happen to see or speak with you, please do not take personally any sort of moodiness or tension you sense. It's the exam. It's study stress. It has nothing to do with you.

I know you respect how tough this is and how much stress I'm under, but I hope this letter makes it a bit more concrete just how much preparation this exam will take. I will be gone during June and July [January and February], but I promise to resurface in August [March]! Above all, I want to thank you so much for your unequivocal support.

[signed]

____

FAMILY/FRIENDS LETTER VERSION 2

Dear Friend, Family, or Significant Other:

Someone close to you will be taking the bar exam in a few months. I want to share what that means for you, from a law professor's perspective. Obviously, each person and each family facing this experience differs, but there are parallels. Here are just some of the challenges your person faces and what has worked for others like you who want to be supportive. Think of this as both a success and survival note—you want your person to pass the exam, and you want to survive this long haul!

Start with the "long haul." The bar exam is a huge challenge. It represents each graduate's "Mount Everest climb." One does not reach the summit without proper gear and training. Your person cannot give the bar exam short shrift. It requires total commitment, 100 percent focus, and a great deal of time.

- Expect your person to be "gone" for the two months prior to his or her exam. If your person is also working and has other demands, he or she may need to start studying early and thus may "disappear" for four or five months before the exam. Note: Your person may be present physically, but in another mental space altogether if he or she is doing what needs to be done to pass.
- Your person will think about exam fact patterns while eating, showering, and sleeping—dreaming (or having nightmares).
- The person you knew as perhaps a slightly crazed law student will be taken over totally by a disease that I call "bar examitis." The good news is it's temporary!
- Your person is in a fierce and exhausting competition. Many of those your person is competing against come from generations of professionals who support them fully in their effort, pay for their bar studies, bring them food, and even do their laundry!

- Most people studying for the bar exam do not work at all for two full months. They do nothing but study. Bar preparation is their full-time job.
- Bar takers also hibernate socially for two months. Some call everyone they regularly talk with to say, "Goodbye until August [March]." One former student added this to her "gone" voicemail, "If anyone wants to know what to do to help me pass the bar, please feel free to contribute to my bar fund. I am taking off two months from work, so I will accept any and all gifts and loans; no contribution is too small. Thank you for your support!" Another left a message simply asking callers to send prayers and good thoughts his way until August [March].
- Plan a fun after-bar trip, something to which you (and your family if you have one) can look forward.

After the bar, your person will return mentally as well as physically; it will be a time to reconnect. In the meantime:

- Say "No" in advance to all social commitments for your person. (One student told me about an event he reluctantly agreed to attend where he ended up sitting next to a lawyer who berated him the entire evening for being out rather than studying.)
- Be flexible and willing as much as possible to play every day by ear. If at the last minute your person has put in a productive enough study day that he or she is able to join in a social event, be welcoming. But understand that even if your person has finished studying for the day, he or she may need to sleep, exercise, or just unwind.
- Preparing for success on the bar exam involves much more than simply studying; it requires being ready in mind, body, and spirit. Think of your person as a warrior preparing to go off to battle. Help your warrior get ready to win!
- Delay any important decisions, significant changes, major purchases, and arguments until after the bar. (Bar-prep is not the time to buy a new house,

refinance a home, or remodel.) Anything that can wait, let it wait.

- Make life during bar review as easy as possible. Some bar takers who are parents of young children ship their kids off to grandparents for the summer (or for winter break for February bar takers). Many use paper plates for every meal. And, unfortunately, some choose to save time by eliminating showers. (Kidding there! But you get the point!)
- Help your person get on and stay on a routine study schedule. If you have a family, it will often be helpful for your person to be available on a consistent and predictable basis, even for thirty minutes. Encourage your person to set and keep "family hours." It will help to know that "Mom or Dad is studying but will be there for you at least a few minutes at 7:00 p.m. every night [or for breakfast every morning]."
- Study schedules also help your person to make time for practice tests, simulated exams, and downtime when he or she can afford it.
- Participate, if there is any interactive studying that would help. For example, be willing to test your person with flash cards or listen to bar review lectures in the car or while cooking. Be open to listening if your person needs to vent.
- Accommodate your person's needs as fully as possible during the week of the bar exam. If he or she needs to be alone, respect that. If he or she needs you there, try to be there.
- Note: If your person is not clearly expressing what will make him or her the most well prepared, well rested, and confident going into the exam, ask. Remind your person that you are not mind readers. Especially if you have never taken a bar exam yourself, your person must be clear in articulating how you can best help.

- Last but not least, do not take personally any moodiness and tension. Stress comes with bar exam territory. This too shall pass.

Sincerely,

____

As weird as these letters may sound, they work. Countless relatives of bar takers have approached me at alumni functions to say how much they appreciated these, how the letters helped explain what was going on and how they could assist. Especially for those who have never done this or something similar, it's hard to grasp just how challenging this preparation is. The bar exam is more than just time consuming; it is *all* consuming.

Using these letters or your own words, take the time to explain the situation to those you want to support you. Let them know in advance what you are facing and what you need.

Think of Analogies to Explain Your Challenges to Family or Friends

A student recently told me that she had been working hard (putting in many hours), but not yet getting it right. (She was missing lots of practice questions and was stressed.) What you already know well, but your family may not, is that hard work alone is not enough; the work must produce results. The law is detail oriented. The bar exam is not an "A for effort" kind of test. For that matter, the legal profession generally is not a holistic, feel-good world. In litigation, there are winners and losers; a judge won't render an "A for effort" verdict.

If a family member needs an analogy, try this cooking one. I shared this with a student, who took it right back to her family, and said it helped enormously in getting the nonlawyers in her family to help understand what she was going through.

> *Ever try baking a cake without measuring the ingredients? A lot of cooking, great cooking, can be done by eyeballing, estimating, truly winging it. Desserts typically are not that way, especially baked goods. Pastry chefs resemble chemists in their kitchens; they are*

> *not Grandma, whose cooking thrives on a pinch of this and a dab of that. Performing well on the bar exam is more like baking a fancy, seven-tiered cake than simmering a forgiving soup or stew where you can throw a mess of vegetables and meat into some water, cook it long enough on slow heat, and something fabulously tasty will usually emerge. For a cake (and bar success), you must put in all the right ingredients (reliable study materials from a trustworthy bar review, time, concentration, etc.). You must measure them precisely, add them in the right order, and bake the mixture at the right temperature for the correct amount of time (study actively, take daily practice tests, and learn from every mistake; honing and refining, doing them over and over again) until you get just the right passing recipe!*

If you or the person you are trying to explain this to is not into cooking, you might ask the person to imagine working at a high-pressure job that requires logging in to hundreds of different websites each day. Concerned with computer privacy and security, the boss uses passwords that are complex and insists they all be committed to memory. Imagine how alert one would need to be and remain all day long. One digit off, and access is denied. It takes a similarly extraordinary amount of time, focus, and energy to learn the quantity of information tested on bar exams, memorize it, and develop the skills of applying the law in thousands of different factual scenarios. What nonlawyers also don't get is that much of what you are learning in bar review you either did not learn in law school or do not remember.

YOU WANT YOUR LAWYER TO BE ATTENTIVE

Betty was meeting with her lawyer. They were getting ready for settlement negotiations with Betty's former business partner, and a costly trial if the parties could not agree. Betty's lawyer proposed meeting over lunch and offered to order in sandwiches. In a phone call the day before the meeting, Betty told her lawyer she wanted a turkey sandwich. Her lawyer asked Betty what she liked on her sandwich. Betty replied, "Everything except cheese." Betty arrived at the appointed time. Her lawyer rushed in a half-hour late carrying a briefcase and a bag of sandwiches. The lawyer sat down, turned on her computer, and handed Betty a sandwich saying, "OK, here's your turkey and cheese sandwich with nothing else on it." Would you want to hire Betty's lawyer?

Another student told me it was the fact that a law professor (me) compared the bar exam to climbing Mount Everest that finally got his family to understand and stop saying, "You always do well, son. You'll do fine on this, too! Don't worry." Well-meaning family can cause additional stress by the "you've always done well" comments. It can also be horribly stressful for a first-generation student to feel as if he or she must succeed on behalf of the entire family. This often increases the pressure to the point where you might have to say something. This is one possible way to phrase a response: "I am doing my very best, and I have explained what I believe I will need to pass this exam. So, I'll keep my confidence as high as possible, but I also want you to keep your expectations in check. Lots of really smart people fail the bar exam the first time around—many from my law school. I am going to fight to beat the odds and not let myself be a statistic, but I want you to help me to focus on just doing *my* best and not feel like I am carrying the weight of everyone else's expectations, hopes, and dreams on top of it all."

However you express yourself, it may help to put your thoughts into words, even if you don't end up sharing them with anyone else. Bottom line, whatever words, images, or analogies you use to explain what you are facing, try hard to acknowledge your own needs and to help those who support you to appreciate the extent of the challenge and understand how they can best help you.

SAYING "NO" TO SUPPORTIVE PEOPLE WHO STILL WANT YOUR TIME DURING BAR STUDY

You may have the most supportive friends and family in the world, but they may simply not get how intense bar exam preparation must be to succeed. Even if you tell them clearly or send them a letter like those above, they still may not leave you alone. So, keep "in your pocket" some ready responses should you be faced with having to say no to some request. Consider the following sample dialogues.

"Can't you come to just this one birthday party?"

- Mom: "You studied all day. Now, you'll just take off tonight. I insist. It's your uncle's eightieth birthday, you know. You can't miss that!"
- Bar applicant, *in your head: "But then next week is someone else's birthday, and before you know it, the exam is here. My uncle is not taking the bar for me. Neither are you, Mom. I have to go in there and do it myself. Can't you just give me a break?!"*
- Bar applicant's *actual reply*: "I would love to come, if I could. But these are the high-gear months and I have to give everything to this exam. I thank you in advance for supporting me in that. After I pass the bar, I'll go to family events. But I cannot take time away from my studies now."

HEAVY GUILT VARIATION OF "Can't you come to just this one birthday party?"

- Mom: "You have always been such a good student. Please just take off tonight. It's Uncle Joe's eightieth birthday. You know he's not doing well. It could be our last chance to see him. And, Aunt Bessie, she'll be there with all the cousins. They will all ask where you are. Besides, you study every day. I am sure you will pass that test. What are you worried about? You are so smart. You've always done well at everything. You'll be fine. This is family."
- Bar applicant, *in your head: "If Uncle Joe were dying, I would go visit him in the hospital. But he's having a party! He can't be that sick. I know what all those people will say if I don't pass this bar exam. I just cannot break this commitment to myself. I've got that John Wooden quote on the fridge. I can't go into the bar knowing that I took off for family parties and didn't work as hard as I could have!"*

"Success is that peace of mind that comes from knowing you've done everything in your power to become the very best you're capable of becoming."

—JOHN WOODEN—

- Bar applicant's *actual reply*: "I want to come, Mom. I love you, and I know it's important to you. Family is important to me, too, Mom. But this is different. The fact that I've succeeded before does not help. I'm playing in the big leagues now. People who don't step up now get left behind. You know how hard I worked to get into law school, how much you and everyone else have sacrificed to see me get here. I have to step up now. I have to study tonight, and basically every waking minute until the end of July. It just has to be that way. That's how I have to do it.
- *You might add, if you need to*: "Imagine if you had to go see a lawyer, Mom. Let's say, God forbid, you were wrongly accused of a crime and your lawyer came to court unprepared to defend you. As you are being taken off in handcuffs, she says, 'I'm so sorry, but I had a family birthday party last night, and I just couldn't get to researching your case.' "

Family expectations can be particularly demanding in certain cultures. Many parents expect their grown children to attend long weekly dinners and other family events, regardless of how much studying they have or whether they are no longer even living at home. If this is your situation, work on it ahead of time. You must find a strategy to protect as much of your time as possible.

Let's look at another dialogue that might help you with family commitments during bar review.

"I need you to take me to the doctor."

- Mom: "I have an appointment with the doctor on Friday. I'm counting on you to take me. You know I can't take the bus anymore."
- Bar applicant, *in your head: "We talked about this before bar prep. I asked you to make as many nonurgent appointments as possible before June or after July. I know you're not going to like it, but you will have to make other arrangements."*
- Bar applicant's *actual reply*: "If this is something that can wait until August, please reschedule the appointment. If you must go now, let's try to think of someone else in the family who could take you." Even if this is your role in the family—you are the one who always takes your parent to the doctor—speak up and ask someone else to help this time. You owe this to yourself. If no one else is available, perhaps you can pay for your parent to take a taxi or use a rideshare service to get to the doctor for any urgent appointments. The price of making alternate arrangements may be far lower in the long run than the price of missing bar review lectures or valuable study time. Note: If you must go to doctor or other appointments (for yourself or others) while you are studying, bring notes and work to do so that you do not get annoyed or frustrated with having to wait.

It is amazing that even lawyers sometimes forget how much time and energy the bar exam really takes. If you are clerking for an attorney, stop for the summer (winter, if you are taking the February bar exam) unless working just a couple of hours in a law office will help keep you motivated. Make sure your colleagues and boss understand your commitment, though. If the lawyer begs you to come in and research something when you know you must be studying for the bar, stick to your studying. (If there is a case you just don't feel like you can let go for the summer or winter if you are taking the February bar exam, let go anyway. Say "No.") Trying to prove yourself worthy by doing extra work when you cannot afford the time will backfire if you don't pass the bar exam. Pass first; then go the extra mile.

The happy-hour dilemma

- Friend: "Happy Hour Friday. Be there!"
- Bar applicant: "Dude, you know I can't. Studying for the bar."
- Friend: "Chill, dude. You study all the time. You're gonna lose your friends. Pretty soon we're not going to invite you anymore. You say no all the time."
- Bar applicant, *in your head: "Just because you're there drinking your weekend away doesn't mean I should. In ten years, when I'm a successful lawyer and a member of the real bar, you may still be sitting here drinking at this bar. Yeah, but who am I kidding? I so wish I could go! Maybe just this one night? I could take off just tonight? But I shouldn't. I really have to focus. Do I want to take this damn test again? No way!"*
- Bar applicant's *actual reply*: "Keep inviting me! I'll try to stop by Friday if I can, but this thing is over in July, and Fridays in August I am all over it. [Pause.] Thanks for supporting me through this! You might need a close friend who's a lawyer someday—ha! Kidding, dude! But seriously, I'll be back after July."

Remember that friends later become referrals. Don't be shy or embarrassed about your priorities. Whom will all these friends come to when they need legal advice?

The unhelpful study buddy

- Friend: "Want to come study with me at the library today?"
- Bar applicant: "No, I think I'm better off studying alone today."
- Friend: "Come on. A bunch of us are going. We'll all help each other. Then we'll go out for some beers after we work."
- Bar applicant, *in your head: "Your idea of studying is 80 percent chitchat and 20 percent study. Working with you is not productive for me, and I know it. I*

end up helping you. I explain things to you, but all you really do is distract me."

- Bar applicant's *actual reply*: "Thanks for asking. Maybe another time. Today I need to study on my own. If I get enough done, I'll text you and see where you guys went and maybe meet up with you. Otherwise, I'll see you at bar review tomorrow."

Sometimes you slip. You know it would be best to say "No" and get back to work (or sleep, for that matter), but you think, "Well, just this once." Try not to succumb. Understand that commitments you make to yourself are as important as those you make to others. Would you flake if you were going to an appointment with a doctor or specialist you had waited months to see? No, of course not. You wouldn't even think of canceling. Your studies must be as important to you as any appointment with anyone on the planet. Follow through. No excuses. Don't be a "no-show" on yourself!

Enlist your supporters to help you stay on track. Post your study schedule so they don't distract you during your "study hours." If you do slip and end up doing something unproductive, get back on track ASAP. Don't waste any more time feeling guilty. Just get back to work.

Remember, some breaks are helpful. You may return to work able to be more productive. Allow yourself that possibility. Although the warnings about people and activities eating your time should be heeded, you may find that some distractions replenish the well and boost your energy. It can be good to take a couple of hours off here and there. Limit the number of these breaks, but don't feel guilty for taking a little time off if the diversion will ultimately help you be more productive.

Father's Day hits right in the middle of summer bar review, so does the Fourth of July. If you are a dad or have a dad, stop for a moment to acknowledge Father's Day. And go to a barbeque or fireworks on the Fourth of July. Some people feel comfortable taking that whole day off. Others feel better putting in a good study day and then enjoying the evening out. Whatever time you do take off, enjoy it! You are doing a good thing in recharging your batteries and preventing burnout.

BEWARE OF THE NAYSAYERS AND SABOTEURS

We discussed people who mean well but don't know how to be supportive. There will be others who are not supportive at all, some intentionally and others inadvertently. You must cut these people loose for the summer (winter, if you are taking the February bar exam).

To better deal with people who may try to sabotage you, it can be helpful to divide them into competitive classmates and others who are generally negative (acquaintances or strangers).

Competitive Classmates

Classmates should not be competitive with each other on the bar exam. A forced curve and class rankings may have created "winners" and "losers" in law school, but *everyone* in your class *can* pass the bar exam. Everyone *can* be a winner on this test. And, if your entire class did pass, you would all benefit. You would forever be known and admired as the "one hundred percent class."

But, alas, some stay stuck in law student competitive mode, even after they graduate. These are the people I call the "blowhards." They are full of themselves. Some may just be so self-absorbed that they make comments they don't even realize are insulting. Ignore them. Others intentionally intimidate. Ignore them too. Tune it out when someone casually claims that they're doing all-nighters every night or completing hundreds of practice questions daily (and getting top scores). First, they're probably not telling the truth. It's tough to do that much, especially if you're also sleeping (which you must—and if they are not, they are not helping themselves). Next and most important, focus on your own work. Run your own race. Stick to your schedule. Trust your bar review and your mentor or coach. Also, don't let yourself get psyched out if classmates say they got a higher score on a practice test than you did. What will move *you* forward is consistently taking practice tests, studying sample answers, understanding why *you* missed questions, and working to improve each and every day.

Don't be angry with yourself for missing questions in practice. Every mistake you make now is an opportunity to get it right on the actual exam. (Repeat this with me out loud: *"Every question I miss now and learn from helps me get the right answers on the bar exam."*) The only score that counts is at the end of the game.

So don't let competitive classmates throw you. Use positive peer pressure *if* it helps motivate you. But negative peer pressure is usually a complete and total waste of your time, a drain of your precious energy. It is not about what or how someone else does; it's all about you. It's *your* bar exam.

Negative People—Friends or Strangers

When faced with a negative person during bar preparation, the best advice is to get away. Don't answer calls or texts. If someone speaks with you in person or you inadvertently answer a call, politely cut off the conversation. One line that works every time is simply, "Gotta run. I have to go to the bathroom."

There will be people who are just dying to tell you about everyone they know who failed a bar exam—from their neighbor's son to famous people. They are similar to people who accost pregnant women to share horrifying birth experiences. (Stay away from them if you are expecting.) Others may want to tell you about dismal legal employment statistics. If it feels negative, it's best to not listen.

Sometimes it can be even more stressful when people make seemingly positive comments, such as, "Oh, I know you'll pass." That may just pile on more stress with expectations you must live up to. How to respond? One of my students shared that she would simply reply, "I'm doing my best," and either walk away or change the subject.

Whatever the comments, have a response ready so you don't feel cornered into talking about the exam with anyone who does not have a positive effect on you.

Build a Protective Wall Around Your Self-Confidence

As we talked about earlier, it's normal to feel some doubts. But remember, if you were not the kind of person who thrived when challenged, you likely wouldn't have started, let alone finished, law school. Some of your classmates failed out after their first year. You did not. Look at all the alumni from your law school who passed the bar exam. Are they *all* smarter than you? No!

Relatives and Others Making Destructive Comments

Far worse than simply "not getting it" is when people share destructive stereotypes or biases that undermine you. Note: *Please do not be offended by this section. I just keeping it real based on decades of work with students.*

- Did you grow up in a family where your mom (or grandma or another relative you love and care about) believed that "girls like you" should "find a good man, get married, and raise a family," and not "waste time" in school? (And, if they don't say this explicitly, do they make comments like, "You're never going to find someone with all that time in the library.")
- Does Mom think her son should be in business and making real money, not spending all his time in school racking up debt?
- Does Dad think that college and graduate schools are only for rich white people?
- Do you have family members who think that all women who want to become lawyers are aggressive and overbearing?
- Does your family believe that lawyers are liars?

Some people truly believe negative stereotypes of lawyers, unfortunately, and will say so unapologetically. Others will give you their full support, but only if you put family commitments first. This mentality might not explicitly undermine, but the effect is just as negative.

To "compete" on this exam, you must give the same intensity to your studies as everyone else is—and not be taken away physically or emotionally from your full and total commitment to success.

Others make comments that are less direct, but equally destructive. For example, the student whose partner says:

"Look, you know I think you are the smartest person I know, but we can't ignore the state pass rate. Just look at the pass rate at your school. All I'm saying is that I'll still love you if you fail."

And, consider the parent who says:

"Honey, I love you and you know I'll be proud of you whatever you do. Becoming a lawyer is a great goal, but it's just that you have never been the best student and I don't want to see you get hurt." Ouch!

Alas these are real stories. If you are getting similar messages, steel yourself and find your support elsewhere.

A note for women whose families do not support your becoming a lawyer: law school will not make you aggressive in any sort of negative way. The rigors of law school should help all law students learn to write and speak persuasively, as well as think critically—both of which are essential to being an effective professional. Passing the bar exam provides credible evidence that you can perform effectively under extreme pressure. These skills will help you manage, lead, and be responsible for the lives and livelihoods of others, if you so choose. That is a good thing. There is nothing unfeminine about being a lawyer or a leader.

Bottom line, if you have negative folks in your life, don't try to change their minds right now. First pass the bar exam, with the help of supportive people, and *then* try to bring them around.

Special Law School Challenge: Professors Who Doubt You

If you believe a professor thinks that you aren't smart or capable of passing the bar exam, this may hurt your confidence. If you have a negative encounter with such a professor, especially in class, first try to shrug it off. There is a good chance he or she doesn't really think less of you and was deliberately trying to prepare you for tough judges and opposing counsel. If it's still bothering you, though, you might want to try talking with that professor during office hours. You might have an altogether different impression after meeting with him or her one-on-one. At the very least, be sure to talk with other professors with whom you do feel comfortable, and let yourself feel respected by the way they treat you. Don't let the judgment or perceived judgment of one person sink in or dictate how you view yourself.

The Naysayers Are Wrong

There are plenty of people who weren't "the best student" who passed the bar exam and are now thriving as lawyers.

The bar tests basic competencies: it is not a test of genius or legal scholarship. With (1) basic knowledge of the law (remember that you have two full months of bar review to learn or relearn the rules); (2) basic analytical and writing skills (which you will train intensively to develop); and (3) the will to succeed, you *can* pass the bar exam. This is not a test of whether you are headed for the Supreme Court!

Reflection: Supporters and Saboteurs

Thinking about who is and who is not supportive in the spaces below. You don't have to show anyone, and it may be best not to. You can delete these lists up after you write them. But clarifying this for yourself will increase your productivity and save you from stressful time and energy vampires. (OK, that may be harsh, but the point stands. Be strategic about who you spend time with, until after the exam.)

Part A: List your supportive troops (Write the names of and contact info for people you know "get it," whom you can call or reach out to when you need a boost.):

1. ____________________
2. ____________________
3. ____________________
4. ____________________
5. ____________________

Part B: List people who are supportive, but don't yet "get it":

1. ____________________
2. ____________________
3. ____________________
4. ____________________
5. ____________________

Part C: List potential saboteurs (You can name individuals or classes of people such as those from a particular student organization who tend to distract you—or who are unsupportive in any other way.):

1. ______________________________
2. ______________________________
3. ______________________________
4. ______________________________
5. ______________________________

Part D: List people to avoid, or, at the very least, whose messages need to be diluted (Name individuals who have intentionally or inadvertently made destructive comments or engaged in undermining actions.):

1. ______________________________
2. ______________________________
3. ______________________________
4. ______________________________
5. ______________________________

Chapter hashtags: #PasstheBar, #NotGoingtoNegativeTown, #AreYouWithMe, #ProudLawyerToBe, #ICANandIWILL, #LoseTheNaysayers, #Self-Care, #BarExamSuccess

CHAPTER 7

WRITE AND POST YOUR SCHEDULE, THEN ADAPT IT TO MAXIMIZE PRODUCTIVITY

- Sample Schedules for Traditional and Nontraditional Students
- Bar Review
- Days When You Do Not Have Bar Review Lectures
- Daily Schedules Versus Weekly Schedules
- The Ingredients of a Successful Schedule
- Law Study: Bar Review Lectures and Outlines
- Self-Care (Including Good Nutrition, Exercise, and Sleep)
- As You Plan Your Schedule, Think About When and How You Learn Best
- Variety
- The Daily Grind: Stick to Your Schedule of Daily, Disciplined, Focused Work
- Dealing with Anxiety (It's Normal to Be Nervous)
- Anxiety While Taking Practice Essay Tests
- Worry While Reading a Sample Answer
- Anxiety-Reducing Tools to Use Any Time Nerves Hit
- Work Hard, but Work Efficiently: Reassess Your Schedule
- Is My Schedule Maximizing My Efficiency?
- Adapt Your Schedule as the Bar Approaches and Make More Time for Memorizing

- How to Memorize? Break Out the Flash Cards, Write It Out Fifty Times, Whatever Works for You!
- Preventing Burnout: Add Incentives and Levity
- Reward Yourself
- Bar Exam Burnout
- Humor: You Gotta Laugh a Little
- Motivate with Music
- Finalizing Your Schedule

"Patience and perseverance have a magical effect before which difficulties disappear and obstacles vanish."

—JOHN QUINCY ADAMS—

This chapter will help you concretize the study-schedule portion of your bar success plan.

One might think that calendaring is something basic. *Everyone* knows how to calendar, right? No, not true. Especially with busy people and even more so if you are in crunch time (as you are in law school and will be during bar prep), it helps immensely to have an effective scheduling system.

Let's begin with some sample schedules to get an idea of what sorts of tasks people do during bar prep and how they fit it all into their day (or week). Then, we'll break down the ingredients of a successful schedule so you can see the pieces and create your own system that works for you.

SAMPLE SCHEDULES

Below are sample daily schedules. You will merge one of these with your bar review course schedule, and build a complete schedule *that works for you.*

You may be asking, "What more do I need if my bar review will give me a schedule?" Your course will include a schedule of lectures and assignments to complete. You want to take that as a starting place and personalize it, committing to target times when you will complete the assigned work, any additional work you must do to cement your knowledge, and take extra practice tests, as well as times you will eat, sleep, exercise, and reward yourself with a bit of fun or social time.

For most people, the more you stick to a routine, the more likely every minute of your day will be productive. (That doesn't mean you are studying every minute. It just means everything you do is working toward passing—including self-care and breaks to recharge. What you don't have time for is "wasting time.")

As you review sample schedules, think about prioritizing. Start with what you *must* get done then build out around what time remains. Your schedule is the embodiment of your priorities.

SAMPLE DAILY STUDY SCHEDULE FOR THE TRADITIONAL STUDENT

- 6:30 a.m.—Wake up, drink coffee, tea, or hot water, take a shower, eat breakfast. (Wake at 6:00 a.m. if you want to exercise before breakfast.)
- 7:00–7:30 a.m.—Complete daily set of practice questions.
- 7:30–8:00 a.m.—Review answers.
- 9:00 a.m.–1:00 p.m.—Listen to bar review lectures. (Many people prefer doing this work from 6–10p.m. Experiment with what timing works best for you. More on most least productive time later in the book.)
- 1:00–2:00 p.m.—Lunch and learn. Take 20–30 minutes to relax and enjoy a healthy lunch. Before or after you eat, take another half hour to identify and review any rules or concepts you didn't understand from the lectures. You can also star or highlight key points you do not want to forget such as helpful examples or areas the professor said would be heavily tested.

- 2:00–6:00 p.m.—Complete bar review reading assignments and practice writing tasks. (During the first month, you can look up rules you do not know when taking practice tests. Don't wait to complete practice tests until you think you know the law. More on that in later chapters.)
- 6:00–8:00 p.m.—Take a break to exercise and eat dinner. Maybe have a lovely meal and take a long walk after you eat. This can also be a time to connect with family or friends.
- 8:00–10:00 p.m.—Do passive work. Review lecture notes and flashcards or answer a few practice questions on your phone, while lying down, resting, and winding down.
- 10:00–10:30 p.m.—Relax, maybe with some nonlaw reading, and complete your pre-sleep, self-care routine (teeth brushing, etc.)
- 10:30 p.m.—Go to sleep.

Bar Review

Nearly all bar review is online. This brings many positives:

- The ability to listen to a lecture or part of a lecture more than once. This is fine so long as you are **actively listening and fully engaged**. (Note: don't "half-listen" with the expectation that you will come back and listen again. It's OK to *selectively* re-listen to parts of lectures you did not understand, but it's essential to be all in the first time.)
- The ability to listen to lectures **at** whatever time of day is most productive for you.

But having all your work online for two months can, for some people, be lonely. You do not have to fully isolate. If you find it more effective to work when surrounded by others, or if you need or prefer the accountability that comes from having to show up somewhere, considering forming a study group or completing your independent online review work in a room with others at your law school.

As with all learning, know yourself and be honest with yourself about what you need to learn most effectively.

As of the writing of this edition, many bar exams are still administered on paper, but nearly all review materials are online. There are advantages to practicing in the same format in which you will take the bar exam. So, be sure to take at least some exams in the format your exam will be in.

Days When You Do Not Have Bar Review Lectures

As noted above, bar reviews will provide schedules. And, there will be days with no assigned lectures. Plan these carefully so you don't waste time. (Remember that exercise and self-care are not wasting time.) Make sure to include practice tests and time to learn rules and concepts you don't understand well or at all. (Don't hope they won't be tested; learn them!) Schedule time to work on memorizing rules and plan to increase that time as the exam approaches. Note: it is much easier and more effective to memorize rules that make sense to you; so focus first on learning.

Most important are practice tests. Practice questions will help you to both learn *and* memorize the law. Studies show that active learning is the key to success. And, learning in the context of fact patterns helps you recall the rules. Think: *"Oh yeah, that's like the one I did before in which the only ten acres of land with access to water were specifically not included in the deed."* Or, let me remember how I analyzed which law applied in that *"contract dispute with a photographer selling her time (services) and her photographs (goods) or the question with the redwood fence where the builder was selling both the wood and service of building the fence."*

Your mind will recall particulars of practice questions that you can then draw on to help you apply similar rules to new situations.

WORKING STUDENTS AND OTHERS WITH LIMITED TIME

Start early. Two months may simply not be enough. During your last semester of law school (or last two semesters if your LGPA puts you in the bottom quarter of your class), devote some chunk of time (perhaps 5–10 hours per week) for early bar study. Devise an early start schedule, perhaps with the help of your ASP faculty, that includes time to:

- Get familiar with your bar review's website and resources.
- Take practice tests in all testing formats and study sample answers. PTs are excellent for early start because they are skills-based and not memory dependent.
- Create your own flashcards and/or create or update your own outlines, with at least some focus on writing out rules that are difficult to understand or tough to remember.
- Review main concepts and get fluent in the terminology used in all testable subjects.

Tip for Working Students

While some people can work a full day, eat dinner, and then study productively for four to five hours straight, many working students find it easier to spread tasks throughout the day, putting in for example an hour before work, an hour at lunch, and an hour right after work (with maybe an additional hour or two after dinner). This would total five hours a day on workdays, without working five hours straight. Working students can also plan on full study days on weekends, for example from 9:00 a.m. to 6:00 p.m.

Daily Schedules Versus Weekly Schedules

Most people prefer daily schedules. For those studying full time, daily schedules leave no time to waste deciding what to do next. You get up, do your various studying tasks at the same time each day, and develop a productive routine. Even if you are working, a daily schedule is useful if your work hours are consistent each day. But, if your work commitments vary from day to day, a weekly schedule may be most effective.

One former student had an erratic work schedule that interfered with accomplishing daily bar review tasks; he felt like a failure even though he had multiple engineering degrees and decades of experience in demanding jobs. I suggested he switch to a weekly schedule; completing more bar prep on lighter workdays and less on busier ones. He realized that he got everything on his list done by week's end and once again thought of himself as the success story he was, and still is!

Simply changing *when* you do things may make you think of yourself in a different light. Try out scheduling variations as early as you can before or in the very beginning of intensive bar review so that you can hit the ground running immediately after graduation.

APPLYING FOR A JOB DURING BAR REVIEW

Students will often ask, "Shouldn't I still be applying for jobs during bar review?" You should definitely work actively with your career services office and on your own to find a job *before* you graduate. But, if you don't have a job lined up by graduation, you may be best served by turning your full attention to bar review and then back to job hunting after the bar. Bottom line: Have a current resume and form cover letter on hand, ready to go, so that if you hear about a job, you can quickly apply. But don't spend active time job hunting during bar review.

THE INGREDIENTS OF A SUCCESSFUL SCHEDULE

What goes into an effective bar schedule? Law study, practice exam training, self-care including exercise, sleep, and good nutrition, and some relaxation and fun to recharge your batteries and replenish the well.

When you get your bar review lecture and assignments schedule, edit it to add the following:

- Time to meal prep, exercise, sleep, and relax (some of these, like meal prep and exercise, you can do while listening to audio of lectures);
- Time after each lecture to review rules you did not understand and make flash cards (or other memory tools) for heavily tested areas;
- Time to complete extra practice tests and study sample answers. (Remember, bar review courses are floors not ceilings; plan to complete your course and then some); and
- Time to complete a full simulated bar exam.

Law Study: Bar Review Lectures and Outlines

Listen carefully to and engage fully in all bar review lectures and workshops. Make sure you are awake and alert. If you are watching lectures at a time of day when you are exhausted, consider scheduling these another time when you are more energized. On the other hand, lectures help keep some people awake. If you are one of them, you might want to build your bar review schedule so you watch/listen when you are a little tired but still awake, and do even more active, independent work such as taking practice tests when you have more energy. For example, if you are most alert in the mornings, you might choose to listen to bar review lectures from 6–10p.m.

Just because your friends are listening to their bar review lectures at a certain time does not mean you need to do so. Run your own race.

I have noticed that most of my students default to morning bar review lectures. When I bring up the possibility of shifting the timing (something they had never considered), a whole new perspective opens. They can then consider when would be the best time for them to do this work.

Getting the Most out of Bar Review Lectures

- Bookend the videos:

  1) *Before each lecture,* review the table of contents of the outline covering the topic of that lecture and look up any terms you are not familiar with, and

  2) *After each lecture,* review the main points and anything that you didn't understand during the lecture.

- Take notes efficiently. For some students, taking notes while listening to a lecture helps them learn the material. Others get more out of a lecture by listening intently and then going back and creating notes by either condensing the main outline or expanding the table of contents. Determine which approach to notetaking is most effective for you.

- Watch your speed. Bar reviews allow you to listen to lectures at double or triple speed. *Use these settings sparingly and strategically*. For example, listen to a speeded version when you are repeating an area that you have already heard, just for review. Do not listen at double speed the first time you watch, especially if you don't understand the lecture. That will not save you time in the long run.

Self-Care Including Good Nutrition, Exercise, and Sleep

Are you running? Jogging? Lifting weights? Boxing? Playing tennis? Taking a Pilates or yoga class? You may think it's nuts to suggest that your schedule allows you to take time off for such "leisure." But exercise is not leisure at this stage; it is a critical component of your stamina building as you prepare for the bar exam marathon. You must let off physical steam, release stress, and keep your body in shape. Exercise is not time "off." It is a key piece of your ultimate study effort.

If you feel guilty any time you are not studying, you can listen to bar review lectures or recordings of rule statements while you exercise.

If you have a regular sport or exercise, do it daily during bar review, if you can. If you are not "an exercise person," add a half-hour walk to your study day. If you can push that to an occasional jog or swim, all the better. Do whatever exercise your body is able to so that you burn off stress if possible.

During each session of your bar exam, your mind will be *on*. It will work better if oxygen is flowing efficiently through your body. Some nervousness—that which keeps you sharp and alert—is good. But you must shake off the excess nerves that can send you into panic or paralysis. (Remember my saying, "Turn *panic* into *power*, not *paralysis*.") Exercise helps you lose the bad stress while keeping the good energy.

As You Plan Your Schedule, Think About When and How You Learn

Research indicates that we all use a mixture of learning styles. So, do not allow yourself to be pigeonholed—or pigeonhole yourself—into one style of learning.

For example, I continue to recommend reading bar exam question fact patterns aloud under your breath (subvocalization), while pointing at each word. This employs sight, touch, and hearing simultaneously.

Think back to other situations when you had to learn and memorize a great deal of material (perhaps a math class with many formulas or a language class with extensive vocabulary). What helped you the most? Learning how to learn (metacognition) is key.

Take the quiz below to spark some thoughts on how you learn best.

Reflection: How I Learn

Q: When studying for class, I learn well by:

1) Silently reading my notes, rereading the casebook, studying flowcharts etc.
2) Listening to a lecture, reading my notes aloud, and having someone test me aloud.
3) Drawing diagrams to track issues and rules, writing notes, and outlining material on my computer.
4) All of the above.

Q: When I go on an interview, what stands out most in your mind afterward?

1) How people looked
2) The names and qualifications of people I spoke with
3) What rooms I was in, what I said and did, what I ate, and so forth
4) All of the above

Q: When studying in a library, coffee shop, or bookstore, I am most distracted by:

1) Looking at things on the walls or the people nearby.
2) Listening to the conversations of people nearby, music playing, and other sounds.
3) My feelings, whether I am thirsty or tired, how comfortable my clothes are, and so on.
4) All of the above.

Q: When I am trying to figure out some concept I don't understand, I:

1) Read until I get it. Read it, think a bit. Read it a day later, think some more. Read it again a few days later.
2) Ask someone to explain it to me.

3) Review the problem in my mind and diagram it out.

4) All of the above.

Q: When I need to memorize a list (of factors, elements, or even a grocery list), I:

1) Write it out five times.

2) Say it out loud or make up a song and sing it out loud.

3) Draw pictures next to mnemonics to help me remember the items on the list.

4) All of the above.

Think about all sorts of ways of learning. Having options can be empowering.

You can't change the way a bar review lecture is conducted, but you can adapt your own independent study. Make time if it would be helpful for drawing charts and diagrams, using flash cards, and color-coding material. Build in listening or talking time, if you want to replay part of a recorded lecture or talk it out aloud. You may want to get up and move around, sing the elements of a cause of action, or study with a study buddy.

Allow your study time to work for you and with you. (Google the song, "I fought the law." Hum the tune changing the lyric from, "I fought the law and the law won" to "I fought the bar, and *I* won.")

Based on what we have talked about so far, begin to fill in tasks/activities you can commit to complete in the Draft Schedule below. (You'll have a chance to refine it. Just start by getting down what you want to include, and begin thinking through what times of day are best suited each action item.)

Draft Schedule

5 a.m.

6 a.m.

7 a.m.

8 a.m.

9 a.m.

10 a.m.

Noon

1 p.m.

2 p.m.

3 p.m.

4 p.m.

5 p.m.

6 p.m.

7 p.m.

8 p.m.

9 p.m.

10 p.m.

11 p.m.

Variety

Studying in different ways can help appeal to the diverse ways you learn. Shaking things up can also prevent burnout and get you through the long, tough days.

Change locations once or twice a week. As a reward for studying well in your regular study spot, take a stack of practice exams outdoors or somewhere with a great view. Bring work to a favorite coffee shop or bookstore and sit in a comfy chair. Make sure it's a place where you can focus, though do occasionally force yourself to focus in a place with many distractions to mimic what it will feel like to take the actual bar exam in a room full of the noises, and stress, of other bar takers.

Vary your studying techniques. As we said, variety alone may help you stay on course; adding a little fun may help even more. Working in a different manner may enhance your learning, for example:

- Talk through concepts or rules you don't understand with a friend, study buddy, or mentor (perhaps over coffee). If it is someone who will stay focused and not distract you, the person doesn't have to have a legal background. If you can explain something clearly to a non-lawyer, you probably understand it well. You can talk to yourself or even explain rules to your dog, if you don't want to be around others.

- Set some of your mnemonics, checklists, or summary outlines to music. Memorize rules by singing them to the melody of a popular tune. (One of my professors set all of civil procedure to music and my section performed a singing review session for the other sections.)
- Make charts and diagrams.
- Include some funny images (perhaps a cartoon that makes you laugh) in your study materials, or maybe place a picture of your favorite action movie actor near the portion of your crimes outline that mentions the deadly-weapon doctrine.
- Make a recording of yourself reading key rules out loud. Hearing your own voice confidently stating rules will have an empowering effect, even if you were reading the rules when you made the recording. A former student shared a unique bar study strategy: recording her own voice reading rule statements, but in a thick, funny New York stage accent. She recorded every subject on the Florida bar this way, and listened on a cross-country drive from California. Adding the accent triggered her memory such that it helped her retain all the rules. Not only did she learn the material and pass the bar the first time, she also laughed along the way.

Do you still think preparing for the bar exam has to be torture? Come on. Really? Try to make it as enjoyable as possible. Yes, you must take this time seriously and be fully committed to success, but that doesn't mean that it has to be painful, or you must feel sorry for yourself. Try recording yourself stating rules in a British accent. (Just saying "rule against perpetuities" in a British accent is funny—at least for an American!) Find ways to see the light at the end of each day, and each week; add some light and levity of your own to the process!

Making Study More Enjoyable

In the space below, list three things you can do to switch up your studying to make it more fun for you. Use the suggestions above or your own ideas.

1. ______________________________

2. ______________________________

3. ______________________________

THE DAILY GRIND: STICK TO YOUR SCHEDULE OF DAILY, DISCIPLINED, FOCUSED WORK

I know we just talked about making studies more enjoyable. But, even when you add levity, it's still a "daily grind" in some respects. If the sample schedules above look doable, that's great! Often people follow them fairly easily the first few days, but fall behind within a couple of weeks and get discouraged. (Others stay on pace, but get exhausted.) "Keep at it," I tell students so often and so loudly they hate it. But they thank me later. *After* their exam, they say, "I needed those reminders to keep on going." When they pass, they say, "I heard your voice in those dark moments when I was tired and drained. When I was ready to give up, I just kept moving forward."

You may also hate me for this chapter, perhaps for the entire book. But if any of it helps to keep you studying and taking practice tests, and to pass your bar exam, you too will be thankful that you did not give up when you are celebrating your success.

(Please drop me a note any time to share your success stories.)

"Rarely do we find men who willingly engage in hard, solid thinking. There is an almost universal quest for easy answers and half-baked solutions. Nothing pains some people more than having to think."

—DR. MARTIN LUTHER KING JR.—

Don't expect each day to be miraculous. Expect it to be hard work. A lot of your preparation may seem like drudgery, but every bit of effort is worth the spectacular payoff down the road. Expect to be tired. Keep pushing forward anyway.

Be determined. Keep your goal, your "endgame," in mind. You are in training. It's not supposed to be easy. Learn as you go, one day at a time. Trust that if you put in what it takes, you will get where you need to go.

Use every good moment available to study, sleep, or otherwise prepare. Don't waste anyone's time fooling yourself. If you are not effectively using your time, get on the ball. Don't spin your wheels. When you hit a wall (and you will!), change gears or stop and take a break.

Don't quit or get discouraged at the first signs of losing focus. You need to build your stamina. Push yourself. It's not easy. But when you find yourself reading the same thing over and over, looking out the window and not "hearing" yourself, take a break. Maybe take a nap. Sometimes after even a short sleep, you can get back in gear and be more productive. Above all, remain patient. Keep moving forward.

Work hard. Work steadily. Work smart. Work when others are goofing off. And do not waste one moment feeling sorry for yourself that you *have to* work while others play. You *get to* work. And you will get to reap the future rewards of that hard work.

Pace yourself and don't burn out. Do what it takes to keep moving forward, slowly but steadily, on this road to success.

Dealing with Anxiety (and, It's Normal to Be Nervous!)

When I describe study schedules to students who are still months away from the bar exam, they are usually fine and able to calmly think through things. When I have the same discussion with people about one week into bar review, they panic: "There is too much material to learn. I can't do it. I will never learn all of this."

Of course you can! And you will. How? One day at a time, improving slowly but surely. This is the same technique writers use when they ask how they could possibly finish a book; one page at a time—or some might even say one sentence at a time.

Put your nerves in a box. And get to work. Instead of spending time and energy on worrying, put it into studying. It's too early in the first weeks of June to stress out. That is the time to focus on getting into a study routine. Don't expect to get practice questions right! Just keep answering them and studying the sample answers.

Walk away from every study session having learned something. Keep improving. Keep moving forward. And you will be fine.

I understand that it's easy for me to say, "Just don't worry." I tell myself that every day, and I still worry! But there are tools to help you "put the worry in boxes" and keep it contained when it does surface. Ultimately, if you can actually learn to channel your nerves into adrenaline, they can become powerful tools rather than paralyzing traps. That's the goal!

"Courage is a special kind of knowledge: the knowledge of how to fear what ought to be feared and how not to fear what ought not to be feared."

—DAVID BEN-GURION—

What should you do when you're blocked by anxiety? That depends on when the nerves hit. Let's consider different strategies for different times you find yourself getting nervous.

Anxiety While Taking Practice Tests

If you freak out while completing a set of multiple-choice questions, try breathing, and as you read the rest of the questions, just focus on seeing if you can even rule out one incorrect answer. When you have done your best, review the explanatory answers and try to just soak up the learning from them—with no self-judgement.

If paralyzing anxiety prevents forward movement while you are taking a practice essay test, the immediate mission is to get the intellectual flow going again—take the edge off. Try simply reading and outlining if answering the question in full right now feels too stressful. Read the sample answer, possibly aloud.

Some jurisdictions release sample passing answers, and your bar review may offer model answers. After trying to analyze a question (and preferably writing out your own answer, unless you are too panicked to do so), read the sample answer. See how your answer compares.) Now take this one step further. *Copy the sample answer.* Write it out longhand or retype it, word for word.

Copying quality sample or model answers can be especially helpful when even looking at those answers stresses you out (when you fall into "I could never write something like this" thinking), or when you are too tired to fully analyze an answer. It is easy. It is simple and low stress.

As you write or type, your mind will sync with your hands, and your brain will register what a "complete" and passing answer sounds *and feels* like. What often happens is that you begin typing and you see that this answer adds one more sentence where you might have stopped, helping you correct a problem of writing in too conclusory a manner. Or you may find the opposite; you see that the answer stops after making a point when you would have gone on and on—writing in a too-verbose or disorganized manner, sometimes even undermining your own logic that would have scored points had you written more clearly and succinctly. Take what you learn into your next closed book practice tests.

When you are nervous or overtired, copying essay answers is one of the best tools. It is not stressful; it just involves retyping. It calms students down because it's not demanding, but it often works wonders to bolster their understanding.

Copying certain sample or model answers as a study technique can also help tremendously for nonnative English speakers or first-generation law students who might worry they are not saying things in the appropriate style or wording.

Worry While Reading a Sample Answer to a PT or Essay or Integrated Set Question

You might find yourself overwhelmed or intimidated when self-assessing a completed practice question by studying a model or sample answer. It may feel like you will never be able to write that thorough of an answer. You must lift yourself out of that thinking. If it's an essay, or sometimes even a PT, copying the answer, as noted above, is one way to begin to believe that you *could* write something like that.

Another effective way to unblock these sorts of nerves is by "reverse engineering" the question. This can work for all sorts of practice questions. This sort of "looking backward" approach involves deconstructing your thinking. There are different ways of doing this with bar study. With an essay or other written response question, for example, one approach is to start by reading the fact pattern and model answer aloud. Then, *look at and outline the answer*, asking yourself, "What would I have needed in an outline to write this kind of answer?" Then look back at the facts and ask, "Where in these facts do I see words that trigger the points I put in my outline?" Sometimes studying answers and working backward helps you see what was important in the question.

Outlining sample answers may not only help you relax and see how certain facts were significant (building your factual analysis muscle) but should also help you recognize logical ways to organize issues on future questions.

Copying answers and reverse engineering are tools that will help you get the juices flowing again when you feel stalled. They seem easy because you are working from answers, so they tend to reduce anxiety. But somehow they often empower people. The very act of retyping and understanding the words coming from your own hands will build skills you need to learn to write similar answers on your own. Likewise, seeing both how an answer flows from a question and how pieces of the question trigger components of the answer helps build your test-taking skills. This process works effectively to deconstruct multiple-choice questions and performance tests as well.

As you work, tell yourself, "I can do this. I see the organization. It makes sense." Remind yourself, "When I'm in the exam, this is how my analysis will flow." Smile and force yourself to take a deep breath. Keep yourself in as positive a frame of mind as possible to keep your brain energized.

Anxiety-Reducing Tools to Use Any Time Nerves Hit

Some techniques work particularly well during specific times, as noted above (during a lecture, while reading, or when taking practice exam, etc.) Other strategies such as those below are helpful any time you feel anxious.

Because intensive bar preparation lasts for two tense, crazy months, these simple steps will help when nerves hit:

- Breathe deeply and slowly. Slow, steady, deep breaths will often release the nerves and "paralysis" that comes from them. We tend to tense up when we are nervous, and often forget to breathe properly. You will read more clearly and think more logically when the oxygen is flowing freely.
- Visualize yourself in the exam setting. Picture yourself thinking and your words flowing. As you take practice tests, imagine taking them in a room full of palpable stress (perhaps picture the place you took the LSAT, SAT, or any other standardized test). Recall the nervous energy and how you prevailed in spite of it. (Maybe part of you thrived on the challenge!) Envision yourself now and on your upcoming exams reading questions; selecting answers to multiple-choice answers; drafting answers to PTs and other written response questions, and feeling calm, confident, and in control.
- Talk to yourself, calmly and positively. Positive thinking is critical! Tell yourself every day that you *can* do this. Say it aloud several times each day. Banish from your mind any past test-taking experiences that were not positive. Replace them with empowering images of you conquering challenges. Go back to Chapter 1 and study the "rephrasing" examples. Ban phrases such as, "I'm not good at standardized tests." That is hogwash (B.S. if you prefer), and you know it!

  You got into law school and may even have successfully completed law school by the time you have read this chapter. You are not only good—you are excellent at test-taking. Rid your speech (and mind) of all that is not positive and strong. Ultimately, remember that you will be alone on the exam. So, figure out how to talk yourself down from the ledge.

One former student said she got through mini panic attacks during the bar exam by telling herself that it was "just another practice test." When she felt the pressure mount, she whispered to herself, *"This is just another practice test. You've been doing these all summer. You've got this. It's OK. You know what to do. Just keep reading and thinking. It's a puzzle. It all fits together. Just breathe."*

Notice that the strategies above can be employed without "props." There are many things you can do to de-stress in June and July (January or February), *before the exam*, such as drink a cup of tea, take a walk, go to a yoga class, meditate, take a hot bath, or talk with someone who loves and supports you. But none of those work *during* the exam.

It is important to develop some effective calming habits that you can employ if you find yourself panicking *on the actual exam*.

Breathing and self-talk techniques help a lot. But by far *the most effective tool to combat nerves is adequate preparation*. The better your training, the more prepared you are, the less your nerves will hinder you. If you do feel nervous, which is normal no matter how hard you have studied, you will be much more able to turn the nervousness into adrenaline so that it serves rather than defeats, you. (Remember the three Ps: turn *panic* into *power* not *paralysis*.)

CONTAGIOUS ANXIETY

People who tell you, "Just don't be nervous" or suggest that it is stupid to feel anxiety are either ignorant or full of garbage. It is *normal* to be nervous. If you are not a little nervous, you likely do not appreciate the seriousness of the bar exam. You might find it helpful when others share that they too are nervous. It makes you feel you are not alone. That's great, unless then nerves are contagious and cause you to stress out further. (If that's the case, do not talk about being nervous with classmates. You must protect yourself as you prepare for success.)

WORK HARD, BUT WORK EFFICIENTLY: REASSESS YOUR SCHEDULE

After a week or two of intensive bar preparation, ask yourself whether the location and timing of your studying are maximizing your productivity. Where you study can mean the difference between focusing well and not focusing at all, or anywhere in between.

Selecting Study Spots

1. Are you studying at the law library? Many find their law school libraries distracting because classmates stop to chat. How is it working for you?

2. Are you studying in your home? Is it quiet? Do you have a dedicated study space?

3. Is the place you are studying helping you focus? Why or why not?

Some people simply cannot focus at a cluttered desk. Some determine their homes are not conducive to study, so they find a good spot elsewhere. You don't have to move out or rent an office to focus effectively (though those things work for some people). Just find a place that works for you. It may be a coffee shop or public library.

"Adapt or perish, now as ever, is nature's inexorable imperative."

—H. G. WELLS—

Your goal is to find a place where, and discover the times when, you are most focused. It is excellent training, though, to take at least a few practice tests or try to study at least a few days in *the most distracting place imaginable.* I urge my students to do this so that they don't get so used to the quiet of their home or a library that they are unable to concentrate during the actual exam, when keyboards will be clacking and other applicants will be coughing, sneezing, sighing, groaning, or making other noises. (Even with earplugs, exam rooms can be noisy.)

One former student who passed the bar the first time was determined to overcome his concern about being distracted on the actual exam. How did he do this? He decided to train by completing practice tests each week at the noisiest place he could think of—the top of the stairs in one of the most crowded shopping malls in Los Angeles. He figured (correctly) that if he could focus there, he could focus anywhere. And he did! (By the way, the exam he took and passed the first time around had a rule against perpetuities issue!)

Is My Schedule Maximizing My Efficiency?

Not getting done each day what you need to? Look critically at your schedule. What is, and what is not, working? When are you getting distracted? Are you a working student whose daily schedule varies? If so, try a weekly schedule so you can fit more into days when you have more time, do less on busier days, and still keep up.

Think about when and what you are eating on study days, and whether you are exercising. Those are factors that can help you work more efficiently or slow you down.

Are people interrupting you? Is your phone still out when you are studying? Put your phone in the other room while you study. Are you too tired to focus? Maybe shifting the time of day can help you focus. Or change locations. Every challenge can be surmounted if you see where the hang-ups are.

Adapt Your Schedule as the Bar Approaches and Make More Time for Memorizing

Though called "bar *review*," much of the process is about *learning*. Practice exams help to learn the law in context and recall rules when you encounter analogous fact patterns.

Your goal when you walk into that test is to know each element of each important rule as well as you know your most frequently used password. (I believe this is true even on exams that indicate you will not need to memorize a concept because it is extremely difficult to quickly and sensibly analyze and apply the elements from a statute provided in a fact pattern if you do not know and understand the rules and concepts that statute governs.) Your schedule must therefore include adequate time for memorization. The more simply you can phrase rules, the easier they will be to memorize and use on the exam. So, a main goal throughout early bar review and the first weeks of intensive bar review is to assemble and organize all key rules into memorizable form.

How to Memorize? Break Out the Flashcards, Write It Out Fifty Times, Do Whatever Works for You!

Read rule statements aloud, listen to them, write them out repeatedly, test yourself, and have others test you. Create hypotheticals that illustrate the rule in context. Engage fully in the memorization process. In the smartphone age, our memories take a back seat. We don't need them much, if at all. But by the end of July (February), your mind needs to act as a sort of Siri for legal rules. When you need the definition of *homicide* and forms of malice, or a statement of Rules 10b–5 or 16b, or UCC Section 2–207, you need them right away. You need instant recall.

Sometimes we need a kick (or trick) to help us recall rules for an exam. Mnemonics are memory-aid techniques that have likely been helping people since ancient times. They can be verbal—perhaps a short rhyme or a key word that helps you remember something. Memory tips can be in song form. (How many people sing the alphabet song when they alphabetize?) They can be based on lists. People often choose the first letter of each word in a list; for example, IRAC is a common mnemonic for Issue, Rule, Analysis, Conclusion. They can also be visual, such as associating arrows to recall how one concept stems from or links to another.

Reflection: How Do You Memorize?

You are a student or were for years. This is not the first time you have had to memorize. Think back to science (memorizing the periodic table), math (memorizing formulas), history (memorizing dates and names), and foreign languages (memorizing vocabulary). What worked best for you? What made things stick? Did you:

(1) Write out, maybe even fifty times, whatever you needed to memorize?

(2) Create a flash card and test yourself, or have others test you?

(3) Say it out loud?

(4) Put it to song or rhyme, or create a mnemonic?

(5) Chunk larger quantities of information into groups of three?

What are your favorite memory tools?

1. ______________________________

2. ______________________________

3. ______________________________

Preventing Burnout: Add Incentives and Levity

Studying for the bar exam is a test of endurance. You have to put in many high-gear days and pack into your brain more learning than you ever thought you could absorb, and you have to do this day in and day out for a minimum of about sixty days. This section provides suggestions to help stay on course.

Reward Yourself

During intensive bar prep, give yourself a small but consistent reward *each day* for doing your best, and a slightly bigger one each week.

What makes you smile, feel happy, or comforted? What works for you?

If it's music, spend at least fifteen to twenty minutes listening (and singing or dancing) to your favorite tunes each evening after you have honestly put in a good, solid day's work. Once a week, maybe give yourself an hour or two off to listen to live music somewhere.

Is it movies or TV? Allow yourself a half hour of mindless TV each evening, and watch a movie at home once a week, with popcorn!

Is it food or wine? Give yourself some special treat once a day, something at the end of a hard day's learning—chocolate, ice cream, sautéed mushrooms in truffle oil? (Well, I said whatever works for you!) Once a week, go out to a special restaurant or cook, or have someone else cook, a special meal at home.

The point here is to positively mark and acknowledge your hard work each day and each week. You need to stay in the game and not get worn out too early. Expect these months to involve hard work. Do that work with as much energy and focus as is humanly possible. Then acknowledge and give yourself credit for what you have done.

This also helps you count down the weeks and pace yourself. Studying for the bar exam is a long haul. (Note: It is a long haul for your family or significant other, too. If you are a person who uses good food as an incentive, think about possibly taking your family or significant other out for a great meal once per week—a reward for you and them!)

Reward Yourself for Your Hard Work

List how you might reward yourself for a job well done.

What works for you?

____

____

____

After enjoying your reward, get a good night's sleep so you can get back to work the next morning. Slow and steady wins the race.

Above all, be kind to yourself all the way through bar review. This is one of the hardest times in your life, one of the steepest mountains you will have to climb. The good news is, once you pass the bar, you'll have a lifetime license. You'll never have to take the exam again.

Pay your annual dues, complete your jurisdiction's continuing-education requirements, and remain ethical, and you'll keep your license for life.

GIVE YOURSELF A SPECIAL REWARD OR INCENTIVE ON JULY 1

One nice thing about seeing June become July (or January become February, for February takers) is that adrenaline will kick in. But the last week of June (January) can also be particularly rough. People are normally drained, and sometimes a little depressed or discouraged, as June (January) ends. Prepare for a jolt when you see the calendar change. It can freak you out if you are not ready for it. (You have been saying the date of your bar exam for years. It felt so far off, but suddenly it's nearly here.) You must make that July 1 (February 1) rush one of adrenaline, not panic. So, treat yourself with extra kindness on that day.

Bar Exam Burnout

We talked earlier about anxiety and how to combat nerves. What about fatigue and burnout? First, let's address the differences between these. It is one of degree. If you are just tired, sleeping more may help. For anxiety, try the tips discussed earlier. (Note that you are apt to be more nervous and less able to conquer anxiety when you are tired.) If you are suffering from burnout, recharging your batteries may be a bit more difficult.

Are you burned out? Some people *start* bar review burned out. Others are really dragging by the end of June (January). What can you do about burnout? First, admit it. Face it so you can correct it. Allowing yourself to be so "done" that you are blocked from putting in further effort will not result in success.

Next, assess whether it's a major burnout. Do you need a half day or full day off? Some people need an entire weekend away. If you know that you are too fried to focus, take time off. Get some fresh air. Change the scenery. Clear your mind.

For minor burnout, the best solution is giving yourself consistent small rewards and breaks that you know you can look forward to after every productive study day. It can also be helpful to break up the day. Put in a focused four-hour block in the morning; then take a good, long lunch break. (Most bar exams actually have long lunch breaks.) You can eat and maybe get in some exercise or even a nap if you need it. (At least a few of my former students power-napped during the lunch break at the actual bar exam! They set two alarm clocks and arranged for a wake-up call, of course.)

Take a similar break following afternoon and evening study sessions. Spend time with someone supportive, if you have someone in your life who is helpful. If not, spend any downtime with a good book or movie! (Do not spend time with anyone who saps your energy or keeps you from meeting your goal.)

Humor: You Gotta Laugh a Little

Some people like to watch a comedy every so often or listen to silly jokes.

This is my "Top Ten List for *How You Know You Are Taking a Bar Exam.*"

10. Your desk and bookshelves are filled with software and books about bars, but none of them tell you where to get a drink.
9. You care how many multiple-choice practice questions other people answer.
8. You study flash cards at red lights.
7. Your phone has a playlist called something like "Get that Study Groove On."
6. You dream about real property fact patterns.
5. You wake from those dreams wondering what the answer is.
4. You know the differences between Notice, Race-Notice, and Race Statutes, and you care about those differences.
3. You have spent more money in the past few months on bar prep than most of your nonlaw friends spend on car payments.
2. Whenever you have to wait for something, you find yourself calculating how many multiple-choice questions you could have done in the time spent waiting.
1. You spend serious time thinking about whether you will be able to make it through anxiety-filled testing bar exam time blocks without having to go to the bathroom.

If you don't find my bar humor funny, watch a few short videos of comedy sketches from your favorite comedians. Laughter is extraordinary medicine! So is music.

Motivate with Music

Every time you feel overwhelmed, overloaded, tired, fearful, or discouraged, play music that makes your spirit sing. Music will lift you right out of whatever you are feeling (those feelings, by the way, are totally normal just prior to taking the bar exam).

Sure, there are some people who one week into July (February) are saying, "Just bring it on. I am tired of studying, tired of waiting, and I am as ready as I'll ever be." But they are few and far between. Most people feel overwhelmed and overloaded just before the exam and want every extra minute possible to prepare.

It's a long haul, the bar exam. If you're tired or feel yourself slowing down, play some inspiring music. And sing along! Find the artists that move you. Even on the actual exam, should you find yourself in an afternoon lull or a moment of panic, humming an uplifting tune in your head may be just the secret weapon to pull you through.

What Is on Your Bar Exam Playlist?

____

____

____

FINALIZING YOUR SCHEDULE

You have the pieces now to create an effective study schedule. Take a look back at the draft you wrote earlier and update it or start fresh. Be sure your schedule includes regular disciplined study *and* regular breaks to recharge your batteries. And, remember this is a living document that you will adapt as needed during bar prep.

6 a.m.

7 a.m.

8 a.m.

9 a.m.

10 a.m.

11 a.m.

Noon

1 p.m.

2 p.m.

3 p.m.

4 p.m.

5 p.m.

6 p.m.

7 p.m.

8 p.m.

9 p.m.

10 p.m.

Chapter hashtags: #PasstheBar, #PanictoPower, #GottaLaugh, #PaceMyself, #NervesAreNormal, #NoDoubters, #Calm ConfidentinControl, #BarExamSuccess

CHAPTER 8

PRACTICE TESTS: THE HEAVY LIFTING

- Passing the Bar Exam Requires Knowledge, Skill, *and* Training
- "I Wish I Had Started Earlier!"
- Overview of Bar Exam Testing
- Active Reading Equals Bar Reading
- What Is Bar Reading?
- Where to Get Practice Tests?
- MCQ Strategy and Preparation
- Practice by Completing a Consistent Number of MCQs Every Day, Under Timed Conditions
- How to Self-Assess MCQs
- Reading Error?
- Didn't Know or Understand a Rule?
- Didn't Finish in Time?
- MCQ Tips and Strategies
- Essay Testing Tips and Strategies
- Crossover Questions
- Practice Essay Writing
- Essays: A Closer Look at How to Read and Write Them
- Bar Writing Is Logical Writing, and It Differs in Some Key Ways from Law School Exam Writing
- Bar Reading and Its Relationship to Bar Writing
- Writing Example #1
- Writing Example #2

- Do Not Assume: Prove It and Say Why
- Conclusions
- How to Self-Assess Your Practice Essay Writing
- Self-Assessment: Improvement Area Action Items
- Persistence
- Reality Check: Getting Your Exams Graded by Someone Else
- Self-Assess Through Reverse Engineering
- Performance Tests
- About Performance Tests (PTs)
- Key Differences Between PTs and Essays
- How to Complete Performance Tests
- Overview of This System: Why It Works and Why It Makes Sense
- Adjust the Timing to Fit Your Strengths and Weaknesses
- A Closer Look at Each Step in the PT Approach
- The Instructions
- The File
- The Library
- Remaining Steps in the Approach
- Performance Test Practice: How to Self-Assess
- PT Strategy Tips
- Practice Test Scores for All Types of Bar Testing

The previous chapters discussed many success factors, including planning, preparing, knowing what to expect, protecting your time, and learning the law. In this chapter, we'll look at practice exams.

This is the hardest chapter of all. You have done your planning and mapped out your study schedule. You have put yourself in the right mindset. From here, it is just plain hard work—the "heavy lifting" phase, completing practice test after practice test, and reviewing sample answers so you see where to improve.

You are in training, so think of this as athletes do their preparation for a high stakes game. Picture a basketball player, for example, watching replays of every game. They don't just compete and forget about it, hoping they'll do better in the next game. No. They dissect every piece of every game, looking for ways to improve.

After you self-assess practice exams, you must take affirmative steps to implement any changes that are necessary. This is part of what is referred to by learning scientists as "self-regulated learners."

Completing practice questions without assessing your performance is what I call "*Doing the Ostrich.*" It's like people who think bad news will go away if they just ignore it. Not true. Do not put your head in the sand here. Seize these precious opportunities, after completing practice exams, to improve.

The road to success is yours, but only if you drive. Don't be the passive passenger. Take control. Get to work. After you read this chapter, review your study plan. Make sure it includes sufficient uninterrupted time blocks for taking *and self-assessing* practice tests on top of bar review.

And protect your practice exam time. Don't be seduced into thinking that passively attending bar review is enough. It isn't.

Bar prep will fly by. You will be taking the exam before you know it. How you choose to spend your time will determine how you go in—confidently, knowing you have done everything in your power to achieve success, or sheepishly, knowing you could have done more. It's your choice.

PASSING THE BAR EXAM REQUIRES KNOWLEDGE, SKILL, *AND* TRAINING

- You must know and understand the legal rules and principles tested on the exam.

- You must be skilled in critical reading, clear and effective writing, analytical and logical reasoning, and time management.

  The kind of critical reading you need I will call "bar reading." This is the first and most important of the skills required for bar success. If you are not reading precisely, *and understanding what you read*, your analysis will be off, usually leading to incorrect or incomplete conclusions. When you fail to read critically, you miss or misinterpret words, assume information not in the question, and make other egregious yet wholly preventable errors, errors you would not have made had you read carefully enough.

- You must prepare by taking practice tests under timed conditions, self-assessing your performance, and following specific steps to steadily and continuously improve your results.

Overview of Bar Exam Testing

Bar exams typically include some combination of multiple-choice questions, integrated set questions, performance tests, and/or essays. There are samples of each of these in the Appendix.

Below, for common testing formats, we will consider:

- what the format is;
- how to practice this type of test;
- how to self-assess practice tests; and
- exam-taking tips and strategies.

Just as you will need to become fluent in each heavily tested area of law, so too must you become skilled at each testing format. Don't go into the bar hoping they won't test a certain sub-topic, and don't go in saying things like, "I'm great at multiple-choice but not so good at those performance tasks." **Get good at everything.**

THE POWER OF MIXED TESTING FORMATS

On a visit to New Orleans, I sampled dishes reflecting Southern chefs' penchant for flavoring with onions, peppers, and celery. The key is the combination. That flavor would not result from a preparation with boatloads of peppers, but no onions.

Not a foodie? Think of your body's need for diet, exercise, *and* rest. All the exercise in the world won't help if you feed your body poorly or are too tired to function. Likewise, on bar exams, all of the pieces are critical. Resist the temptation to favor one form of practice testing over another. Slap yourself if you are tempted to fill every hour with practice multiple-choices or shorter questions because you can complete more of them in less time. **Take the time you need to strategically prepare; be ready for all testing formats.**

If you catch yourself thinking you don't need practice in a certain format or that you can't afford the time to engage with practice tests, think again. I assure you, you cannot afford to *skip* them.

Different exams have different testing formats and different amounts of time to complete each part of the exam, so train under timed conditions. Below is a bit about some common formats.

Bar exam multiple-choice testing.

Some exams still include the legacy multistate bar exam (MBE), a 200 multiple-choice question exam in torts, contracts, criminal law and procedure, constitutional law, evidence, real property, and civil procedure.

Some exams include state-specific questions. (Check you state bar's website to see if your exam will include these and study any sample questions.)

Forty-nine percent of the NextGen bar exam that launches in certain jurisdictions in 2026 is based on multiple-choice questions. Many of these will resemble MBE questions. Others may differ. (The NextGen bar will include some where applicants must select the two best answers from six possible answer choices.) Sample NextGen MCQs are included in the Appendix to this book.

While more law professors are incorporating multiple-choice tests into law school, most students are not exposed to the rigor of taking so many complex (tricky) multiple-choice questions in a variety of subjects under significant time pressures.

Like essays (discussed below and a familiar law school testing format), multiple-choice questions (MCQs) are based on a factual story. This similar structure is why we will develop a similar strategy for approaching MCQs as one might employ taking essay exams: read the question first; then read the facts. With both essays and MCQs, it is essential to read every word carefully. Unlike essays, though, you will be asked to select the answer (or answers, in some NextGen formats) from a set of choices.

MCQs are challenging because 1) there is only one *best* answer (at least on traditional MCQs that will still be heavily tested even on the NextGen exam), 2) the questions tend to focus on narrow points of law, and 3) students are given only a short time to reason to the best answer. Success requires detailed knowledge of many legal rules but does not demand the skill that essays do of articulating those rules in your own words.

Bar exam essays.

Essay questions on bar exams that still use that format (there are no traditional essays on the NextGen bar exam) are similar to law school essay exams. They typically tell a factual story about two or more parties who have some conflict or problem. Your job is to apply the law you know (and have memorized) to these facts, and reason through to logical conclusions that answer the question(s) asked. The ultimate question may be who prevails, why, and what damages may be awarded; with what crimes may a defendant be convicted; how provisions in a will should be interpreted to determine how property will be distributed; or who will be awarded which assets or incur which debts following a divorce proceeding.

Note that many sub-issues (additional questions) may need to be resolved in order to reach the ultimate conclusion. (Think about it: to decide whether P may prevail against D in a cause of action for negligence, you must resolve any issues relating to duty, breach, actual and proximate cause, and damages, and then discuss possible defense theories, and each of these may have discussable sub-parts.)

Bar essays differ from law school essays in that they typically test or can test greater number of issues within a wider range of legal subject areas than law school exams, but bar essays usually test in less depth and often have shorter fact patterns than law school essay exams.

Even if you have taken essay exams all through law school, if your bar exam tests using essays, practice writing out test questions in full under timed conditions during bar review.

Performance tasks or performance tests ("PTs")

PTs are practical exams during which applicants are placed in legal role-play scenarios. As of this writing, nearly every jurisdiction incorporates some form of performance testing on their exam. They differ in timing but strategies for completing them will remain the same:

- NextGen PTs are 60 minutes,
- MPTs and PTs in California for example are 90 minutes,
- Nevada PTs are 2 hours, and
- California used to test with 3-hour PTs.

Some sample questions appear in the appendices to this book and samples of PTs varying in length from 30 minutes to three hours appear in the appendices of *Bar Exam PT Success: Strategies and Practice*, another book in the West Academic Law School Success Series.

Though the quantity of material differs, PTs are similar in that they simulate a lawyer working with a client file (which provides source documents to digest the factual situation), a Library (where relevant rules are provided, often in cases and/or statutes), and applicants are asked to draft one or more "real-world" documents based on those facts and legal rules.

You may be asked to draft briefs in support of motions, memos, client letters, settlement offers, affidavits, closing arguments, discovery plans, or other documents.

PTs are "open book" in that the legal principles are provided in a "library." You, of course, have to extract the rules from primary or secondary sources (e.g., by pulling holdings from cases; analyzing statutes; and reading jury instructions, law review articles, or treatises).

PTs would be relatively easy for most law graduates *if* they were given more time in which to complete them. But to provide a complete enough answer to pass within the allotted time is *not* easy; it requires mastering an approach and extensively developing the requisite PT skills.

THE PT PRACTICALLY WRITES ITSELF!

I cannot discuss PTs without being transported back to the voice of a most-charismatic law professor who lectured nationwide for decades. In bar review, he practically danced with enthusiasm as he pounded the podium declaring that because it was open book, the PT was the easy part of the exam; he joyously concluded, "Why, it practically writes itself!" I had 1L professors who incorporated performance tests into a doctrinal and legal research course, so I knew better. Though I appreciated his desire to calm and reassure the crowd, I knew PTs were tough. They were also fair in my view, but in no way easy. (This professor, it turns out, took a bar exam without a PT. Easy for him to say they write themselves. They do not!)

Active Reading Equals Bar Reading

Before considering how to tackle specific types of exams and improve your skills (and, ultimately, your scores), let's first focus on *the most important habit to develop for bar success*: becoming an effective bar reader.

What Is Bar Reading?

Bar reading certainly includes careful reading, but it also involves being deeply engaged with the material, *analyzing and thinking* while you read. Bar reading includes bar thinking which essentially requires superimposing a mental template (issues and rules in a logical structure) on top of the facts so that you immediately see their legal significance and begin reasoning "random" facts into a logical order. (West's *Step-By-Step Guides* to contracts, torts, and criminal law provide excellent examples of logical templates to answer questions in those subjects. For most law students, these are free using your West Academic login.)

You know from law school that facts are not relevant in isolation. You *use* facts to prove or disprove *elements* of identifiable causes of action, crimes, defenses, or other legal theories.

Please understand what I just said: when you do not know and understand the law well enough, you will not see the significance of words you are reading. But when you do know the law really well, just reading a certain word or phrase will trigger rules in your mind.

For example, if you see a "broken" door or window in a criminal law fact pattern, you might ask yourself if there was a burglary? When you see facts indicating someone was driving or doing some other action "carelessly" or "without paying attention," or "while distracted," you know you might have a negligence issues. And, the minute you see a fact pattern involving "police" where a suspect "blurted out" something, you should have a sense that *Miranda* might be at issue.

Then once you have identified the appropriate area of law, to answer a question, you must know and thoroughly understand the rule itself and the many exceptions to it. In a criminal procedure question involving *Miranda*, you cannot just know the TV version in which any time a cop and a suspect are on screen together, *Miranda* rights are read. No, you must know and understand the rule well.

Unless you have a photographic memory, bar reading also involves note-taking. If you are taking practice questions online, find a way to take notes either on scratch paper or on the screen while you read. If you can, highlight on the screen or underline key words, do so. If you are taking a practice test on paper, jot notes in the margins or on top of words on the exam itself.

You will want to note any word or words that appear to trigger a discussion or analysis of some particular area of law. (This is sometimes called *issue spotting*, as we'll discuss in detail below.)

For example, suppose you are reading a criminal law fact pattern and see that the defendant was diagnosed with schizophrenia. You would immediately underline the word *schizophrenia* and jot in the margin something like "Insanity defense?" Why? All of the tests for insanity require that the defendant suffer from a mental disease or defect, so although this one word does not necessarily mean that insanity is a *discussable* issue, it may be, and you need to be alert to the possibility. The word "schizophrenia" is therefore an insanity issue trigger.

Consider another example: if a criminal law fact pattern indicated a defendant was engaged in some other crime at the time a death resulted, what might that suggest? Yes, that's right: it's a tip-off that felony murder might be a discussable issue. Again, you might *ultimately* conclude that the felony murder rule does not apply. Perhaps it's not a dangerous felony, or the rule is inapplicable for some other reason. But felony murder still may be a relevant (and in any essay question, a discussable) issue. Remember, *it is often just as important to recognize that the rule is implicated though not satisfied, and analyze why the moving party will not win, as it is to prove when the moving party prevails.*

The main point of bar essay testing is not to demonstrate that you know the best answer; that is the goal of multiple-choice questions. Rather, essays allow you to demonstrate that you know a) what questions or issues the facts give rise to, and b) how, given the law you know and can articulate, these facts tend to prove or disprove related claims or defenses.

While every essay will be different in some respects, there are often parallels in essay exams. Writing answers to many practice exams will help you see which issues tend to arise in similar fact patterns, and it will help you easily spot words that suggest or trigger particular issues.

Tip: Keep lists of "trigger words" for every bar-tested subject!

Torts Trigger Test

Test yourself quickly here below: what cause of action, rule, theory, or sub areas of torts do you think of when you see the following words?

1. Extreme and outrageous
2. Rescue
3. Child
4. Premises
5. Product
6. Not paying attention
7. Intentionally

When you are engaged in active bar reading, you will also want to:

- Circle or put a box around certain words, such as party names the first time they are introduced in a fact pattern.
- Circle the connecting words *and* and *or* when reading questions and answer choices.
- Underline the words "not," "most" and "least."

  Do this as well when reading documents such as contractual provisions in an PT file and statutes in an PT library. You cannot afford to miss even one *and* or *or*. Missing one such word may change the entire meaning. As such, you will also underline, highlight, or otherwise clearly mark the holdings in cases in the PT library.

What do all of these examples have in common? The most important part of bar reading is *thinking* while you read.

- Bar reading requires asking yourself *why* each word in a fact pattern is there and whether it triggers some legal issue.
- Bar reading involves recalling previous fact patterns as well as discerning how the new facts are analogous to or distinguishable from other scenarios or examples you recall, so that you can

readily determine if a legal theory is or is not applicable and why.

Reading with Three Senses

To ensure that you read in this fully engaged manner, lean forward and sit up straight when you read, and develop the habit of simultaneously reading with three senses: touch, sight, and hearing.

- *Point* to each word with your finger or pencil (touching the screen or paper you are reading on), while you
- *Read* with your eyes, and at the same time
- Softly *say* the words aloud. (Don't read loudly enough to disturb others or be kicked out of the exam room, but just loudly enough so that the words enter your consciousness, a sort of mumbling process called *subvocalization.* If you are concerned about disturbing others, you can mouth the words without a sound.)

Practice this three-sense reading strategy—reading with your eyes while touching and saying each word.

Bar reading also involves reading certain parts of these exams several times.

Essays: When approaching a bar essay question, read the interrogatories (or "the call of the question") first, and then reread them. Read the essay fact pattern closely and, if necessary, more than once as well. Circle, underline, or highlight trigger words and other words or phrases that seem important. Write notes to yourself in the margins and/or on scratch paper or in your answer file.

PTs: When starting a PT, read the instructions several times. (We will talk later about specific strategies for reading PT files and libraries.)

MCQs: Multiple-choice testing requires such fast responses that time may not allow for repeated readings, so you must develop a strategy to read those initially with the utmost attention to detail. That said, too many students rush through

MCQs without taking all the time allotted. This can lead to sloppy reading and careless mistakes. So, do not rush. Instead, focus on reading each word of MCQs and learning the law so well that when you see (and touch and hear) key words, you will know how to analyze the choices and reason to the best answer.

Where to Get Practice Tests?

Much of the rest of this chapter is directly or indirectly related to taking practice tests: why to take them, how to take them, and how to self-assess and improve the quality of your answers. This may feel like extra "busy work" that you don't have time for, but it is the most important part of bar preparation.

Studies repeatedly link active preparation to success. So, I repeat, taking practice tests is the most important part of bar prep.

Where are these practice tests located, and how do you get ahold of them? For practice bar exam questions, go to your bar review course materials, your state bar's website, or other reputable sources referred by ASP faculty. You can sometimes buy practice exams from the examiners directly, and examiners often have a number of sample exams posted (and freely accessible) on their websites. You can also find older, used materials from bookstores, law libraries, or online sites. Two caveats: First, the material may be dated and some of the law may have changed. Second, exam formats may have changed. That said, as long as you are aware of these possible deficiencies, certain old bar review materials can be very useful, especially for early start, when much of your goal is more general exposure than the intensive training, and especially in subject areas that don't tend to change much (such as real property).

SAMPLE VERSUS MODEL ANSWERS

Simply put, a sample answer can tell you what you will need to do to pass; a model answer can show you what to strive for.

Many jurisdictions release student answers. These are sample passing answers and may contain errors. (Bar exams are pass/fail tests. Bar examiners do not expect perfection!) By *model answers* I mean those written by professors in a reliable bar review or ASP program. Model answers should not contain substantive law errors, though they occasionally do. Sample answers are written under timed conditions, whereas model answers may have been crafted and edited for days or weeks. Both can serve as learning tools just be aware of their limitations.

The Multistate Bar Examination (MBE) and Other Multiple-Choice Testing Formats

Note: While the MBE will not be part of the NextGen bar exam, it will still be in place for a couple of years in some jurisdictions. Some of what follows below is unique to the MBE, but most of it applies to all multiple-choice questions.

If you are taking the NextGen bar exam, get familiar with the MCQ portion of that exam by reading the information on the NCBE's website. If you are taking an exam with the legacy Multistate Bar Examination (MBE), the NCBE describes this as a "six-hour, 200-question multiple-choice examination developed by the NCBE and administered by user jurisdictions as part of the bar examination on the last Wednesday in February and the last Wednesday in July of each year." The MBE tests civil procedure, constitutional law, contracts, criminal law and procedure, evidence, real property, and torts.

MCQs, like essays, begin with a short fact pattern. The facts are followed by an interrogatory (question) and four answer choices. Applicants are to respond by choosing the best of the four choices. (As we will discuss below, the "best" answer is not always the "correct" answer choice!) Some multiple-choice questions on the NextGen bar exam may include the two best answers out of six possible choices.

MCQs on bar exams require fast-paced reading and thinking. On the MBE, applicants with standard time limits must answer 200 questions to be answered in six hours: 100 in three hours in the morning, and 100 in three hours in the afternoon.

MCQs tend to test fine distinctions in points of law. Otherwise stated, they can be picky and confusing. The more you engage with practice, the stronger you will become and better at seeing the tricks.

As noted, some jurisdictions also include state-specific multiple-choice questions. These vary a great deal, so be sure you are taking a bar review that is dedicated to helping students in your jurisdiction. Below we will focus on multiple-choice questions as tested on the MBE, though some of the strategies for other multiple-choice tests may be similar. Practice NextGen MCQs are included in this books Appendix.

To understand MCQs, you must have mastered a great many detailed legal rules. You will need to choose the *best* answer for each question. Therefore, *a single-most accurate* answer choice must necessarily be included for each question. To make it possible that one answer is clearly the best, questions are often crafted such that the answer turns on a rule of law rather than a factual analysis. Essays, by contrast, often focus more on facts from which differing inferences may be drawn. In other words, taking the same essay facts, applicants may reason through them differently or draw varying conclusions from them. Thus, applicants may write essay answers with different outcomes and still be correct and pass the exam. Because you are writing your own answers, you can present arguments from different points of view (e.g., using "defendant would argue" or "plaintiff would argue" language). However, there is no room to argue the facts when answering an MCQ.

To illustrate, let's take a simple hypothetical criminal law scenario:

> Defendant Dan is approached by Vicious Victor, who is wielding a knife. Dan does not know for certain that Victor intends to kill him, but Dan responds nonetheless by pulling out a gun and shooting Victor, aiming at Victor's toe. Victor dies as a result of the injury.

Assume an MCQ posed a question that asked applicants to give the best defense theory presented by this scenario, with the following as answer choices: (a) deadly weapon, (b) insanity, (c) self-defense, or (d) intoxication. Let's think it through: There are no facts to help Dan establish either an insanity or intoxication defense, so rule out choices "b" and "d." Next, although it isn't certain that Dan would prevail in asserting self-defense as a justification, it is likely the *best* of the choices given. Why? The focus of the question is on defenses, and Victor's use of a deadly weapon does not in and of itself provide a defense theory. In fact, it might help the prosecutor to convict Dan of a more serious offense, as discussed below. Note: This is tricky, as MCQs often are, because Victor's use of a knife, a deadly weapon, is necessary to justify Dan having responded by defending himself with deadly force. But because the question asks what Dan's best defense theory will be, the best response appears to be "c."

The best answer would be less certain, however, if this same fact pattern were an essay question asking, "Of what crimes, if any, might Dan be convicted—and why?" You would certainly strive to analyze the issues as clearly as possible, but you might point out how drawing different inferences from the facts in this case could lead to different results. Let's look at this more closely. The prosecutor would assert that Dan committed murder, and, unless Dan successfully argued a defense or mitigation theory, Dan would be convicted of either first- or second-degree murder. A murder is a homicide committed with malice aforethought. Dan killed Victor; therefore, Dan committed the homicide element of murder—that is, the killing of one human being by another. Dan's use of a deadly weapon allows for an *inference* that Dan possessed the intent to kill, which would prove malice and satisfy the mental state element of murder. (This means the judge or jury *could* find that Dan intended to kill Victor just because Dan used a deadly weapon in a deadly manner, without other evidence of Dan's actual intent. This does not have to be the conclusion, but it is permissible.)

Law students will correctly recognize that for a first-degree murder conviction, the prosecution would also have to establish that Dan's shooting was premeditated and deliberate. Both premeditation and deliberation would likely be more difficult to prove under these facts, as Dan's actions appear to have been unplanned. But before we even address these concerns, is it crystal clear that Dan had the required mental state? Not at all.

The prosecution *might* be able to show by virtue of using a deadly weapon that Dan possessed the intent to kill, but that is not the only reasonable inference one could draw. (And the judge or jury would not have to come to the same conclusion.) The defense could counter (or rebut) the inference that Dan intended to kill Victor, for example, by stressing that Dan aimed at Victor's toe.

What inference would be drawn from the fact that Dan shot at Victor's toe? Well, one who intends to kill typically aims for the head or a vital organ, rather than the smallest of extremities, right? So, Dan's having shot at Victor's toe might tend to prove that Dan did not intend to kill.

The prosecution might in turn contend that aiming to shoot at any part of a victim's body evidences an intent to kill or, at the very least an intent to seriously injure, a mental state that would suffice for second-degree murder.

The defense might go on to argue that Dan's actions were justified, that he was acting in self-defense. After all, Victor was the first to draw a weapon, his knife. But in order to prevail in a complete self-defense justification, the defendant must prove that at the time of action, he or she reasonably and in good faith feared being attacked with imminent deadly force. This could pose a problem for Dan. Why? Well, although it's true that Victor was wielding a deadly weapon himself, the facts specifically state that Dan was uncertain as to whether Victor was intending to kill him. (Maybe Victor wanted to show Dan his knife to prove how vicious he was, without intending to *use* the knife at all.) Unless Dan could establish that he himself believed, and that a reasonable person in his shoes would have believed, that he was about to be attacked by Victor with deadly force, it is doubtful Dan would prevail in claiming self-defense.

Therefore, a logical conclusion to the analysis might be that Dan would *likely* be convicted of second-degree murder because he shot Victor with what can be established was the intent to seriously injure him. But it's *possible* to have logically concluded that despite aiming at Victor's toe, Dan still likely possessed the intent to kill, especially given his use of a deadly weapon.

From this short scenario and the fact that we were able to reason to more than one plausible conclusion, you can see how much more room there is for gray areas in essay questions than in MCQs. Learning the differences between the two and taking many practice tests of every format of tested question, will help you gain a command of effective test-taking strategies. On MCQs your sole task is to find the *best* answer, but on essays you may reason to different conclusions depending on the inferences you logically draw from the facts, and whether the facts prove or disprove the existence of legal elements.

MCQ Strategy and Preparation

How to approach MCQs? When you complete an MCQ, do the following:

- Cover the answer choices so you don't get suckered into selecting a seductive-looking answer before you even know the facts, and so that you do not become biased while reading the facts.
- Next, read the interrogatory or "call of the question," at or near at the end of the facts. (This will help you know what area of law you are in so that you can "call up" the relevant rules in your mind's search engine.)
- Then read the fact pattern *and reread the interrogatory*. Remember to use bar reading technique described above: read with pencil in hand, touching and subvocalizing each word as you read. Underline words that trigger legal issues. Based on the law you have memorized, reason through the facts to draw a conclusion that you believe best answers the precise question asked. (Read and analyze this part of the MCQ in the same manner you read a bar essay question.)
- Only after completing these steps (including carefully rereading the interrogatory) should you then take your hand off the answer choices and read through the first choice carefully, asking yourself: "Is this choice plausible?" "Is it responsive to the question?" "Does it mirror the answer I reasoned to?" "Is it even a correct statement in and of itself?" If the choice contains an incorrect rule statement, does not answer the question asked, or answers it incorrectly (applies the law incorrectly

to these specific facts), immediately put a line through it and go on to the next choice.

- Ask yourself the same questions regarding each of the three remaining answer choices, crossing out any that are wrong or don't answer the question. Do this clearly so that you don't mistakenly think an answer choice is still on the table if you have ruled it out. (Some people find it helpful to play a sort of "find the wrong answers" game with themselves. The more you rule out, the better. If you like puzzles, this might be a good strategy for you.)
- Now, what are you left with? If only one answer choice remains, select that one and quickly move on to the next question. (Always keep in mind that the MCQs test speed as well as knowledge and accuracy, so keep moving.)

  In questions where you must select the single best answer, if you have two answer choices that are both consistent with your conclusion but for different reasons, read each one again carefully and isolate what exactly differs between the two choices. Then see if one includes faulty reasoning, an internal inconsistency, an incorrect rule statement, or fails to answer the exact question posed. Reread the interrogatory to be sure you understand the exact question. Reread the facts as necessary. By process of elimination, choose the best of the remaining answers.
- Note that the best answer might not be perfect. Sometimes the best answer is supported by a minority rule rather than the prevailing majority rule. In such a situation, if the other choices are flat-out wrong, then the minority position will be the best answer. Select the answer that seems to reason to the best conclusion when applying appropriate law to resolve the issue asked in the particular question.

- When you study answers, you should strive to determine why you chose the answer you did, and, if you didn't choose the correct answer, why it is best. (More on the self-assessment process below.)

Practice by Completing a Consistent Number of MCQs Every Day, Under Timed Conditions

"How many should I take?" Students always ask this question—a difficult one to answer. The key is consistency. When I sit down with students to plan their schedules, I don't tell them how many to take each day. Rather, I ask them, "How much time do you have each day to commit to a dedicated block of MCQ practice?" Once we have a time slot, we can figure out how many they should take each day.

Let's say a student replies, "I can devote a half hour to MCQs every morning. I'll complete them while having coffee or breakfast." Or, "I can devote 30 minutes for my 'daily MCQs' before bed (after brushing my teeth, so that it becomes an automatic habit)." We would then calculate the number of daily questions that fit into that time slot, accounting for time to review explanatory answers.

If you are taking the MBE and can devote only 15 minutes each stay, start with your "Daily 5." Complete 5 questions in 9 minutes and, in the remaining 6 minutes, study the explanatory answers for any questions you got wrong or guessed on.

Commit to increasing the number of questions you complete and time dedicated for those practice questions as you get closer to the exam. (MBE takers, know that you will eventually have to complete two sets of 100 questions, each within a three-hour block, on your actual exam.)

So, for example, if you begin earlier than May, complete just five questions each day in nine minutes (your "Daily 5") and you will be making MCQs a habit. At the beginning of May, you might increase to ten questions per day in eighteen minutes, with fifteen minutes to self-assess and review questions you missed or guessed on. Work up to seventeen questions daily in thirty minutes by the beginning of June, with another thirty minutes or so for self-assessment.

Your bar review schedule may include a set number of MCQ practice sessions to be completed on certain days. Complete those *along with your extra daily practice. (Remember, bar review is a floor, not a ceiling!)*

By the end of June, most people find it helpful to be answering thirty-three questions in an hour every other day. You can alternate, doing seventeen one day, thirty-three the next, and so on, but always completed at least your Daily 5. In July, make time for at least a few simulated exams in which you answer full sets of 100 questions in three-hour blocks. You do not want the actual exam to be the first time you have tried to do three hours' worth of MCQs in a row. (More on simulated exams below and later chapters.)

Be sure to include ample review time whenever you take MCQs. Immediately after you complete a set of questions, study explanatory answers. Many people review answers to questions that they got right *and* questions they got wrong. Others find it most productive to only review questions they missed or guessed the answer.

Note: In practice, a guess is equivalent to a wrong answer. If you guess right, you got lucky. Do not bank on luck to pass the bar exam. Bank on knowledge, skill, and preparation.

So definitely study every single answer you got wrong or guessed. And, if you find it helpful and not confusing, study each explanatory answer you got right as well. Use this opportunity to learn and or review the rule of law at issue in the context of the particular question to be sure you answer correctly the next time it appears. (The fact pattern may not be exactly the same, but it will be analogous.)

Another different timing strategy is this: when you first start taking practice MCQs (during early start or at the very beginning of bar review), slowly and methodically work through *one question at a time* in each subject. See how the questions are phrased, look carefully at each answer choice, and read the explanatory answer right away before moving on to the next question. After you take at least a small number in such a careful way, then begin taking them under *timed conditions* in sets. Continue taking them under timed conditions until the exam, studying explanatory answers to each set just after you complete that set.

Again, study every answer choice or only those you missed or guessed—whichever you find most helpful.

The key here, like so many of the other study and test-taking strategies in this book, is to figure out how you learn best and what makes sense to you. Also, realize that what you should do in early start differs from how you must train in intensive bar preparation.

MORE THAN ONE EXPLANATION: HELPFUL OR CONFUSING? YOU DECIDE

Let me tell you a story: Eighth-grade algebra. I was doing well; my best friend wasn't. I noticed that my friend would diligently listen to every word the teacher said. I tuned out as soon as I understood a concept. My friend didn't realize that our teacher explained each concept repeatedly, in different ways. Listening to another explanation once I understood something confused me. I convinced my friend to stop listening after "getting" a concept, until the teacher moved on to the next area. (Belated apologies to my teacher, though my motives were purely to achieve self-regulated learning, I too often facilitated this by passing notes or chitchatting.) Remarkably, though, within a week of trying my approach, my friend's grades shot up. We both ended up with an A in the class, and I ended up with a lifelong learning lesson: not every explanation makes things clearer. I applied this strategy in bar review. Once I "got" something, I moved on.

That said, many of my colleagues urge students to review every MCQ answer, right or wrong. And it certainly is important to know when you get the right answer but for the wrong reason! So, you decide.

In addition to asking how many practice questions to complete, students also ask what subjects they should study. "Should I focus on areas on which I am weaker?" "Should I do sets that assess the same subject, or a mix of subjects as will be on the actual exam?"

Again, it depends when you start. You may benefit from starting with subject-specific sets, at or around the same time your bar review lectures cover those subjects. Begin weaving in previous subjects as you complete a topic. By July, complete mixed sets (questions in different subjects) so that you have at least a month of training to handle them since this format will be tested on the bar exam: questions will be fired at you in random subject order. It takes mental dexterity to switch subjects that rapidly. You must be ready!

Some people focus during the week on whatever subject or subjects their bar review is covering that week and do mixed practice questions on weekends to get acclimated to switching subjects.

Once you have trained in all subjects, if you have identified one or more subjects that you are weaker in, spend more time on those areas. You do not want to go into the exam "exposed." Knowing you are prepared for everything will make you feel stronger on test days. Conversely, you will feel particularly vulnerable if you go into the exam hoping an area won't be tested.

Don't *only* answer extra practice questions in weaker areas; you should still be training in all of the subjects. Improving weak spots while maintaining strengths will maximize your ability to do well on every part of the exam.

ARE YOU AVOIDING REAL PROPERTY OR SOME OTHER SUBJECT?

Real property questions tend to have the longest MCQ fact patterns; they also test areas that tend to throw people such as future interests and landlord tenant rules. Others loathe the constitutional law MCQs. Whatever your Achilles' heel, if you have one, train for that area even harder than for the other subjects! A student came to me in January to create a study schedule for the following July's bar exam. She had taken all the bar subjects in law school, listed her grades in each course, and sorted them from lowest to highest. We plotted an early-start review based on that information so that she attacked her weakest subjects first and then progressed to those that were stronger, covering every subject once before bar review even started. She went into bar review knowing that her weak areas had been strengthened and it would truly be a review. More important, she went into her bar exam prepared and confident.

How to Self-Assess MCQs

First, be sure to keep track of which answers you felt fairly certain about and those on which you guessed. Be honest! Again, a guess in practice is equivalent to a miss.

When you finish your set, study the answers. Don't just score yourself and add up the totals. The learning is what is critical. (Don't think about the score at halftime. *Focus on winning the game.*)

Work through every question you missed or guessed the answer (or every single question if that helps you). Read the explanatory answers. Figure out *why* you missed the question. Note: You may miss a question for more than one reason.

Self-Assessment: MCQ Diagnostic

Check all boxes that apply:

[ ] I read the question (the interrogatory) incorrectly.

[ ] I missed a key word or words in the fact pattern.

[ ] I read one or more answer choices incorrectly.

[ ] I didn't understand what the question was asking, or I didn't see the issue.

[ ] I didn't know the law that I needed to apply to the issue to reason to a conclusion.

[ ] I memorized the rule, but I didn't understand the underlying principles the question was testing (so I narrowed it down to two possible choices, but I missed the best one).

[ ] I knew the correct answer, but I entered it incorrectly.

Note: This is just one way of self-assessing. Your bar review or ASP faculty may suggest a different system. All good. Do what works for you.

Next, use this information *to improve. Don't spend a minute being down on yourself or frustrated by the fact that you got the wrong answers.* That's a waste of time. So long as you know *why*, you are winning this game. (The word *game* does not suggest this is easy. But it can be helpful to view these as challenges, puzzles you are determined to solve.)

Practice tests are learning opportunities; your bar reading skills will become more refined and your reasoning more strategic with every set you do. (They are like weightlifting. Train consistently, and you will get stronger.)

Be very pleased with yourself simply because you are *taking* daily practice tests. Do not obsess about scores. Just keep doing the work and self-assessing. Your goal is to develop strategies to strengthen different skill or knowledge gaps.

Reading Error?

If you read something incorrectly, ask yourself why. Did you read too fast? Did you drift off while reading? Did you assume some fact that was not in the fact pattern? Did you not understand the meaning of one or more words that turned out to affect the entire question? Which part of the question did you read incorrectly: the call, the facts, or the answer choices? (And, again, why did you miss that part? Were you rushing?) Once you know why you missed a question, you can then take steps to change the behavior. Reading incorrectly is one of the most common reasons for missing MCQs, and the easiest to fix. Remember your bar reading skills. Touch each word and say it out loud under your breath as you read with your eyes. It works.

Didn't Know or Understand a Rule?

If, after studying explanatory answers, you can see that you did not know or understand a rule, go look it up and either write it in your outline, on your paper, or electronic flash cards, or say it out loud several times, or both. (If you want to be sure you understand it, try explaining the concept to someone else.) *Expect* to be learning some new rules from practice MCQs, even up to the day before the exam.

USE EXPLANATORY ANSWERS TO CONTINUOUSLY UPDATE FLASHCARDS

Often an explanatory answer may phrase a rule more clearly or succinctly than in your outline. The explanatory answer may also include an instructive example. That is a gift. And whenever you come across rule statements that are easier to memorize or you find helpful examples, you hit gold! Get out your flashcards and rewrite your card for that rule, replacing your old definition with the newer, clearer version. (Again, *flash cards* here refers to whatever you have chosen as your "memory tool.")

Didn't Finish in Time?

If you didn't have time to carefully complete each question or didn't finish in the allotted time and guessed on a number of questions, ask yourself why. First, are you timing yourself? On the bar exam, you have approximately 1.8 minutes per MBE question. (In early start and the first part of intensive bar prep you can take longer, but you should wean yourself down to bar timing by mid-June.) Did you lose time by focusing too long on one question? Guess, and move on if you find you have spent more than the time allotted on a question. Did you drift off while reading? Did you get distracted answering a phone call or going to the bathroom? Each set of questions is an opportunity to incrementally improve your accuracy and speed and your ability to focus for longer and more concentrated periods of time.

USE QUALITY PRACTICE QUESTIONS

Be sure you are practicing with sufficiently difficult exams. Sometimes older exams are easier than newer ones. And sometimes one bar review's questions may be easier than the questions in another course. Mix it up. (Ask your law librarian or ASP faculty where to find extra questions.)

Chart to Track Wrong Answers (Including Guesses!)

Complete this assessment for every question you missed, checking the reason(s) you erred and writing an improvement plan, so that you do not repeat the same mistakes.

Question # ___

[ ] I read the question (the interrogatory) incorrectly.

[ ] I missed or misunderstood a key word or words in the fact pattern.

[ ] I read one or more answer choices incorrectly.

[ ] I did not understand what the question was asking or did not see what was at issue.

[ ] I did not know the law that I needed to apply to the issue to reason to a conclusion. (If you missed a question because you didn't know the rule, write it now in the space below.)

[ ] I memorized the rule but didn't understand the underlying principles the question was testing. (So, I narrowed the answer down to two possible choices, but didn't choose the best one.)

[ ] I knew the correct answer, but I entered it incorrectly.

Other: ____________________

To improve, I will:

____

____

____

Rule(s)/concept/area of law tested in this question that I need to learn/memorize are:

____

____

____

Chart to Track Correct Answers

If you are someone who benefits from reviewing questions you got right, complete this assessment for every question you answered correctly.

Question # ___

[ ] I understand why I chose the answer I chose.

[ ] I chose the correct answer for the right reason.

Note: If you chose the right answer for the wrong reason, write out here why your reasoning was flawed:

____

____

Rules/concepts tested in this question and tips to remember this area of questioning in the future:

____

____

____

MCQ Tips and Strategies

Keep this list of tips handy to look at the morning of your exam, and perhaps again during the lunch break. These were written with the MBE in mind, so they will need to be adapted for the timing and strategy of NextGen MCQs.

- If you have ruled out one or more answers and reviewed the facts and interrogatory and still don't know the correct answer, guess and return to this question at the end if you have time. You need to complete thirty-three questions per hour.
- Watch the clock. After one hour, be sure you are on or near question thirty-three, and after two hours, question sixty-six. If you stick to this pace, you should be finished or nearly so after two hours and fifty-five minutes. Note: if during your actual bar you are seated where you cannot see the clock, ask the proctor politely to be moved, if at all possible.
- Be a smart clock-watcher during practice tests and on the actual exam. Be sure to bring in an approved timepiece, if allowed. (Carefully verify the rules on watches and clocks in your jurisdiction.) Note the exact time each of your sessions starts. Let's say your day consists of an approximately 9:00 a.m.-to-noon block in the morning and a 2:00-to-5:00 p.m. block in the afternoon. If the afternoon session starts at 1:55 p.m., you will finish at 4:55 p.m.; it is therefore important not to think you have until 5:00 p.m. to finish the test. Look at and confirm the exact time when the proctor says, "You may begin." (If that's 2:05 p.m., write on your answer booklet, *"End at 5:05 p.m.—begin guessing at 5:00 p.m."*) Note that you may begin the morning or afternoon session at a slightly different time each day. Some people reset their watches to noon during practice testing (and if allowed during the actual exam) at the beginning of every session (that way, one hour will have elapsed at 1:00 p.m., two hours at 2:00 p.m., etc.).

- Have a guessing strategy. If you can't rule out any of the four answer choices for a question or questions, or if you run out of time, select a predetermined letter and quickly put that in each blank answer. Pick your favorite letter, and have the plan in place—all Cs, for example. If at ten minutes before the end of the session you are more than a few questions from finishing, get ready to implement your guessing strategy. Don't leave questions blank.
- Be sure each response you bubble in corresponds to the question you are actually answering. Due to exam day nerves, it is easy to inadvertently bubble in an answer on the wrong line. If you catch this early, you can fix it. So, every few questions, verify that you haven't skipped any questions or answers.
- Be sure to bubble in the circles on the Scantron completely. Make sure the whole circle is darkened.

Each of these tips comes from actual incidents. You might think it impossible that someone failed the bar exam because of a bubbling mistake, but this and other equally preventable errors happen with every bar exam. And, on every exam, there are applicants who only fail by one point. Every point matters. Do not make careless mistakes.

BAR ESSAYS

First a note: the NextGen bar exam will not have essay formats. This book includes an extensive section on essays for a few reasons. Some jurisdictions are not adopting the NextGen exam, or are doing so in a few years so current readers will still have essays on their bar exams. Additionally, because essays are a primary law school testing format, understanding them strategically and comparing and contrasting them with other testing formats can help improve performance all around.

Like MCQs, bar essays are made up of relatively short fact patterns, often only a half to single page of text. Compare that with some law school finals that are several pages long. Some bar essays are designed to be completed in thirty minutes such as the multistate essay exams (MEE) that appear on the legacy

UBE. Some jurisdictions such as California, test with one-hour bar essays.

Regardless of the length of an essay, in essay answers, applicants must identify issues, state the applicable rules of law (typically from memory), logically apply the law you stated to the given facts, and accordingly resolve the issues you identified in a way that comes to a reasoned conclusion, thereby answering the specific question or questions posed.

Depending on the jurisdiction, the law you are to apply on a particular essay question may be state-specific, federal, modern-majority, or common law. You may pick up additional points for noting influential minority rules, or for comparing a modern trend to the common law rule. Your jurisdiction's website and your bar review will explain which law is to be applied to answer essay questions. Your ASP faculty at your law school can also help you with this.

Bar reading is a critical success skill for essays, just as for MCQs. Because you must produce an *organized* written product rather than just identify the best choice, you must also include time (during and after you read the interrogatory and facts) to *order* what you intend to say in a logical manner—in other words, to *outline.*

On essays, you must not only understand the rules and how they apply to the facts, but also to articulate those rules in your own words and analyze in writing how the facts prove or disprove the elements of those rules. On MCQs, you must see those connections, but you don't have to write out anything yourself. (This is one reason why doing many practice MBEs is not a substitute for writing out practice essay questions in full under timed conditions.) If your exam includes both, you must do both; they test different skills. This is also why some people find essays more difficult. And non-native English speakers may have a tougher time with essays than with MCQs—yet another reason for additional practice.

YOUR WRITTEN ANSWERS ARE LIKE PAPER INTERVIEWS

Think of your written bar answers as a sort of paper interview. The graders need to see that you are "lawyer material." After all, it is in their hands now whether to grant you a license that puts you in charge of people's lives and livelihoods. In addition to sounding intelligent and answering responsively and thoughtfully, you must present yourself well—in a clear, organized manner.

It helps if your paper looks good, too. Self-assess your work product the way you would your appearance before going to an interview. You would wear a clean suit that makes you look professional, right? Similarly, your paper should be neat, with an obvious, logical organization. Clear headings and subheadings provide graders with a roadmap to your organization—a way to quickly and easily see that you are a logical person. Avoid typos and especially misspellings of key legal terms. (If you handwrite, write legibly. Don't scratch through or cross out too many words.) Students who fail often show me their exams and say, "But I had it in there." To which I reply, "But the grader could not easily see and understand what you wrote." You are the interviewee. Present yourself as well as you can. And remember, the burden is on you to write clearly, not on the grader to decipher what you might have meant.

We saw previously that traditional MCQs have one correct or best answer choice; your mission is to seek and find it. (Some NextGen MCQs will have two best answers out of six choices.) On essays, however, you may not need to find a certain answer. There may not even be one single answer to an essay question. Rather, the facts may provide a vehicle for you to give reasoned arguments as to how both sides would resolve the issues. Think about a personal encounter with someone who saw something happen in a completely different way than you saw it. (If you have time or want a break, check out the 2008 drama *Vantage Point* or the 1950s Japanese film *Rashomon*, which both illustrate this vividly.) As you reread, think, and outline, ask yourself both how the plaintiff would use these facts to prevail *and* how the defendant would use them.

You may find essays liberating, in that the burden of having to know the exact "right" answer is lifted. In a recent alumni seminar, a former student was discussing his first years in law practice. He noted as the biggest change having to *know* (or be expected to accurately predict) who would win, as compared with law school—where he could nearly always just argue for both sides!

Essay-Test Tips and Strategies

The tips below focus on strategies within a single essay. (Note that some of these tips will also apply to other written testing formats including parts of integrated question sets on the NextGen bar and PTs.)

Before we explore exam strategies, let's talk about how to answer sets of several essays in a row. First, answer them in the order they appear. Most everyone else will, and your exam will be compared with others' exams. For example, if everyone does an amazing job on #1 and a poor job on #3, you will not benefit from going out of order and doing a superlative job on #3 to the detriment of #1. Your goal is to write a passing answer for *each* question. Answer the questions out of order only if you find yourself blocked when you see question #1. If that happens, take a deep breath; if that doesn't help, just move on confidently to the second question and return to the first one later when you have your "flow" back.

Second, answer the questions within the suggested time. If you must answer six thirty-minute essays in three hours, you must budget your time accordingly. (Proctors generally do not notify applicants of how much time has passed.) Cut yourself off (wrap up and conclude) if you exceed the suggested time on any single question. Finish all the questions, and then and only then return if there is extra time to edit or add to one of your completed answers.

Third, make sure you answer every question; do not skip any.

Now here are tips for strategies within a single essay (and again, some of these apply equally to short answer portions of other testing formats):

Answer the questions asked and only the questions asked. Many students waste time on nonissues. Careless reading is often the culprit. Lawyers must be detailed.

Approach essays as follows: (1) read the interrogatory and then read the facts. Then reread the interrogatory; (2) read every word using the three-sense technique we have talked about (reading aloud but under your breath, so you can hear yourself while not disrupting others around you, and touching each word with your pencil, pen, or finger—touching the screen when you are reading on a device).

Slow down. Expect that people next to you in the bar exam will be typing while you are still reading the question! No worries. They are not smarter than you. They may well be failing the exam, writing nonsense, or writing something irrelevant because they do not yet have a handle on the law, facts, or interrogatories. Do not let them throw you. Make certain *you* understand what is and what is not asked of you, and see how the facts fit the analytical steps of resolving the specific question or questions *before* you write your answer. Have confidence in yourself. Even for a thirty-minute essay, you may want to take a full ten minutes (or more) to really understand the question and outline your answer before clacking away at the keyboard.

Before you write, organize and outline. At a minimum, your outlining goal should be to note the main headings (and subheadings) you will include in your answer. There is often more than one logical way to organize. The best and easiest organization is usually to mirror the call of the question. But if the question is general or for some other reason you need another strategy, just be sure that you discuss the issues in some reasoned order, for example, you might organize a torts answer by party, lawsuit, or cause of action; a contract answer by communication or event; a family law essay by asset or liability; a criminal law essay by crime or by defendant where there are multiple defendants. Any systematic, logical organization is usually fine. Your outline is the framework for your organization, and your outline is often the first draft of headings that will serve as the graders' road map in your answer. Note that graders will judge you only on your answer, so writing an elaborate outline will waste time. Include in your outline what *you* need to write an organized answer.

Determine how much time to spend on each call of the question if there is more than one interrogatory or if the interrogatory poses a multipart question. Make this determination by how complex each part is and how many facts relate to each part of the question. As you read the body of the question, put brackets around facts that relate to specific issues, and then arrows pointing back to the interrogatory asking about those issues. Generally, the more facts that relate to a part (or particular call) of the question, the more time you should spend writing that part.

Cross out words in the fact pattern after you write about the issues they raise in your answer. Then, look back at the fact pattern periodically to see if there are words you have not crossed out. Might they be useful? Why? Do they raise new issues? Do they bolster arguments in support of or against issues you have already analyzed?

Use every fact they give you! This does not mean every word must be restated in your answer. (In fact, if you quote, do so selectively and using quotation marks.) It means you should *think about* each fact to see if it triggers an issue, and include it in your analysis/argument if it supports or refutes some element of a rule of law, or otherwise affects some relevant argument (perhaps a policy argument).

Write in plain, simple English that spells out your reasoning so clearly that even a layperson could understand you!

Focus on the most serious issues first (unless you are writing in another *logical* order, such as chronological order where appropriate). For example, if someone has battered a victim, and that victim dies as a result of the battery, start with the homicidal offenses before mentioning battery (if that is even relevant). Likewise, write about a lesser included offense within the larger crime; for example, if there is a larceny and robbery, discuss a robbery first, and write about the larceny within the discussion of the robbery, since the larceny elements are essentially "subsets" of the robbery elements.

Quick Test

What are the elements of robbery?

What are the elements of larceny?

- Discuss what *is* a problem or most "at issue" first and then quickly address (if time permits) why something is not an issue given the particular facts. An example of this might appear in a criminal procedure essay about a warrantless search. You want to hit the most likely exceptions to the warrant requirement, thoroughly discuss those, and then—if you have time—perhaps show why the other exceptions would not suffice under these facts; for example, "Here the defendant did nothing to suggest that he explicitly or implicitly *consented* to the search." Students always ask whether they should discuss all the potentially relevant exceptions when the prosecution would need only one exception to proceed. My answer is, "Yes, because exams are not the real world." And you typically get points on exams for hitting all of the relevant issues, if you explicitly state why they are relevant. (Remember, do not limit yourself to discussions where the plaintiff [or prosecution in a criminal fact pattern] prevails. Discuss both "winning" and "losing" arguments, if suggested by the facts.)

- Write in complete sentences, thoroughly analyzing the facts to resolve the issues. Bullet points can sometimes be helpful, such as when noting a list. But, don't expect a grader to follow your shorthand. Fully "spell out" your thinking.

- Provide a key to any terms or party names that you abbreviate. For example, if you abbreviate "contract" with the symbol "K," write out "contract (K)" or "contract (hereinafter 'K')" the first time you use that abbreviation. You might think this association is so obvious that it's unnecessary to identify it, but the abbreviation "K" is also used to mean "$1,000," so even something so seemingly straightforward may be misconstrued.

- Avoid hammering on one point of view. Essays are about analysis not advocacy. Each issue may lend itself to both a defense and plaintiff/prosecution perspective, as the facts can and frequently do cut both ways. If you get stuck trying to advocate in a manner that's too one-sided, you may miss points to be gained from analyzing the opposing party's perspective. Note: If you write about two opposing arguments, conclude your thoughts by noting which side has the stronger position *and why* before moving on to your next area of discussion.
- Write complete (but succinct) rule statements, and then prove up (analyze) each element of each rule—piece by piece. Lawyers break complex thoughts down into logical parts. Elements are components of the bundle that is a rule, and each part must be proved. This is also true for defenses, as defense theories often have multiple elements that must be discussed. (Always consider defenses when analyzing crimes or causes of action.) Know the difference between tests that include *factors* (all of which need not always be established) and *elements* (each of which must be proven by the requisite level of proof).
- Make sure your exams are reader friendly! Don't underestimate the importance of style. Am I suggesting form over substance? No! I am urging you to pay attention to form *in addition to* substance! The best essay answers tend to identify main areas of discussion with descriptive headings that provide a roadmap for graders to quickly see that the applicant identified the key issues and relevant rules. At a glance, the grader should be able to see that your answer is set out clearly and

logically. (During early start and intensive bar review, work on polishing form and style, as well as mastering content and substance. The best way to do this is to study sample and model answers.)

- **Tip:** Even if you don't plan to handwrite, write out at least one or two essay or PT answers in full by hand during bar prep so that you know you can do it should an emergency require you to do so (e.g., a computer problem or power outage). If you are handwriting your answers, make sure your writing is legible.
- Write using lawyerly language. I don't mean that you should use formal, ritualistic language ("the party of the first part heretofore contends . . ."). I mean that you should write in a clear and professional manner. Below are some examples I have seen frequently when students are concluding essays.
    - Do write: *For these reasons, the plaintiff is unlikely to prevail.* (Do **not** write: *The plaintiff's argument is really not going to fly.*)
    - Do write: *It is therefore possible for the plaintiff to prevail; however, for the reasons stated above, it appears that the defendant has the stronger argument here.* (Do **not** write: *This is a wash. It is up to the jury. The jurors could decide either way here.*)
    - Do write: *The police arrest may have violated the warrant requirement.* (Do **not** write: *The cops here did not follow the rules, and the defendant was busted without the warrant they should have gotten.*)
- Avoid writing in the first person (do not use "I" or "we"). *Exam graders do not care what* you *think or what* you *believe.* What matters is whether the facts prove, or fail to prove, the particular legal theories you have articulated.

- Do write: *For the reasons stated above, the defendant will likely prevail.* (Do **not** write: *I think the defendant will win.*)
- Do write: *After weighing the facts on both sides and for the reasons stated above, it appears that the plaintiff has the stronger argument on this question because the plaintiff has more evidence and that evidence is more credible.* (Do **not** write: *I believe the plaintiff has the better argument.*)
- Do write: *The defendant's spitting on the plaintiff/victim is an offensive action. Reasonable people find spitting to be a rude and even demeaning gesture.* Do **not** write: *The defendant's spitting on the plaintiff/victim is an offensive action. I would be horrified if someone spat on me that way.*

READ YOUR ANSWERS ALOUD

I often ask students to read their answers to practice questions out loud. I do this in class and during office hours. Some students will read a paragraph and then stop themselves and say, "This doesn't make any sense." Or, "I'm not sure what I meant here." What you write must make sense to you if you want it to make sense to a grader. Reading answers aloud will help you see if what you wrote was logical, clear, and responsive.

Crossover Questions

One of the many differences between bar exam essays and law school essays is that bar questions may contain testable issues in more than one area of law. (This will likely be an even more important part of the NextGen bar exam.) In law school, your evidence professor will give you a final exam that tests evidence rules. A bar essay question may involve a litigation scenario that includes both pretrial civil procedure issues (perhaps a jurisdiction question) and trial issues that concern evidentiary questions, such as whether a document or statement will be admitted and why.

A fact pattern that includes issues from more than one subject still usually tells a single story, so certain subjects cross over more naturally.

Crossover Quiz

What subjects do you think cross over most naturally?

Some answers: 1) criminal law and criminal procedure, 2) wills and trusts, and 3) civil procedure and evidence.

Crossovers tend to be unnerving; they are often unfamiliar because law school exams don't test that way. (You didn't walk into your torts final to find a family law issue on the exam.) But the idea of subjects crossing is not odd at all when you think about it. The law is not isolated, and neither are people's problems. A client may come to you about a divorce, so she definitely has concerns relating to family law; but, she may also have financial concerns that dip into bankruptcy law, there may be a related criminal matter, or she may own intellectual property for which you have to understand a patent or copyright issue. You don't simply do one search (or open one book), find an answer to one of your client's questions, and let the rest go. Yes, you may end up referring part of a case to an attorney who specializes in that area of law, but you will often need some basic knowledge in multiple areas to even know where to refer the client.

Bar preparation is similar. You are no longer studying one subject at a time. You are preparing to answer any question that they throw at you in any of the bar-tested subjects, or combination of those subjects.

Working with numerous subjects simultaneously helps you see how disparate pieces fit together. As we've noted, most law school courses focus on the details—the veins on the leaves on the trees. Bar preparation allows you the opportunity to pull it together and see the bigger picture. Don't let this freak you out; you might actually find it intellectually exciting to start seeing parallels and intersections that likely didn't occur to you when you were studying subjects in silos, one at a time.

Practice Essay Writing

Set aside a certain number of hours per week to write essays in full and under timed conditions, as well as additional time to study sample or model answers and self-assess.

Self-assessment may be a quick process if you readily see where and how you need to improve. But, if a question asks about rules that you don't know or understand, you should take time immediately or soon after completing the question to look those up. Invest that time while the fact pattern is fresh to learn and see how these rules apply. Don't procrastinate. Why? (1) You may never get back to this question, and then you will remain exposed—with a weak area. (2) The closer it gets to the exam, the harder it is to make time to look things up. (3) Learning a rule in the context of a fact pattern will make it "stick" in your memory more effectively than simply memorizing words in a vacuum.

How will this help? Imagine you are in your bar exam. You read a question and say to yourself, "There's a rule here. I know I learned it at one point, but for the life of me, I cannot remember it." If you then take a deep breath and just think, "Well, is the fact pattern similar to one I remember practicing with. What rule applied there?" That might either allow you to remember or help you analogize enough to "make up" a rule that is likely close to the actual rule. (On most bar essays, you will get some points for analyzing the facts and applying them to a rule, even if that rule is not completely accurate.)

After completing your self-assessment and looking up any rules you don't know or remember, add those rules (or memory tips or examples illustrating the rules) to your outline, flash cards, or other learning and memorization tools.

In addition to writing out essays in full under timed conditions, set aside additional time to outline essays and review sample answers. If you do a lot of writing in full under timed conditions and develop your skills during early start and the first six weeks, you can focus mainly on outlining the final weeks.

How many essays should I write out in full, and how many should I outline? If possible, complete all of the assigned work in your bar review course. Then do more. (Early start makes this much easier.) Try to complete an essay every other day or so. Don't worry about running out of new questions. You can easily get new questions and it's fine and can be very helpful to rewrite essays you previously completed to see if you have improved and to cement concepts and rules in your memory.

Make sure you write practice essays in every tested subject. Students often tend to take exams only in the subjects where they are comfortable. Do not fall into that trap. Be sure to hit every subject, *especially* weaker subjects. By exam time, you should have written out in full several essay exams for each essay tested subject. Plan to complete essays slowly and steadily, writing some essays every week rather than cramming in a bunch of practice essays right before the test.

At first, in early start, look up rules if you cannot write your answers from memory. Closer to the exam, you will need to train under *closed-book and timed conditions*, but early practice that is open book is perfectly fine and often very helpful. In July (or February), write closed book practice tests; open your bar review outlines to help you self-assess after you finish if you need to look something up.

Note: When you are quite close to the exam and time is running short, you will gradually shift to writing more essay outlines instead of writing essays in full—still, of course, studying the model answers. Days before the exam, you can even practice by just reading questions and issue spotting in your head and then studying the sample answers. Going through many fact patterns and sample answers will help you review and memorize, as well as see how testable issues tend to arise and repeat themselves. At a certain point, you will hopefully find a great deal of overlap and catch yourself saying, "This question sounds a lot like. . . ."

As you review questions and answers, you can edit your one-page "cheat sheet," ideally so that the main issues in each subject are set out in a logical order that you can memorize.

MAKE SURE YOU CLOSE THE BOOKS

Often, people who fail the bar confess that they never wrote practice tests, or, that they wrote them only open book.

Consequently, they never got their timing right and never memorized all the rules they needed to know. (You must have as many rules as possible memorized for instant recall by the time of the exam.) When you begin taking practice tests, spend as much time as is allotted and try to recall everything you can. Then when you are stuck, look up the information you need, close the books again, and return to finish writing the exam. But, by early July, **finish your practice essays entirely closed book**. Force yourself to answer the questions as fully as you can, without looking anything up, as if you were taking the actual bar exam. Only *after* you finish to the best of your ability should you study the sample or model answers, self-assess, and look up rules you do not know or understand.

Essays: A Closer Look at How to Read and Write Them

Start at the end of the fact pattern with the "call" of the question. That's what you must answer, so start there. Then read the fact pattern. Then reread the question. Read slowly and carefully, touching each word and mumbling it aloud under your breath, circling and highlighting key words.

Take notes. Jot down (on paper or start a "notes" section at the end of your draft answer file), noting any words that raise "discussable issues" (more on issue spotting below). As part of notetaking, you might want to also create a quick chronology, listing key facts in the order in which they occur. That can be especially helpful in certain subjects. For example, in a torts negligence fact pattern for which you are analyzing proximate cause, tracking the chain of causation requires knowing what happened and when. Bar essays often tell the factual "story" out of order. (Pay attention to dates.) Looking at your own ordered list of events on scratch paper or in a notes section of your draft answer, you will readily see if an event came between the defendant's actions and the victim's injury. You can then assess that intervening event to determine if it was foreseeable or not, and complete your proximate cause discussion. Another example is a contracts question in which there are numerous communications between the buyer and seller or between the employer and employee. In order to know the legal significance of each communication, you may need to know exactly what was communicated, and when (think "mailbox rule"). Another example of when chronological notetaking is helpful is in a family law or community property exam. Depending on the relevant law, when property was earned or when debts were incurred (before, during, or after marriage) may change the characterization of that property or obligation, and thus who will be awarded certain assets or have to pay certain debts in a divorce proceeding.

Next, create an outline. The best bar exam essay outlines are those that help you create a logical order without taking too much time, because most bar graders will not look at or consider your outline but only your completed answer. Think of your outline as a table of contents to your essay. Start by making sure your outline includes the main discussable issues and possibly relevant sub-issues, organized into a logical order (often, but not always, tracking the calls of the question). If you type your outline into your essay answer file, you can often turn your outline into headings in your actual answer. (Again, headings serve as a road map for graders.) For example, a question asks, "Of what crimes, if any, may the defendant be convicted?" Your headings may be each of the crimes you intend to discuss. When a question asks about the division of assets in a divorce, the headings may be an asset-by-asset list. In a torts question involving multiple parties, the headings may be the various lawsuits: *A v. B*, *B v. C*, etc.

Remember: Before you upload a bar exam essay, delete any of your own internal notes and your draft outline.

Bar Writing Is Logical Writing, and It Differs in Some Key Ways from Law School Exam Writing

Earlier you learned that "bar *reading*" is active critical reading. Bar *writing* is clear logical writing. It is often recommended that first-year law students and bar takers write using a style template known by the acronym IRAC: issue, rule, analysis, conclusion. For bar writing, as I will detail below, the acronym IRPC—issue, rule, *proof*, conclusion—may be more helpful.

When law students first hear about IRAC, they sometimes think it stands for "I Really Am Crazy" and wonder why they went to law school in the first place. But IRAC is just a tool—a template or system—to help students write logically.

IRAC forces the writer to move through steps (like A + B + C = D) and to remember to use the facts to prove or disprove the elements of the rules of law. In law school exams, as distinct from bar exams, the analysis portion is typically richer, deeper, and more thoughtful. On law school essays, you will want to weave into your analysis discussions of cases (with analogies and distinctions), policy concerns, and subtleties or relevant changes within the law itself, noting how those affect the resolution of the issues at hand. You may mention both majority and minority positions in evolving areas of law, or you may compare older case law to more modern trends you have studied. Of course, you must reason to a logical conclusion.

Bar writing is similar, but often simpler. Once you understand what is expected and practice every single day, you will likely find bar writing to be rather straightforward.

CRAC OR CRIAC? START WITH CONCLUSIONS?

I suggest writing in an IRAC (or what I call "IRPC") style unless you know your jurisdiction prefers CRAC. CRAC (conclusion, rule, analysis, conclusion) or CRIAC (conclusion, rule, issue, analysis, conclusion): Some jurisdictions prefer that bar applicants state their conclusion first and then follow that with a full "proof" or analysis of how the rule is or is not satisfied. This does not change the basic logical structure. If you are advised to write in CRAC style and you are not sure who will prevail, write in IRAC style and then cut and paste your conclusion at the top of your discussion.

IRAC OR "IRPC"

Some people hear the word *analysis* and think of complex and varied wrinkles in legal theories and reasoning; they picture lengthy, Socratic questioning in law school classes—exchanges that are designed to break apart and promote an understanding of case law. Others hear *analysis* and think of a layered literary analysis from a college English class, reflecting perhaps on the meaning, style, and value of a novel or poem. As you will see below, a more useful mental picture for effective bar writing may instead require a flashback to middle school geometry and the simple logic contained in a basic proof.

For many students, the term *analysis* conveys a more complex, and often longer, written discussion than is required for most passing bar answers. The word *analysis* may well represent what law professors expect on law school midterms and finals. Many law professors wish to see students weave relevant cases into their discussion as they reason to thoughtful conclusions, drawing analogies or distinguishing between the facts in the exam and facts from cases or hypotheticals studied throughout the term. Your professor may also expect a rich policy discussion, possibly noting relevant implications the issues you are discussing might have for third parties, society at large, past precedent, or future evolution of the applicable law. But, bar writing is often simpler than law school writing. Thus, the term "proof" many be more useful in this context than "analysis"—hence IRPC.

Let's look at the following example as a useful (albeit oversimplified) analogy for effective bar writing.

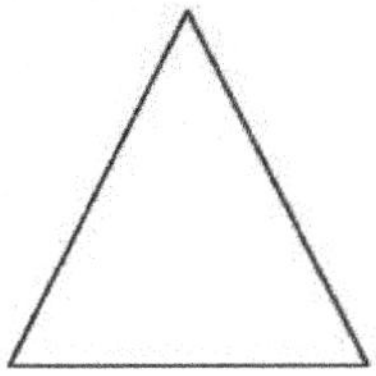

What sort of figure does the shape above represent? **[ISSUE]**

Three-sided figures with sides coming together at three corners are generally known as *triangles*. An equilateral triangle is a three-sided figure in which all three sides are equal in length and all corners have the same degree angle. **[RULE]**

Here, side A measures *x* inches, side B measures *x* inches, and side C measures *x* inches. The three sides are touching and meet at three corners. Each angle measures *y* degrees. **[PROOF** (or analysis)**]**

Therefore, the figure represented above is an equilateral triangle. **[CONCLUSION]**

This logic may sound more mathematical than legal, but it is highly instructive for bar writing. Let's consider another IRPC example, this one using an everyday driving scenario in which you will see the same sort of logic but in a situation that more closely resembles a law-type fact pattern. Note here that we will also add a policy consideration to our logical writing ("IRPPC"). Policy concerns, while not essential in bar writing, can be helpful in improving your score. As long as you have written about all the discussable issues, correctly using the basic components of an IRPC—*and you finish answering the entire question*—adding policy considerations may indicate a further mastery of the application of the rule of law that a grader may appreciate.

> The defendant and his passenger, Witness X, both testified that the defendant's car was in the left-turn lane, the green arrow was blinking, and it was 3:00 p.m. when the turn was made. Did the defendant's turn from Elm Street onto Main Street on December 1 violate traffic regulations?

Now let's say you know (because you have learned the relevant rule of law) that left turns are permitted from the left-turn lane at the intersection of Elm and Main when the green left-turn arrow is blinking at times other than 4:00 to 7:00 p.m. on weekdays. (From 4:00 p.m. to 7:00 p.m. on weekdays, such turns are not permitted even if the arrow is green.) Now, using an "IRPC" format, how would we logically deconstruct the legality of the turn in question?

Did the defendant's 3:00 p.m. left turn at Elm and Main violate traffic laws with respect to turning? **[ISSUE]**

Left turns are permitted at the intersection of Elm and Main from the left-turn lane when the green left-turn arrow is blinking and at times other than between 4:00 and 7:00 p.m. on weekdays. **[RULE]**

The defendant was in the left-turn lane (the proper location to make a left turn). He saw the turn arrow blinking (the signal that it was safe to make his turn). The defendant made the turn in question at 3:00 p.m. (an appropriate time for this type of turn). Since it was 3:00 p.m., it did not matter which day of the week it was, as the only restrictions on turning are from 4:00 to

7:00 p.m. **[PROOF or analysis]** Last but not least, policy would dictate that even if the defendant had followed the technical requirements for turning, he must have also confirmed that it was generally safe to make the turn—t hat is, that there were no other obstacles, emergency vehicles, or unanticipated conditions that would make the turn unsafe. Assuming the defendant did confirm this, there is no indication that the turn was unlawful. **[POLICY** (optional)**]**

Therefore, the defendant's turn from Elm onto Main appears to have been lawful. **[CONCLUSION]**

This is straightforward, right? It makes sense. It is not mysterious or intriguing. It is not eloquent. It is simple and direct, logical and organized.

One of my law school professors once explained bar exam writing something like this: "Many of you came to law school from lofty colleges where you theorized and studied literature and history and the like. You read poetry and wrote beautiful essays. You sought to include metaphors and alliteration, so that your words would flow. You want to continue that sort of writing now, in law school. Your minds are creative. You *want* to think, 'Well, I'll start by discussing A; but then let me foreshadow Z; then I'll get back to B; and maybe then toss in a bit of H and J to make things more vibrant.' " He then hollered, "No!" in such a booming voice that everyone in the class jumped. "Cut that out right now! From here on, instead of flowery prose, it's A + B + C = D. Period."

Bar Reading and Its Relationship to Bar Writing

Both to issue spot and to prove your points, you must read carefully, *and think*, as you read. Let's look at a couple of examples in the context of criminal law. Criminal law fact patterns often include one or more defendants who will have done a series of actions that arguably amount to criminal offenses. You must *use* the facts to demonstrate the proof or lack thereof of the requisite conduct, mental state, or any other elements of those crimes, and to demonstrate which, if any, defenses apply. As with all law exams, the most important skill needed to successfully answer a criminal law question is careful bar reading. Start with the call of the question, or interrogatory (often presented at the end of the fact pattern). This way, you immediately discern what the question is asking so that you can answer that question or questions—and *only* that question or questions. The questions themselves may also provide an effective organizational structure for your answer. Reading the call of the question first on a bar exam essay also often reveals what area(s) of law is or are being tested in that fact pattern. Knowing what subject(s) you are dealing with allows you to read with your "subject-specific antennae" up. Attentive to the types of issues you know arise in that subject and with that subject's rules in mind, you will more readily see the "trigger" (or buzz) words that point to discussable "issues."

The interrogatory in a criminal law essay may ask something like this: *With what crime or crimes, if any, may the defendant be charged?* or *Of what crime or crimes may the defendant be found guilty?* or *Did the court err in convicting the defendant of any crime or crimes?* By reading the interrogatory first, you will know just a moment into the exam that you are dealing with criminal law.

Bar exam questions will not be labeled by subject, so the very first step to take in approaching a bar exam essay or multiple-choice question is to determine what subject or subjects are being tested so you can recall the relevant rules while you read the facts.

After reading the interrogatory, go to the top of the page and read the entire fact pattern, slowly and carefully. Use the active bar reading techniques discussed earlier. Read simultaneously with three senses: touch, hearing, and sight. Put your finger, pen, or stylus on each word as you read it with your eyes and say it in a barely audible voice. Circle, underline, highlight, and write notes on or near words that seem significant. If a word or phrase triggers an issue or leads you to see a point you might want to discuss in your writing, note it right away so you do not forget. Mark directly on the question using online annotation tools, jot your thoughts on scratch paper, or type right into the document that may start as your outline and then become your essay answer. (If your outline is made up of your headings, then you can simply type each section under the appropriate heading.)

Let's practice with the following short essay question:

> Defendant Dufus wanted to burn Vicki's cottage. Dufus walked to the cottage, carrying matches and kerosene, and lit a match, setting fire to a chair in the living room. A neighbor smelled smoke and called the fire department. Firefighters came within moments and extinguished the flaming chair. Of what crime or crimes may Dufus be convicted?

What did you read first? Hopefully, the last sentence, "Of what crime or crimes may Dufus be convicted?" That reveals critical information, that you are being tested on criminal law. Next, read the short fact pattern. "Burn" is a trigger term for a criminal law question. What crime do you think of when you heard the word burn? The minute you saw the word *burn*, you might have recited the definition of arson in your mind and asked yourself, *Do these facts prove that the defendant committed arson?*

Which definition would you recite? Good question! As with most good lawyer answers, "It depends." The common law definition of *arson* is the malicious burning of the dwelling house of another. You might have thought of that, or of modern-majority variations that relax some of the traditional elements. For example, modern jurisdictions have extended arson to include most any protected structure, not just a "dwelling," and a defendant can, in certain circumstances, be convicted of arson for burning his or her own house down, not just the property "of another." Your bar review course will help you determine which rules to memorize.

You might not have every rule memorized yet, but you must have all the main rules committed to memory by the time of your exam. Knowing the rules is necessary to effectively issue spot. All the relevant crimes, causes of action, defense theories, and other testable principles must be as accessible to you during your bar exam as the passwords you use every day. The applicable rules must be memorized succinctly enough that you can spit them out quickly on essays. If you see the word *burn* in a criminal law fact pattern, you want to automatically recite the elements of arson, and then read and think through the facts *with that definition in mind.*

Unlike typical law professors, bar graders usually do *not* want to see treatises on the legal rules. Writing too much on particular rules may prevent you from finishing your proof discussion (the most important task!) and reasoning to a conclusion. Shoot for short, clear rule statements. You will not get extra credit for knowing and listing all the exceptions to a rule, for example, if those exceptions do not apply to the facts at hand.

Law professors often want to see that you listened in class, read the material, and learned a lot of law during the semester. Incorporating references to specific cases is one way of showing your professor what you learned. But it is typically *not* advisable to cite cases on bar exams, except in subjects such as constitutional law or where a case has become synonymous with a rule such as *Miranda* or *Hadley v. Baxendale.*

Back to arson—back to the fact pattern and to what you were thinking as you read. (I'll paraphrase your potential thoughts in italics.) For this example, we'll use the common law definition of *arson*: again, the malicious burning of the dwelling house of another.

> With what crime or crimes may Dufus be convicted? (*OK, I'm in criminal law, so I'll think about possible crimes as I read.*) Defendant Dufus **wanted to burn** (*Dufus's desire to burn the cottage proves his willful intent and satisfies the malice or* mens rea *element of arson*) Vicki's cottage (*the dwelling of another*). Dufus walked to the cottage, carrying matches and kerosene, and lit a match, setting fire to a chair in the living room. A neighbor smelled smoke and called the fire department. Firefighters came within moments and extinguished the flaming chair. (*The chair was flaming, but did the flames burn or char any part of the structure itself?*) Of what crime or crimes may Dufus be convicted?

"Issue spotting," and what that really means, can confuse people. Start by thinking of issue spotting as looking for those places where the facts raise *questions* about whether or not an element of a crime, cause of action, or defense has been or can be proven. One leading bar exam expert suggests that after reading the facts, students think about and develop theories based on those facts from one side's perspective. Then "switch hats." Put yourself in the mindset of opposing counsel and look to expose any weaknesses in the arguments you just thought of. Those weaknesses form the basis of many of the issues you should discuss in your answer.

But some of what you must write in bar essays relates to what appear to be non-issues. In other words, you must state whether or not each element was established under these facts and why, even an element that does not seem to be in question. For example, in the arson question above, the facts say that Dufus "wanted to burn." It therefore seems wholly obvious that the defendant possessed the requisite *intent* for arson. But you still have to *prove* he had the requisite intent. Here you might do that by simply referring in your answer to his "wanting" to burn the structure as evidence of his intent. (See sample answers below.)

Reading further, you will notice that from the information we are given, it appears that only *the chair* burned, not the structure. So, you will have to use the facts given to determine whether there was a requisite burning to support an arson conviction. (That's issue spotting.)

Once you read carefully and issue spot, you can start making an outline. Take a moment and write an outline of the Dufus arson hypothetical in the spaces below, and then consider the sample outline.

Test Yourself: Outline Before Writing

Draft an outline of the crime or crimes for which Dufus may be convicted here below.

____

____

____

____

____

____

Crimes of Dufus

ARSON?

a. Malicious? (wanted to burn = willful, so yes)

b. Burning? (the chair burned; need to demonstrate charring or burning of structure, as smoke damage is not enough, so no), of the

c. Dwelling house? (cottage, yes)

d. Of another? (Vicki's cottage, so yes)

Would you be done if you concluded (which you should, after discussing *all* the elements of arson) that Dufus will *not* likely be convicted of arson? No. Remember that the question being asked is: "Of what crime or *crimes may* Dufus be convicted?" You need to discuss *any and all* of the relevant crimes.

So, what should you ask yourself now? You know this! Whether Dufus might be guilty of *attempted arson*. To determine that, you have to resolve yet another issue: whether Dufus's action of setting fire to the chair was sufficiently close to the completed offense to find him guilty of an attempted crime. To reason to a logical conclusion on that point, you must know the rule or test for attempt in your jurisdiction. (There are several, including those that look at whether the defendant "took a substantial step toward" or was in "dangerous proximity of" completing the offense and those that consider whether the defendant did the "last act" before actually completing the target offense tested. The outcome may differ depending on the test used.)

On a law school criminal law exam, you may be expected to analyze a situation using all the tests you studied. On the bar exam, you will need to prove the attempt did or did not take place using first and foremost the test that controls in your jurisdiction, or, on many bar exams, the modern-majority rule. Only if you have *extra* time should you even consider writing about a minority view, for example. (Note: Some bar examiners stress the need to answer according to modern-majority principles, but they may award additional points for noting where your state's laws differ. As part of bar preparation, you will learn what law you are expected to know and use in your answers, and whether any additional points may be awarded for more refined comparative knowledge.)

Let's continue our outline then, adding this second possible crime.

Crimes of Dufus sample outline continued ATTEMPTED ARSON?

a. Acting with specific intent to burn the structure in question? (wanted to burn, yes)

b. Defendant took a substantial step toward completing this arson? (Yes, Dufus "walked to" the cottage, carrying matches and kerosene, a highly flammable liquid, and lit a match, setting fire to a chair in the living room).

Are you done now? *Well, wait a minute!* you say. *If the chair burned, then didn't Dufus permanently deprive Vicki of her property? Surely she didn't consent to that. Should I discuss larceny?* You quickly rattle off the elements of larceny: "the trespassory taking and carrying away of the personal property of another with intent to deprive the owner thereof," and you continue thinking, *Ah, but he didn't move the chair at all.*

Let's finish off the sample outline.

LARCENY?

- Taking and carrying away? (no, the movement or asportation element of larceny is not satisfied here)
- Of personal property of another? (yes, Vicki's chair)
- With intent to permanent deprive? (unclear)

OK, we read carefully. We *thought* as we read, asking ourselves questions about what was potentially in question or at issue while looking at each word. We took notes so as not to lose those thoughts. Then we outlined, placing the points we want to write about in a logical order. Now let's translate this into bar writing.

Note: This is a sample only, using a truncated hypothetical. You may not have time to or need to go into this much detail. This would likely be only one paragraph in a longer fact pattern, and there would be many other main issues or sub-issues to discuss. But this short sample gives you an idea of how to read, think, and write bar essays, hitting each part of IRPC and making your reasoning explicit enough for a layperson to easily follow your thinking.

Reflection: Now Take About 20 Minutes and Write out a Full Answer to This Question

Defendant Dufus wanted to burn Vicki's cottage. Dufus walked to the cottage, carrying matches and kerosene, and lit a match, setting fire to a chair in the living room. A neighbor smelled smoke and called the fire department. Firefighters came within moments and extinguished the flaming chair. Of what crime or crimes may Dufus be convicted?

Answer

Below are two sample answers. Use them to compare and contrast with your answer.

Sample Writing Example #1

Crimes of Dufus

The defendant may be charged with several crimes, but under these facts there is only one crime of which he may likely be convicted. [This is an optional sort of introduction. It shows the grader you read the question and are planning to respond to it. You might write this when you finish and insert it here at the beginning if time permits.]

ARSON

Will Dufus be convicted of arson? Arson is the malicious burning of the dwelling house of another. ("Malice" can be proved by establishing either willfulness or a reckless disregard for the risks.) Here, the facts state that Dufus "wanted" to burn Vicki's cottage and that he "walked to" the cottage with matches and kerosene (the tools necessary to set a fire). His desire to burn the cottage and his going to the target site with those tools prove that Dufus acted deliberately or willfully, therefore establishing "malice" and satisfying *the mens rea requirement for arson.* A cottage is typically a *dwelling house*, and this cottage belongs to Vicki; therefore, it would be the dwelling house of another and satisfy the *structure requirement* of common law arson. The *burning element* of arson, however, would not likely be satisfied here since that requires some burning or charring of the structure itself. Here the flames appear to have been extinguished while only the chair was burning—before the fire could reach the floor, walls, or any other part of the structure. Assuming that is the case and no part of the structure actually burned or was charred, despite the fact that Dufus possessed the requisite intent and took some action toward committing the crime, *Dufus may not be convicted of arson.*

ATTEMPTED ARSON

Will Dufus be guilty of attempted arson? A conviction of attempted arson here would require proof of Dufus's *specific intent to burn* Vicki's home, and evidence that Dufus *took a substantial step toward the completion* of that crime. Here, as was noted in the discussion of arson above, the defendant "wanted" to burn Vicki's cottage. His specific intent is evidenced by that fact. Next, Dufus "walked to" the cottage, with "kerosene" (a highly flammable liquid) and "matches" (incendiary devices), went to Vicki's cottage (her dwelling place), and lit a chair on fire inside the home. These actions go far beyond merely thinking about committing the offense or even simply *planning* to burn the cottage. The defendant went to the site where he wanted to commit the target offense and started a fire in the home, an action very likely to have led to the burning of the cottage had the neighbor and fire department not intervened so quickly. The defendant was thus well beyond the zone of preparation and well within the *zone of perpetration.* Because the prosecution has ample evidence of both the specific intent to complete the arson and his having taken a substantial step toward completing that act, *Dufus will likely be convicted of attempted arson.*

LARCENY

Did Dufus's actions in deliberately setting fire to Vicki's chair amount to a larceny? Larceny is the taking and carrying away of the personal property of another with intent to permanently deprive the owner thereof. Dufus may have deprived Vicki of her chair (a moveable object and thus personal property), and done so intentionally, but nowhere do the facts tell us that Dufus took or carried the chair away. Because Dufus did not move the chair, the asportation element of larceny is not satisfied, and *Dufus will not be convicted of larceny.*

CONCLUSION

For the reasons stated above, and because the facts do not appear to raise any plausible defense theories, Dufus will likely be convicted of attempted arson, but not convicted of arson or larceny.

Notice how the writing sample above tracks the logic of IRPC and is written in complete sentences in a way that a layperson could understand and follow the reasoning. In the example above, we *italicized* elements and conclusions to provide a road map for the grader. It would also be possible to set the same answer up with subheadings, as in the example below.

Sample Writing Example #2

This answers the same question but using a slightly differently style, with shorter paragraphs and more frequent headings and subheadings. Neither is "right." As you read, think about which you prefer.

Crimes of Dufus

The defendant may be charged with several crimes, but under these facts there is only one crime of which he may likely be convicted.

ARSON

Will Dufus be convicted of arson, the malicious burning of the dwelling house of another?

Malice or mens rea requirement ("Malice" can be proved by either establishing willfulness or a reckless disregard for the risks.) Here, the facts state that Dufus "wanted" to burn Vicki's cottage and that he "walked to" the cottage with the tools to do so. His desire to burn the cottage and his going to the target site with those tools prove that Dufus acted deliberately or willfully, therefore establishing "malice" and satisfying the mens rea requirement for arson.

Dwelling house of another

A cottage is typically a place people live (so qualifies as a dwelling house), and this cottage belongs to Vicki; therefore, it would satisfy the structure requirement of common law arson, the dwelling house of another.

Burning

The burning element of arson, however, would not likely be satisfied here. This element requires some burning or charring of the structure itself, and the flames appear to have been extinguished while only the chair was burning—before the fire could reach the floor, walls, or any other part of the structure.

Assuming that is the case and no part of the structure actually burned or was charred, despite the fact that Dufus possessed the requisite intent and took some action toward committing the crime, he may not be convicted of arson.

ATTEMPTED ARSON

Will Dufus be guilty of attempted arson? A conviction of attempted arson here would require proof of Dufus's specific intent to burn Vicki's home, as well as evidence that Dufus took a substantial step toward the completion of that crime such that he crossed over from what might be deemed merely the "zone of preparation" into the "zone of perpetration."

Mens rea: specific intent to complete the target offense

Here, as was noted in the previous discussion of arson, the defendant "wanted" to burn Vicki's cottage. His specific intent to complete the target offense is evidenced by that fact.

Actus reus: the defendant took a substantial step toward completing the crime One test used to evidence a "substantial step" is where the defendant's actions are said to move beyond the zone of preparation and into the zone of perpetration.

Here, Dufus "walked to" the cottage with "kerosene" (a highly flammable liquid) and "matches" (incendiary devices), went to Vicki's home, and lit a chair inside the home on fire. These actions go far beyond thinking about committing the offense or even simply *planning* to burn the cottage. The defendant went to the site where he wanted to commit the target offense and started a fire in the home, an action very likely to have led to the burning of the cottage had the neighbor and fire department not intervened so quickly. The defendant was thus well within the "zone of perpetration."

Because the prosecution has ample evidence of both the specific intent to complete the arson and his having taken a substantial step toward completing that act, Dufus will likely be convicted of attempted arson.

LARCENY

Did Dufus's actions in deliberately setting fire to Vicki's chair amount to a larceny? Larceny is the taking and carrying away of the personal property of another with intent to permanently deprive the owner thereof. Dufus may have deprived Vicki of her chair (a moveable good and her personal property), and done so intentionally, but nowhere do the facts tell us that Dufus took, carried, or even moved the chair. Because Dufus did not move the chair, the carrying away or asportation element of larceny is not satisfied, and Dufus will not be convicted of larceny.

DEFENSES

The facts do not appear to raise any justification or excuse for Dufus' actions, nor are there any mitigating factors.

CONCLUSION

For the reasons stated above, Dufus will likely be convicted of attempted arson; however, Dufus will not be convicted of arson or larceny.

About Essay Answers

Notice in the second example above that there was no need to *italicize* key terms because the headings and subheadings gave the grader a clear road map. The purpose of these basic examples was to take you through the process, from bar reading, thinking and issue spotting, to outlining, and then writing simply in a logical *IRPC* style, proving each element of the rules you stated with facts from the fact pattern.

If you are reading this well before you even start bar review, it should help give you a window into the strategy of essay writing for bar exams. If you are reading this during bar review, hopefully it will help you see strategies to sharpen your essay reading, outlining, and writing skills. Again, these writing examples would not be sufficient for law school essay answers but they illustrate the basic framework of drafting passing bar exam answers under extreme time pressures.

Do Not Assume: Prove It and Say Why

Often one of the toughest things to grasp is how much more straightforward bar exam essays tend to be when compared with the most challenging aspects of classroom questioning in law school. How many times did you go into a law school class having completed *and thinking you understood* the reading only to find the professor threw so many factual variations or subtleties in the law at you that you ended up feeling like you hadn't prepared at all?

It's good to leave law school classes with your head hurting; it means you were thinking! But on bar essays, you mostly work with the stated facts, which are presented in a fairly straightforward manner, and show how they prove or disprove elements of rules of law.

Note: I did not say bar essays were easy. There are many rules, in many subjects, and you have to read and see the relevance of every word in the fact patterns—and do all of that quickly and in a high-pressure situation. What I *am* saying is that the level of analysis is fairly superficial compared with most law classes. Again, that is why I prefer the mnemonic IRPC for bar exam essays rather than IRAC. Bar essays more often require simple *proof* rather than complex *analysis.* But you cannot skip steps in your logic; you must at least note points that may seem obvious to you. (Remember the equilateral triangle example.) In the Dufus example above, the facts convey that Dufus "wanted to burn" the cottage. How much more obvious could his intent be? It is clearly stated. Nonetheless, in your answer, you must state that the intent element was proved and why (even if that "why" is because the facts stated that "he wanted to burn").

Let's say you read a fact pattern and determine that the main crime the defendant may have committed is burglary. (First, of course, you would recite the rule, "At common law, a burglary was the breaking and entering of the dwelling house of another in the nighttime with intent to commit a felony therein.") One element of burglary is *breaking* into the structure. Even when a fact pattern explicitly states that the defendant "broke the door to go inside," you would need to say something to briefly indicate that the facts prove the existence of that element. For example, you might write, *The breaking element is satisfied here because the facts state that the defendant "broke the door" to go inside.* While that may seem self-evident, points are often given on bar essays for stating the obvious in a clear and organized fashion. This shows that you see the relevance of the particular facts and can apply the facts to that law. (This is precisely how litigators help jurors see how evidence presented at trial proves or disproves elements of the causes of action or crimes in question.)

What you do not want to do is *assume*, here meaning to arrive at a conclusion without saying why—in other words without making your reasoning explicit. This sort of assuming is what law professors and bar graders call *conclusory*. (You would not expect a jury to convict a defendant without believing beyond a reasonable doubt that there is sufficient evidence of each and every element of the charged crime, right? So why write law essays without proof of (or against) every element of every crime or cause of action?)

Let's look back at the example of Dufus's attempted arson above. We did not just write, *Dufus wanted to burn the cottage and took a substantial step toward doing so and therefore is guilty of attempt.* We broke down each element (the intent element was easy to prove because the facts stated he wanted to do this, but we nonetheless still noted it explicitly). Then we showed how and *why* Dufus's walking to the cottage with the kerosene and matches (linking these tools explicitly to the target offense) amounts to a substantial step toward the commission of the crime.

You may think this is obvious, so why bother writing it? Of *course* kerosene is flammable. Duh! On a bar essay, though, your job is *to show why* the facts prove or disprove the elements of the relevant rules. I often tell students, "Walk into the bar exam imagining you have a teleprompter in front of you the whole time flashing the question *Why?*" That will force you to always remember to explain your reasoning and make your thoughts explicit. (And picturing yourself writing to a non-lawyer rather than to a colleague or professor will also help you to note every step of your reasoning more clearly.)

"IN MATH AND ON THE BAR: SHOW YOUR WORK"

Law students who are professionals in other fields, or businesspeople used to customers and clients seeking quick answers, often find it challenging to slow down and write each step of their thinking. Some of my former law students who were doctors frequently told me, "The patient doesn't want a long story. She just wants the diagnosis and treatment. Basically, she would be thrilled if I didn't say anything other than, 'Take this. It will make you feel better.' " Clients who are paying for services also often want instant answers. But bar graders are more like good math teachers; they want to "see your work," your ability to reason logically, step by step. Bottom line, don't "jump to conclusions" in bar writing.

Issue-Spotting Exercise

Look at the following sentence: "The defendant entered the Miller office building at dusk through an unlocked door to get the umbrella that he had left, then saw the diamond ring, took it, and walked out into the rain." If the question asks about the defendant's possible criminal liability for burglary, what, if any, discussable issues are raised by the following words? Write the first thoughts that come to mind about these words in the spaces below:

"office building at dusk"

"through an unlocked door"

"that he had left"

"then"

What did you identify as issues? Before identifying any issues, of course, you undoubtedly recited the rule for burglary: *Common law burglary is defined as the breaking and entering into the dwelling house of another in the nighttime with intent to commit a felony therein.* (**If you don't know the rule, it is very difficult to effectively issue spot.**) But, with that rule in mind, you likely went on to ask some of the following questions:

1. Does the office building satisfy the "dwelling house" element of bur glary? (Here, you likely reminded yourself that modern jurisdictions have extended this element to include any "protected structure.")
2. And, do the words "at dusk" satisfy the "in the nighttime" element? Again, this element has been eliminated under modern law.
3. Does entering through an unlocked door satisfy the "breaking" element?
4. Is the defendant's going inside to get the umbrella "that he had left" sufficient to prove he had the requisite *mens rea*, or "intent to commit a felony therein"? He may not have had any criminal intent if he walked in to retrieve his own property.
5. Does the word "then" raise a potential issue? It may be relevant to the question of when the felonious intent was formed, timing being critical to culpability.

I hope this one sentence issue spotting exercise illustrates how both knowledge of the law, and slow, careful reading are indispensable to effective issue spotting.

SOME JURISDICTIONS HAVE SPECIFIC SUGGESTIONS OR REQUIREMENTS FOR ESSAY WRITING

This chapter focuses on broadly applicable guidelines for and insights into effective bar essay writing generally. You must research any unique aspects of your exam. Enroll in a reliable bar course tailored to your jurisdiction and study the website and any information provided by your bar examiners. Be sure to carefully review any past questions and sample answers your jurisdiction has released or, if applicable, those released by the NCBE.

Conclusions in Essay Answers

Finally, a word about conclusions. While it may not always matter so much *how* you conclude or "who wins" on bar essays, it matters that you do conclude. Bar graders want to see that you can answer the entire question (and all of the issues that it raises) within the allotted time. They will not be satisfied if you merely demonstrate that you can *start* answering the questions or outline the answers to the questions. (Do not, for example, write an excellent answer to part one of the question and then run out of time for part two.)

That said, two passing answers may contain opposite conclusions—especially when the facts are "gray," meaning there are good arguments on both sides. When faced with such ambiguity, you may, for instance, conclude in a manner that acknowledges this: *Based on the foregoing analysis, the defendant will* likely *be found to have possessed the intent to kill the victim here. If, however, the prosecution is unable to prove intent to kill, also as noted above, the prosecution may well be able to demonstrate that the defendant possessed the intent to cause serious bodily harm or, at the very least, that his actions showed a reckless indifference to human life.* On most bar exam questions, there is typically nothing wrong with concluding in a way that shows a number of probable outcomes, but you must finish, and do so logically. Again, giving some emphasis to a conclusion, even a brief one (perhaps by underlining it or making it a subheading), shows the grader that you completed the answer.

Note: There are some jurisdictions where bar graders seem, based on the answers that they publish, to want more definitive conclusions. Follow the guidance of your ASP faculty and your bar review for jurisdiction-specific advice on bar essays.

Quick Quiz

When I complete a practice exam, I:

A. Never look at it again, and certainly never show it to anyone else.

B. Study it alongside a sample or model answer, comparing and contrasting the two.

C. Show it to a professor, mentor, study buddy, or academic support advisor to review and critique.

D. Do either *B* or *C*, or both, *and* rewrite that same practice exam at a later date and assess improvements.

Many of you, if you are honest, will choose *A*. Hopefully, I will have convinced you by the end of this chapter to choose D after completing a practice exam. If you picked *B*, that is good; however, be sure at some point to also have someone else critique at least some of your exams, hopefully early on, so that you are not mistakenly thinking your answers are just fine if they aren't. There is also a danger in not studying reliable sample or model answers; you risk cementing your errors and continuing to repeat the same mistakes. The goal is to improve with every practice exam. You do yourself the greatest of disservices if you simply compound your mistakes. That said, if you picked *C*, be sure in the future to *first try to figure out* what *you* think you missed, and *then* let someone else critique it. Hopefully, what they say mirrors what you saw as errors and ways to improve. Eventually, you will learn what you need to from studying reliable sample or model answers on your own. (After all, you will not have someone critiquing or editing your actual bar exam answers. You must get to the point where you are doing them well, alone, but it is a process getting there! And reality checks along the way are important.)

How to Self-Assess Your Practice Essay Writing

After completing an essay, look carefully at your own answer and a model or reliable sample answer (e.g., one released by your state's bar examiners as representative of a passing answer). Sit with both. How are they the same and how do they differ? Pay attention to content, organization, phrasing, and presentation. Note how precise and complete the rule statements are. Are there any rules you can learn more about or rule statements you can memorize more thoroughly? What about proof (application/analysis)? Is there proof of the existence or lack thereof of each element of each rule at issue? Was every key fact used? Review them side by side, and, as a clever detective:

- look for what the sample or model answers include that your answer did not contain, and what you may have written about that was not in the sample answers;
- be sure you understand why the sample answers included what was discussed and why the sample answers left out things you may have thought were important;
- look for content, organization, and style (make sure your answer is reader friendly!);
- look at the rules and be sure you understand them; and

- reread the fact pattern and then look at how the facts were used in discussing each issue in the model answer.

Then, after this basic compare-and-contrast, ask these specific questions and check the appropriate boxes:

[ ] Did I finish within the allotted time?

[ ] Did I spot the main discussable issues? (And did I see which issues were major and required more discussion, and which were minor and called for less emphasis?)

[ ] Did I state the rules correctly and succinctly?

[ ] Did I use facts to show why (to *prove*) each element of each rule was or was not established in the question?

[ ] Did I reason to a logical conclusion for every main issue I raised?

[ ] Was my answer presented in a manner that was organized and easy to read?

After you have done this first part of self-assessing, find concrete ways to improve. The examples below are illustrations. Your situation is unique to you. The key is to figure out where you need to improve and to then create a doable plan of action for your success. Make every effort to leave each practice session with at least two to three specific ideas about how you can improve.

CAVEAT: USE PRACTICE EXAMS TO IMPROVE!

I have said this before but cannot emphasize it enough: *taking* practice exams is not sufficient. You must walk away from every practice session dedicated to *improving* the quality of what you just produced. If you write essays poorly, you get the law wrong or your analysis (proof) or use of the facts is insufficient, or your answer is disorganized—and you just keep repeating the same mistakes on future practice exams—you will just be cementing and compounding your weaknesses. That is why you must study quality, reliable answers and learn how to make your answers look and read more like those passing answers. This is also why it can be so helpful to at least periodically have your answers reviewed and critiqued by someone reliable.

Improvement Area Action Items

Check those items that apply to you.

[ ] I must read the questions more carefully. (Note a specific example of something you did not read carefully enough, for instance, "I wrote about other crimes, but the call of the question specifically asked about homicidal offenses.") In upcoming exams, I will read the call of the question first, then read the facts, and then reread the call of the question before I begin outlining. I will also underline the call of the question, and I will keep the fact pattern and my outline in front of me as I write my answer.

[ ] I need to manage my time better. (I wrote for 20 minutes on the first interrogatory and didn't have time to write the remainder of my answer.) Note: On a simulated bar exam, you will write several essays back-to-back, and you will want to watch your timing carefully to be certain you are stopping after the suggested time for each essay, so that you can finish the whole set in the allotted time.) I will work on my timing. I will keep a small clock in front of me as I write practice exams. During a thirty-minute essay, such as MEE essays, I will note the ten- and twenty-five-minute marks. I will read and try to finish my outline by the ten-minute mark. I will strive to have hit all the main issues by the twenty-five-minute mark and begin concluding. (During a one-h our essay, I will note when I reach the fifteen-, thirty-, forty-five- and fifty-five-minute marks. I will try to finish my outline by the fifteen- to twenty-minute mark. I will strive to have hit all the main issues by the forty-five-minute mark. And I will be concluding by the fifty-five-minute mark.)

TIMING

It is absolutely critical to have your timing down—*nailed*—by mid-July (mid-February) at the latest. You must go into your bar exam knowing you can read and answer each type of question within the time allotted. Remember, when you appear before a judge, your time will be limited as well. It's part of the game. You must train both speed and accuracy. On essay questions, you will often need at least ten to fifteen minutes to read and outline. (That is true whether the essay is a thirty- or sixty-minute exam.) This will help you write in an organized manner and allocate your time appropriately between the issues raised by the question and facts. Note: The times may need to be adjusted if you are a fast reader and slow typist or a slow reader and fast typist. Experiment by varying the amount of time you spend respectively on 1) reading, 2) analyzing, and 3) writing; see if adjustments in timing on one part can help boost your scores. I frequently see bar takers' scores increase significantly when they spend more time reading, thinking, and outlining **before** writing.

[ ] I must type faster. (I have the thoughts in my head, but don't get them out fast enough.) I will work on improving my typing skills. I will type every day, and I will make time to type out model answers in full for at least some of the practice essays I write. (This is another good example of why it pays to start bar preparation well before formal bar review. If you determine early in your last year of law school that you are not typing fast enough for the time pressures of the bar exam, you can do something about it, for example take an online typing course. If this is something that you just realize in mid-June (mid-January) is causing a major obstacle you will have a tougher time making the necessary improvements.)

[ ] I need to understand the law better. (I either did not see issues or I saw what the issues were but did not write applicable rule statements clearly.) I will review the lecture notes and look up areas I do not understand in the outlines. Then I will either say out loud or copy or rewrite the legal rules several times to help memorize them.

[ ] I'm not using enough facts. Cross out words from the fact pattern as you use them in your answer. Learn the law more thoroughly. The better your knowledge of the law, the better your ability to quickly see how these new facts prove or disprove elements of governing rules.

Your Turn to Self-Assess

1. Did I finish the entire essay within the allotted time? [ ] Yes [ ] No

If not, indicate why and what you might do to improve in the space below.

Improvement action:

---

2. Did I spot and write about the main issues? [ ] Yes [ ] No

Improvement action:

---

3. Did I allocate my time well as I was writing? (Did I write too much on any one issue such that I gave short shrift to other issues?) [ ] Yes [ ] No

Improvement action:

---

4. Did I state the rules correctly and succinctly? [ ] Yes [ ] No

Improvement action:

---

5. Did I use facts to show why each element of each rule was or was not established in the question? [ ] Yes [ ] No

Improvement action:

---

6. Did I reason to a logical conclusion for every main issue I raised? [ ] Yes [ ] No

Improvement action:

---

7. Was my answer presented in a manner that was organized and easy to read? [ ] Yes [ ] No

Improvement action:

Bottom line: Troubleshoot now, during early start or intensive bar prep. Do *not* use the actual bar exam to figure out what you need to do better next time. Pass the first time you take the exam. The more practice exams you take, the more opportunities you will have to learn and improve, slowly and surely.

It's normal for improvement to be slow and incremental. Some of you will hit a wall at the end of June (January) and be tired of practice tests. You must keep going, keep plugging away, and don't give up. The breakthroughs and "aha moments" will come, maybe when you're not even expecting them, as long as you keep at it and keep moving forward. By comparing your answers with model answers, you may gain insights that show you where adding even one more sentence or bolstering the factual analysis of even one particular issue would greatly improve the answer. Note those observations. Make them a part of your process. You will get there. Slowly and surely.

Persistence

Keep taking practice tests and keep reading and studying those model answers. Continue writing what you learn from each practice test in your outline. And rewriting practice essays can be helpful. You will see them differently now than you did even a month ago. You will see the ways to improve. Until the exam is over, there is time to improve. Even the day before the bar, you can learn valuable things that may boost your scores. Do not give up. Be dogged, determined, and persistent.

You can also try rereading practice exam answers aloud and handwriting or retyping them in full, to "tune your ear" to a complete response. Often doing that just a few times brings home seemingly small changes that can make a huge difference in how effectively your answer responds to the queries and covers the required material.

Reality Check: Getting Your Exams Graded by Someone Else

Throughout this chapter and book, I stress self-assessment. But be sure to *also* complete and turn in as many exams as possible to your bar review for critique. And check and see if your ASP faculty have time to review your essays. You need to know that you are on track and not continuously repeating problems you didn't even notice. Know, though, that unless you have a tutor standing over your shoulder while you write, there will be a delay in getting feedback—even from the best of bar reviews. Also, remember that you will go into the exam alone. So, the sooner *you* see how to improve, the better. Another reason for *immediate self-assessment* is that powerful learning comes when the fact pattern is freshest in your mind. You will much more readily see exactly where you erred and understand how to improve. (You will quickly notice if you misread a word or didn't see the significance of a key fact. You will easily see if a fact triggered an issue, but you didn't know the relevant law. Look up that rule *while the fact pattern is fresh* so that it sticks in your memory.) If you have to reread a fact pattern, days or weeks later when your graded exam is returned, you will waste time getting back up to speed. And, it may be difficult to recall what you were thinking at the time. Use a grader's critiques to confirm or change your own assessment. When you get an exam back from your bar review, compare the grade and comments to your own assessment. Did they point out things you didn't see, or does the critique confirm what you already figured out for yourself? (If the former, do you see them now? If not, ask for further help.) Either way, you will come out ahead by working to learn from practice tests immediately after completing them.

Self-Assess Through Reverse Engineering

For essays, a useful tool can sometimes be to study the fact pattern and sample or model answer, and then to work backward. In other words, *outline the answer*. Ask yourself what you would have needed in an outline to produce this sort of (passing) answer. Then look *back* to the facts to see how and where the answer got its analysis out of these particular facts. How did this answer use the facts selected to reason to certain conclusions? Usually, we move from question to answer. But turning that process around, and moving from answer (end goal) back to the question, can sometimes help you see more clearly where you need to go. Note: This process can also be used on performance tests, as discussed below.

PERFORMANCE TESTS OR PERFORMANCE TASKS (PTs)

About PTs

PTs serve as a practical portion of the bar exam in most jurisdictions. Though they may vary in time, the work on the PT is similar to what you might do as a beginning lawyer: draft legal memoranda and write briefs to the court, letters to clients, discovery plans, settlement offers, and more. To complete an PT, you will be called upon to read and analyze a case *file* and a *library* of legal authorities, and draft one or more documents based on information you glean from those materials.

Whatever the exact tasks to be drafted, passing PTs requires demonstrating competency in the ability to:

- sort detailed factual materials and separate relevant from irrelevant facts;
- analyze statutory, case, and other legal authorities for relevant principles of law;
- apply the relevant law to the relevant facts in a manner likely to resolve the client's problem;
- identify and resolve ethical dilemmas, when present;
- communicate effectively in writing; and
- complete the requested task(s) thoroughly and within time constraints.

These six skills are described in the NCBE's MPT information booklet. The California state bar also publishes very useful information about its PTs on its website.

ANY LEGAL SUBJECT IS FAIR GAME ON PTs

The PT library may include virtually any area of law. (The NextGen specifies what areas certain PTs will cover.) PTs have involved areas such as health law, sports law, bankruptcy, intellectual property, tax, environmental law, and maritime law in addition to the more familiar torts, contracts, and the like. The good news is that you need no familiarity with the law in advance. The library will have everything you need. And often the law in areas most people are not familiar with is easier to understand than is the law in more routine areas. **As long as you know how to read and brief a case, and read statutes and other sources of law**, you are set. (I bolded that part for a reason. If you used canned briefs throughout law school, you must learn to read and brief cases under timed conditions before your bar exam.)

You must practice writing PT answers in full under timed conditions, rather than just reading and outlining them. They do not involve memorization; they require skills. Training by writing a critical mass of these as practice tests will give you the confidence to approach whatever might be thrown at you on your exam. (More below on the range of unusual tasks that could appear on a PT.)

Plan on completing at least eight PTs, written out in full under timed conditions, before your bar exam. That is a minimum.

To be certain you do at least that many, plan an "PT date" every Sunday afternoon. Schedule ample time after you complete the exam for self-assessing, as directed below. Again, it cannot hurt and may help enormously to complete at least one PT each week.

PTs are among the most productive work you can do to get a head start before you graduate, and, thankfully, more and more law schools are starting to integrate performance testing into the curriculum. If your law school has an PT course, take it; if not, train for the PT independently (preferably, before graduation).

PTs are open book. They don't require memory. So, if you master PT skills early, you will not need to take as much time with practice PTs during bar review—time you will need for learning and memorizing rules for essays and multiple-choice questions.

Key Differences Between PTs and Essays

There are several differences between PTs and essays. These differences affect how one best prepares for these exams.

1. PTs are open book; essays (in most jurisdictions) are closed book. (In law school, they may be open book or closed book depending on the professor.)
2. PTs are predominantly skills based, whereas closed book essays require skill, knowledge, and memory.
3. PTs have a great deal more material that you must sift through before writing. PTs require focus and stamina, as well as better time management.
4. A PT typically includes some irrelevant material and tests in part on your ability to distinguish

relevant and irrelevant information. Essays tend to have all, or nearly all, relevant facts that often trigger or affect your analysis of discussable issues.

5. There is often more variety among performance test answers deemed to be passing than among passing essay answers.

Document Types That Could Appear on Unusual PTs

Are you familiar with—and could you draft—each of these documents? In the space provided, write what each document below is, who it is prepared for, and what is its purpose. Check the box next to each document that you would feel comfortable drafting. You can learn about what these documents are and how to draft them in books such as *Trial Advocacy in a Nutshell (West)* or *Represent Yourself In Court: How to Prepare and Try a Winning Case* (Nolo.com).

Task/Document Type

[ ] Opening Statement:

[ ] Closing Argument:

[ ] Memorandum of Points and Authorities to a Supervising Attorney:

[ ] Opinion Letter:

[ ] Jury Instructions:

[ ] Client Letter:

[ ] Memorandum of Law:

[ ] Trial Brief:

[ ] Appellate Brief:

[ ]	Persuasive Memorandum:
[ ]	Contract:
[ ]	Will:
[ ]	Trust:
[ ]	Affidavit or Declaration:
[ ]	Proposal for Settlement Agreement:
[ ]	Discovery Plan:
[ ]	Witness Cross-Examination Plan:
[ ]	Witness Direct-Examination Plan:

How to Complete Performance Tests

Although individuals think differently, and PTs are set in different contexts with different assigned tasks, it helps to move through the material with a strategic approach. The following is a six-step logical approach to answering PTs. The timing is written in percentages because PTs differ in length.

- **S**tudy the Instructions and Task Memo (5%)
- **S**kim the File (5%)
- **B**rief the Library Authorities (20%)
- **R**e-Read Instructions, File, and Library as needed (15%)
- **O**utline (5%)

- **Write** your answer (50%), going back as necessary to consult your outline and notes in the margins of the file, library, and task memo.

Overview of This System: Why It Works and Why It Makes Sense

PTs are like puzzles. They consist of separate pieces that all fit together. But it takes a while to see how they fit. Though it may seem like the exam provides ample time, the time flies.

I intentionally use this "chicken and egg" approach that moves back and forth between different pieces of each PT. (And they are like puzzles!) This approach will make the time you spend on each part of the PT puzzle more efficient. Why? Because you cannot really understand the significance of facts in the file until you know the law, but you cannot readily see how the law applies to or is distinguishable from your client's situation unless you understand the facts. (Law is not relevant in a vacuum, but in how it applies to a given situation.) Thus, the most efficient system is to fully understand the instructions, and then gather enough of the facts from the file so that when you go to the library you can readily see not just what the rules are, but their significance to your client's situation. Hence, first skim the file. Then review the file after you learn the law from the library. (You can always come back to any part you want. This is an open book test!)

Your goal on this first read/skim of the file is to learn just enough about your client so that when you read the library, you will be able to readily see if the legal authorities support your client's position or not and why. Then, with a basic understanding of the factual and legal backdrop, return to the task memo. You will be surprised how much more sense it makes after you have some context! Also, when you reread relevant parts of the library and file (after also rereading the instruction), your reread will be targeted and focused. You will be less likely to get caught up in what you know is a mass of irrelevant information.

Studying the law in an PT library should be like *going on a precision mission, not a fishing expedition*. PT reading is not like reading cases to prepare for class, during which your professor might ask about any aspect of a case. On PTs, you read to *use* the cases to prepare the documents you are being asked to draft. To this end, your case briefing must also be more targeted.

Once you have a basic understanding of the law and renewed clarity about what you must draft, you can return to the facts and go through the file with a keener sense of what you are looking for. You will much more readily see whether certain factual sources are relevant, and, if relevant, why. When you don't know the law, you will waste time on facts that turn out to be insignificant or irrelevant.

Always, and at every turn (between each step), come back to the task memo (instructions). Such memos are crafted extremely carefully to give you tools to organize and respond to the interrogatory. But again, their importance may not be apparent upon first read. Only after studying the file and library will you really see how helpful these instruction memos are.

Lastly, before writing, think and organize (and outline) carefully so that you can write well. PT answers that are organized and thoughtful score higher than those that are scattered and shallow.

Adjust the Timing to Fit Your Strengths and Weaknesses

The suggested breakdown is to spend half of your time reading and thinking and the other half writing. I suggest you experiment with the timing as you are doing practice tests. If you are a very fast reader and slower typist, or vice versa, adjust accordingly. Many students I encounter need more than half the time to read and analyze and can type very quickly once they understand the PT components and task they must draft.

Bottom line: Watch the clock while completing practice tests. Experiment with a 50/50 split, then with other time allocations. See if there is a timing methodology that enhances your ability to produce quality work. Remember, the time goes quickly but the material is open book, so don't get bogged down anywhere. (You can always come back to the file, library, or instructions.) Keep moving using this logical approach and keep close track of time. You must get through all the materials efficiently to finish in time with a complete and well-organized answer.

A Closer Look at Each Step in the PT Approach

We overviewed the process above; now let's break it down.

The Instructions

The more important part of the instructions is the task memo as these instructions are specific to each PT. The task memo is *not* boilerplate. You should read every word of it, two or three times. Usually, the task memo includes information about your client and specifics on what document(s) you are to draft. The task memo may include or be followed by a separate *format* memo telling you how to set up the assigned document.

As you read, underline or highlight the exact tasks you are to perform, and as you write, check back in with the task memo to be sure you have completely responded to the assignment. Note, too, that the more closely you read the task memo, the easier it often is to write your response, as there are often organizational hints within the task memo.

There are also usually some boilerplate instructions that will be the same or substantially the same as those you have completed in practice. Just take a moment to verify these. They will usually tell you how long you have to complete the exam, what materials are included (usually a file and library—but double-check to make sure they haven't included some other document), and possibly the weight/value of each task, if you are to complete more than one assignment. They might also tell you the name of the fictional jurisdiction(s) where the PT "case" is set. They might also provide information you need to assess the precedential weight of the respective authorities in the library. Know what to look for in boilerplate instructions that might differ; take a moment and glance at them as you begin.

The File

After reading the instructional documents, skim the file. Unlike essays, where you have predigested, fixed facts, PTs provide facts in the form of resource documents such as a letter from a witness, a transcript of a client interview, an office memo, or criminal indictment. Learn who your client is and the issues your client faces. Get a sense of which documents are provided, where they come from, and who wrote them. (Look at the four corners of the document, including letterhead, dates, and footnotes.) Pay attention to whether a document has been redacted or excerpted from something else. For example, there can be a big difference between a *transcript* of an interview and a *summary* of an interview; the former, because it includes every word, usually has a lot more irrelevant information.

Get ready to read the library with some sense of your client and the "characters" in this PT role play. Unlike law school, where you read cases to see all the reasoning and nuances of the opinion, you read cases on PTs to use them to craft your answer. It is much more targeted reading, reading you can only do effectively when you know your client's circumstances.

On scratch paper, the task memo, or on the table of contents of the file, list the major parties and players, their names, and their roles. Get into the habit of writing this in the same place on every practice PT you write. This way, you will know where to turn to immediately verify who people are if you forget while poring through the file. For example:

- My client = the professor, Mr. X
- University of Liberty, "University" = employer and possible D
- Wanda = witness who observed X's relationships with students
- Sally = student bringing complaint

PTs ARE NOT ALWAYS SET IN LITIGATION CONTEXTS

PT instructions might direct you to produce a transactional document (e.g., a contract or a will), so the authorities in the library may not support or negate your client's position, but simply provide information. Nonetheless, your mission in that library is to see how the law relates to your client's situation and helps you draft whatever documents you are to produce.

The Library

After your quick look at the file documents (knowing you will come back to them), go to the library, and read and brief the authorities there. (More on how to brief PT cases below.) Assess whether each case or statute (or other authority) supports your client's position or not. Note which are binding and which are merely persuasive. Pull out rules and try to determine how those rules fit together. For example, if there are three cases, does one represent a rule and the others exceptions to that rule? Is each case providing a distinct theory on which a party might bring suit? Try to step back and see how the library rules (in the various cases and/or statutes) relate to one another.

BRIEFING CASES

If you did not brief cases on your own in law school, master that skill now. If you relied exclusively on canned briefs or those of a classmate, you are not alone. But you will not be happy if you first realize during bar review that you must effectively and efficiently brief cases under timed conditions for the PT. If you are still in law school, check out the resources in the Bibliography at the end of this book, including *Cracking the Case Method: Legal Analysis for Law School Success*. If you are in bar review, read through the rest of this chapter and train by briefing cases in practice PTs.

Don't get bogged down on the PT in long case briefs. You don't have time to brief as thoroughly as you would in school. Read the case to determine the four W's—which, what, why, and where:

- **Which** party is in the position analogous to your client's circumstances,
- **What** the court ruled (consider holdings and possibly dicta) and **why** (the court's rationale), and
- **Where** you will use the case in your answer. (Will it support an argument or analysis in favor of your client or will you distinguish the case from your client's situation?) If a PT is set in a transactional context, you may use case law and other authorities to learn the applicable rules and standards that govern or guide the particular transaction.)

Remaining Steps in the Approach

Now, with the law in mind, review the file and reread the task memo. Again, the documents will make more sense; you will readily be able to note what is relevant and why.

Next, outline the document(s) you are to draft, going back to the library, file, or instructions as needed. (This is the beauty of an open-book exam!)

Outline, but do not write a long or detailed outline. The grader will only consider your final product. I have seen far too many students fail because they tried to follow suggestions of instructors who recommended detailed outlines or charts as "magic" formulas to writing passing performance test answers. These students get so caught up in preparing their special charts that they do not have time to produce quality passing answers. Similar to essay outlines, a good PT outline provides a framework for your answer, which you can turn into headings and subheadings that provide a roadmap for graders. (My favorite place to outline PTs is directly on the library table of content. Often, the most logical way to organize an answer will come from a combination of the library rules and the task memo instructions. Remember, facts are not relevant in a vacuum; they are relevant to elements of rules or factors.)

Finally, draft your assignment. Be sure to write for the proper audience in the appropriate tone, and complete the task or tasks requested in an organized, lawyerly manner. If you are writing to a non-lawyer in a task such as a letter to a client or in a closing argument to jurors, be sure to define any jargon you use. If you are drafting a brief to the court, use more formal language. Note: You are often writing to your employer, typically a partner in your firm, but the document may be intended ultimately for your client, the opposing counsel, a private investigator, or another person or entity. A few points on that: (1) Write in a way that is appropriate for that *ultimate audience*. In other words, if the Senior Partner is directing you to write a brief for her to file with the court, write in a tone you would use for the court; if the Senior Partner is requesting an internal memo for her or someone else in your law firm, write in an appropriate interoffice style. (2) Documents intended for someone on your side (a lawyer in your firm, your client, a private investigator you hire) are typically more analytical. You might reveal weaknesses in your case, whereas documents to the court or opposing counsel are usually more persuasive in tone.

PTs are deceptive. People think they are "easy" because they are "open book," but they are not easy. There is a lot of material to sort through and organize and then use effectively in your answer. The time flies. You *must* practice PTs—lots of them—under timed conditions. I recommend at least one PT each week. (Again, my standard is, "Every Sunday afternoon, you have a 'date' with a PT.") The key to having the time to complete a sufficient number of practice PTs under timed conditions is to start early.

Just as with essays, make sure your answer is grader friendly, easy on the eye with headings and subheadings, so that, at a glance, the grader can readily see your organization. Type or handwrite legibly.

PT Practice: How to Self-Assess

PT practice is more time consuming than essay or multiple-choice practice, so students often procrastinate about making time for them. Big mistake. In addition to practicing in all the other testing formats, be certain your study schedule includes a regular time to complete a practice PT each week.

One trick to get more "mileage" out of each PT practice session is to "spin off" the scenario to review other testable tasks. Let's say you complete an PT that is set in a criminal context where you are the prosecutor filing a motion to suppress certain evidence. After drafting and assessing that motion, talk yourself through how you would have drafted the same assignment if you represented the defendant. Then "dictate" or write a letter to the client, updating him or her about the upcoming hearing on the motion. Next, reclaim your prosecutor's hat and draft a letter to defense counsel proposing a plea bargain. Develop a discovery plan that may be implemented if the motion is denied. Doing such spin-off exercises as practice can give you exposure to different types of tasks (and boost your confidence in your ability to handle anything they throw at you) without having to invest the extra time reading a new file and library. Note: This spin-off suggestion is *not* a substitute for weekly practice PTs but a complement. You can do spin-offs with a study partner. Go for lunch or coffee after doing a practice PT and talk through how other tasks might be drafted using these same facts and law.

PT Self-Assessment

When you finish each practice PT, ask yourself the following questions:

[ ] Did I finish within the allotted time?

[ ] Did I follow the instructions given in the task memo?

[ ] Did I use all the relevant authorities from the library?

[ ] Did I bring in key facts from the file to support all the points I made? (Did I leave out irrelevant facts?)

[ ] Is my answer well-organized and easy to read?

Next, study the model or sample answers. Just as with self-assessing essays, the key is in comparing and contrasting your answer with a passing answer. Outline your answer and outline the sample answer and you will easily see if you missed issues, discussed irrelevant issues, didn't understand or write in enough detail about the law, or if your writing was disorganized. Then review the answers side by side, paragraph by paragraph, to see how you can improve your own answer. Ask yourself what, if anything, you can do to write more clearly and use the authorities in the library in a more precise and more organized fashion. It is also great to have quality feedback from your bar review or ASP faculty. But that is not a substitute for you yourself seeing how to improve. Self-assess immediately after completing each practice PT, even if you are turning your practice exams in for grading.

PT Action Items

Just as you drafted action items to improve your essay writing earlier in this chapter, note below steps you can take to strategically improve MPT skills:

[ ] I finished in the allotted time.

Improvement action (if you did not finish timely):

____

____

____

[ ] I followed the instructions in the task memo and any format memos.

Improvement action (if you missed any instructions):

____

____

____

[ ] I used all the relevant authorities from the library, and I cited all the main cases in the table of contents of the library (I did not have to cite the cases within cases).

Improvement action (if you did not use all main authorities):

[ ] I sorted the relevant from the irrelevant facts, and I incorporated key relevant facts from the file to support all the points I made.

Improvement action (relating to your factual analysis):

[ ] My answer is well organized and easy to read.

Improvement action (if your answer needs work in organization or clarity):

PT SELF-ASSESSMENT THROUGH REVERSE ENGINEERING

Just as with essays, looking backward from the model or sample answer to the task memo, file, or library can be most helpful in learning to improve PT writing. Outline the answer. Study the task memo, then ask yourself what from this answer came directly (or indirectly) out of the task memo? What points were pulled from the file? How did the answer use the library authorities? How was the answer organized and where in the instructions, file, or library were hints as to what would be a logical organization? Doing this sort of reverse engineering can be especially helpful if you feel “stuck” on how to organize PTs.

PT Strategy Tips

The toughest part of the PT is managing the data and your time. There is a lot of material and the time flies. Keep in mind that your notes end up in the trash. You only get credit for your answer.

PT facts are numerous; some are duplicative, and others are irrelevant. You need to read with a logical system that takes this into account and you need to practice extensively with your approach.

Just as I suggest you create your own one-page "cheat sheets" on all substantive subjects tested on your bar exam essay, I also suggest that you draft your own PT strategy sheet. Draft this for yourself only, with reminders of what you want to keep in mind during your PT. Below is a sample.

Sample Performance Test Strategy Sheet to Personalize with Your Own Notes

INSTRUCTIONS: I will read through these quickly checking to make sure there is nothing unusual.

Notes:

TASK MEMO: The task memo is the most important document in the PT. I will read it to find out (1) whom I am role playing and whom I represent; (2) for whom I am writing; (3) what type of writing (analytical, persuasive, transactional) is necessary and the goal of the task(s); (4) what exactly I am expected to produce by the end of the exam (Is there any guidance on formatting I need to follow?); and (5) whether there are any clues to or suggestions for organization.

Notes:

CASE: Who is the client? What does the client want? What is preventing the client from getting what the client is seeking? If the PT is set in the litigation context, who is suing whom over what?

Notes:

LAW: (1) I will try to find the main legal issues and figure out the legal analysis *framework*. How do the library rules fit together? (2) What is the library/legal issues fundamentally about? Is the analysis mainly procedural or substantive, or both? Is it expanding or narrowing a legal policy? Is it building a prima facie case or defense theories? Is it distilling a rule from a long line of cases? Is it arguing why our case doesn't fit some particular statutory scheme? What sort of legal analysis will I have to perform? How can I use the authorities in this library?

Notes:

FACTS: In my initial skimming of the file, *before* I read the library, let me try to determine my client's basic story. In my second read of the file, *after* I read the library, let me think: (1) Knowing what authorities are in the library, and, if possible, breaking down the main legal rule(s) into elements or component parts, I will search for some relevant facts that relate to, by proving *or* disproving, each element. Remember, many facts will be irrelevant or duplicative, so there is no need to use every fact (the way I strive to in essays). Here, I am just looking for some fact or facts that relate to each key component of each main legal rule or principle. (2) Let me take note of inconsistent facts and facts (and sources of fact) that do not seem reliable (credible) and why. I will also keep in mind that I may be looking for additional facts (how to establish and possibly how to prove them.) (3) Again, I must expect irrelevant and duplicative facts. I don't want to get bogged down and waste time in anything I don't immediately see as relevant. I can always come back to anything in the file or library. It's all right here, open book. Things will become clearer as I have more context. So just keep rereading, thinking, and moving between the different pieces of the MPT puzzle. Go back to the task memo.

Notes:

PROFESSIONAL RESPONSIBILITY: There may not be any but here I will keep a look out for conflicts and rule violations—actual and potential—and ways to resolve any ethical concerns. Are any lawyers behaving in an unprofessional manner? (Are the lawyers returning client calls and e-mails promptly? Are they explaining the pros and cons of various courses of action thoroughly?) Is there anything being done or recommended that could be accomplished in a more client-centered manner?

Notes:

SOLVE CLIENT'S PROBLEMS: This may or may not be part of your task. If it is part of the instructions, I will keep the client's objectives and obstacles in mind, present alternative strategies (give at least two choices), and recommend tactics and strategies as well as substantive courses of action that will help the client achieve the client's goals.

Notes:

CONCLUDE: (1) I will finish my answer with a final sentence or paragraph that begins with some obvious concluding language, such as "In conclusion . . . ." (2) I will ask myself, as I am outlining and writing my answer: Did I perform the task(s) I was asked to perform? Did I help whomever I'm supposed to help on this project?

Notes:

INTEGRATED QUESTION SETS

The NCBE states on the NextGen website: *"Just under a quarter of the exam time will be devoted to integrated question sets. Each of these sets is based on a common fact scenario and may include some legal resources (e.g., excerpts of statutes or judicial opinions) and/or supplemental documents (e.g., a police report or excerpt from a deposition) and include a mixture of multiple-choice and short-answer questions. In addition to testing doctrinal law, some integrated question sets will be focused on drafting or editing a legal document; other sets will be focused on counseling and/or dispute resolution."*

Practice integrated question sets (IQS) are included on the NextGen website and some are reprinted with permission from the NCBE in the Appendix to this book.

Because IQS are new and will not yet be widely employed when this edition of this book is published, we will not spend a lot of time on them here. Future editions of this book will cover them in greater detail. A few things come to mind, however, as reading the NCBE's descriptions and studying the sample answers.

- Like with all testing formats, bar reading and taking practice tests and studying sample answers will be key to doing well on this format.
- In some ways, the IQS resembles mini-PTs. They are not testing memory but skills and may require legal analysis, factual analysis, problem solving, and awareness of professional responsibility rules—the core competencies on PTs. Thus, completing many practice PTs may be super helpful in preparing for IQS success.
- In other ways, the IQS differ from PTs. Namely, the IQS will present an evolving fact pattern, where applicants must answer questions as stages as (facts and law) unfold. In contrast, PTs involve an analysis of an entire closed universe.

  What this distinction may mean in practice is that while it is important to employ a ping-pong strategy on PTs, (going back and forth between the File, Library, and Task Memo to see the whole), on IQS, while you *can* return to a previous portion, it is critical *not to* second guess a previous answer

> because of new information from a subsequent portion of the set. The questions are integrated but sequential.

Again, it seems plainly apparent that a) thorough training with other (existing) testing formats, especially PTs, and b) practicing with any released IQS or with IQS practice exams from your reliable bar review course, will be the best preparation technique for success on the IQS.

PRACTICE TEST SCORES FOR ALL TYPES OF BAR TESTING

Notice that nowhere in our discussion of assessment did we mention scores you receive after submitting practice tests for grading. Even when you submit your answers to your bar review (which is really important!), it is also critical to do your own self-assessment as soon as possible after completing that practice test. That is when the exam is freshest in your mind and thus the best time to learn from the experience of writing.

Please prepare for this reality: *you likely will get a lot of practice questions wrong.* Do not worry. This is normal. Just keep working. Students always e-mail in June about how frustrated they are. Many threaten to quit. But it is especially common early on to frequently choose the wrong answer on practice multiple-choice questions. And graders may give very low scores on practice written exams. Don't worry; keep working. Self-assess to find any and every way to improve your knowledge and skills, learn from each practice test, and move on. Every wrong answer is an opportunity to get it right on the exam! #Mistakes=Opportunity

PRACTICE IS ABOUT THE LEARNING, NOT THE SCORES

The value of consistently taking practice tests is not in the scores, but in what you learn from doing them. Think about Michael Jordan's wisdom: "I have missed more than 9,000 shots in my career. I have lost almost 300 games. On 26 occasions, I have been entrusted to take the game-winning shot . . . and I missed. And I have failed over and over and over again in my life. And that is precisely . . . why I succeed."

SELF-TALK DURING PRACTICE TESTS

What do you tell yourself?

Do you say, "Making this mistake now will help me not to make it on the actual exam; making mistakes on practice tests will help me pass the bar exam." Or do you complete a practice test, look at the results, and say, "How could I be so stupid as to miss *that*? I'll never pass."

If ever you catch yourself thinking, "I'll never pass," stop immediately and rephrase. Review Chapter 1 on rephrasing self-talk, growth mindsets, and doubt-busting. You will pass. You are not stupid. You are learning. And if you keep learning, you are indeed extremely smart. The problem is not making mistakes—it's not learning from them! #GrowthMindset #PasstheBar

If your practice test scores are consistently lower in certain areas, *use* that as information about where you need to improve. Do not let practice test scores have a negative effect on your self-confidence. But do not ignore them. Test scores do not just miraculously increase. *You and your hard work* improves your scores. So get busy figuring out what is lacking and how to improve, continually.

Conversely, do not let higher scores inflate your ego or lead you to conclude that you can stop doing them. No! Overconfidence is just as much a problem as lacking confidence. Continue to work to improve until the last "time" is called on your exam. A bar review grader may have inflated a grade on an essay. You may have guessed on a multiple-choice question and gotten lucky. You can always do better. There is always room for improvement. (In an area such as constitutional law, for example, even if you have mastered all the rules, you can still improve by weaving in policy concerns.)

A solidly answer that has hit every discussable issue is like a cake without frosting. It's a good cake, and you must strive to bake that sort of well-prepared cake. (The bar exam is pass/fail. All you have to do is pass. You do not have to "get an A.") But, *if* you have time, go ahead and "frost" that cake with "bonus" issues. Perhaps you might make the point that if some fact were slightly different, an entirely different outcome might result. Or, you might weave in commentary on policy implicated in one or another approach to resolving an issue. Or, you might compare legal frameworks (especially if your jurisdiction awards points for knowing state and federal distinctions). For instance, in a contracts question for services or land that is governed by the common law, there may be an analogy to a UCC provision that, while not binding, is nonetheless instructive. That would be frosting the cake.

But again, only frost the cake *if you have time*. Do *not* go in search of "bonus points." However, *if you have hit everything* that is straightforward and a main issue, and still have extra time, by all means, say something further that is thoughtful and relevant if it comes to mind.

What if you think something might be at issue, but you are not sure? My rule is that if it takes you longer to figure out whether it's relevant than to just get it out logically and move on, write it. You will likely not be marked down if something is not correct. It will simply take time from points that are definitely at issue. (On essays, the more you complete, the more you will see what sorts of points tend to be main issues and which are more "bonus points.")

So, are you convinced? No matter how difficult or time consuming, in order to pass the bar exam, you must practice, practice, practice!

Louis Pasteur said it best: "Chance favors the prepared mind." Of course, it sounds better in French: *Dans les champs de l'observation le hasard ne favorise que les esprits préparés*. (If you don't want to take advice from 1850s France, remember what I mentioned at the beginning of the book about Beyonce's words on preparation and planning in her 2019 film, *Homecoming*.)

Your chances for success multiply geometrically the more prepared you are. Give yourself the best odds possible. If you want to pass the bar exam, prepare as well as you can. The best preparation includes consistently taking practice tests under timed conditions and studying sample answers so that you constantly work to improve.

Chapter hashtags: #PassTheBar, #PreparePracticePass, #Mistakes=Opportunity, #PTSuccess, #growthmindset, #work notworry, #BarExamSuccess

CHAPTER 9

THE HOME STRETCH: ELIMINATE DISTRACTIONS AND EMBRACE SUCCESS

- Bar Review: Eight Weeks at a Glance
- Envision Success to Achieve Success
- Eliminate Distractions and Focus Fully
- Simulated Exams as the "Dress Rehearsal"
- The Days Before the Exam: Getting Ready
- Plan the Event: What You Will Do on Test Days and Nights
- Getting Dressed on Exam Days
- Bathroom Breaks on the Bar Exam
- Listen to Instructions and Pay Attention to What Proctors Say
- Be Careful What You Eat Before and Between Each Testing Session
- Be Careful Where and with Whom You Eat
- Manage Your Stress and Don't Be Thrown by Curveballs
- A Walk Through Your Bar Days
- Handy Tips for Bar Days
- Top Ten Test-Taking Tips: Essays
- Top Ten Test-Taking Tips: MBEs
- Top Ten Test-Taking Tips: MPTs

The saying "It's always darkest before the dawn" applies to the home stretch of bar review. This chapter gives you tools to keep going, even when you feel you cannot. It will help you see that you are almost there and stay the course.

BAR REVIEW: EIGHT WEEKS AT A GLANCE

- **Eight weeks and counting:** Clear your calendar and make your study plan if you have not already.
- For skills training, get on a daily regimen of practice questions. Do not be freaked out by the quantity of material. Two months is a long time if you use it wisely. Book whatever travel and lodging you may need for the exam if you will be taking an in-person exam.

TO STAY OR NOT TO STAY (IN A HOTEL): THAT IS THE QUESTION

Some applicants live far enough from their bar location that they must stay nearby. If you have a choice, stay wherever will make you most comfortable. A student came to me recently trying to decide where to take the bar. (Some states have multiple locations and others only one.) Her parents lived nearby, and she could save several hundred dollars by staying with them. My question was simple: will you feel at your best? The student thought carefully and decided that her parents would be supportive; she would have meals cooked and feel nurtured. And not having to drive a long distance would reduce her stress. Other students come to completely opposite conclusions, realizing that even if they live very close by, they need to be alone in a hotel to totally focus, away from any family or friends. Do what is best for you. And try not to make the decision based on cost alone. I know that everything adds up, and you may feel guilty adding to the debt by something "frivolous" like staying in a hotel. It is not. If you are thrown by coming home on bar nights to an atmosphere that distracts or undermines you, you will pay far more dearly than for a few nights of treating yourself to a hotel. If you need it, do it. You are worth it. Done.

Seven weeks and counting: Assess your skills. Where are you weak? Adjust your study schedule to correct those weaknesses while continuing to follow your bar review schedule. Try not to get overwhelmed by the quantity of material. Think of how much you learned in seven days before certain final exams. You have seven full weeks. Make the most of every day, one step at a time, one day at a time. Reread the parts of this book's earlier chapters that discuss anxiety. Any time it all feels like too much to handle, use the tools you have learned to move through *paralysis to power*.

Six weeks and counting: Stick to your bar review. You chose a reputable bar review. Trust the process. Avoid distractions. Keep your focus. By now, it should be an absolutely dedicated habit to be doing daily practice questions in all testing formats. Don't be concerned about scores; just do them in full (under timed conditions), self-assess, and implement strategies to improve in any way you can. The focus is on continuous improvement.

Five weeks and counting: Combat burnout. You may feel fried. If you have put in three really solid weeks, you should be tired. This is perfectly normal. Still, you have a long way to go, so hang on. Push yourself. Slow and steady wins the race. Take off a couple of evenings to do something enjoyable that will take you away for a moment from bar study, then get back to it bright and early next morning. Stick to your schedule.

Four weeks and counting: July (or February) 1 arrives. Just seeing the new month will kick you into high gear. Pace yourself. Take off July 4 to celebrate. This is also the time to take care of some business. Make sure that all your travel and hotel arrangements are set for the bar exam, that you have your admission ticket, and that you know the rules on what you will be allowed to bring into the exam.

REVIEW AND UPDATE YOUR BAR SUCCESS PLAN

Go back and review your Bar Success Plan; update any sections with any new information. With one month to go, there is still time to take important steps needed to pass.

JULY (FEBRUARY) IS HIGH GEAR

You are in *high gear* now. It's July (or February). Only a few weeks until the big show. Don't be alarmed or freaked out when you see the date. You are getting ready to be at your peak, in both mind and body! Don't forget self-care, sleep, exercise, and eating healthy foods. Being strong is just as important as memorizing rules. At the actual exam, another candidate may know more law than you. No matter how much you study, that is possible. But, when all is said and done, if that person is too tired to be an active, detail-oriented bar reader, all the memorized rules in the world won't help. Yes, you must know your stuff. But you must also begin your exam ready to read critically, understand every word of every question, and use that information to think and reason carefully to logical conclusions. The facts will be new to everyone, and the person who stayed up all night before the exam to pack in more rules may not be awake and alert enough to read the facts critically and intelligently answer the questions asked.

- **Three weeks:** Take a simulated exam—look at it not as a referendum on how you will do on the real exam, but as a learning tool. Work on improving wherever you still need to. Stick to your schedule.
- **Two weeks:** Draft your "cheat sheets." Put each subject on one page. This will force you to identify the most critical areas and master the applicable rules in a logical order. It also gives you something to "hold" during last-minute reviews. (Students frequently say they learn so much just from *preparing* their "cheat sheets.")
- **The last week:** Reread all exam logistics rules on your jurisdiction's website. If you are taking an online exam, verify what you may have out on your desk. If you are taking an in-person exam, verify what you can bring into the exam. Assemble your clear plastic bag (and be sure it includes anything you need for admission into the testing room). Decide what you will wear and eat, and what you will do each day before and after the exam. Even if you are taking an online exam you may have very little time for lunch so you will want to have that meal planned ahead of time. Review your one-page "cheat sheets." Keep doing daily practice questions as you have every day for at least eight weeks. Be

good to yourself. Sleep well, eat well, exercise regularly, and get ready for battle.

With that weekly countdown snapshot, let's pull back and look at the month of July (or February) generally. In no uncertain terms, the key is to use the time you have as productively as possible. Work steadily and confidently, day by day, study session by study session, improving slowly and steadily, the focus still on *improvement.* Also, get in the habit of concentrating for longer stretches. Train in blocks of time that mirror (or are a little longer than) your exam's testing time blocks. Focusing at the level you will need to focus for that long can be a challenge for anyone. It can be physically grueling just to sit for that long. Get used to it. Train. This includes getting enough sleep, eating right, and exercising.

Be sure to continue taking practice tests in all formats and all bar-tested subjects. By mid-July (mid-February), start switching from writing out practice exam questions in full to reading, issue spotting, outlining, and studying model answers. (You can shorten this to mostly just reading the question, issue spotting and organizing in your head, and reading answers in the last two weeks.) Exposure to as many fact patterns during these last weeks is helpful. Review at least one more PT (or read through a few sets of task memos and sample answers if you don't have time to read the whole file and library) a few days before the exam.

Be sure that you have learned rules and can see legal issues in the logical order they tend to arise in each particular testable area of law. A good bar review program will help you to get these in order, but you must tailor them to work for you—make them your own. Remember, this month you are transitioning out of the big outlines into condensed outlines and eventually to your memory alone. You will eventually have to close those books entirely. Your cheat sheets provide a bridge to help you make that transition.

Be sure this month (July or February) to shift your body clock (if it is not already there) to "Bar Standard Time" (BST). If you are a late-night or early-morning studier, know that the hours you must be "on" are loosely between 9 a.m. and 5 p.m.

Make the shift now, slowly and surely, so that by July's (February's) end, you are on BST, and functioning well with it.

Another must this month is to keep the *flow* going. Nerves are good, to some extent. July (February) is the time to turn that *panic* into *power*, not *paralysis*. But if ever the nerves throw you (in practice or on the real exam), have tools handy to calm yourself and get back on track. (Reread sections in previous chapters on anxiety and how to unblock nerves and counterattack with power.)

As you study sample and model answers, envision yourself writing similar answers, responses that flow as logically as the model answers do. Note how much easier it is to read an exam that is clear. Make your answers simple to follow, with key points labeled for the grader. Make it easy for graders to see and understand what you have written. State what you have to say plainly and obviously. Do not try to sound witty or funny. The grader may not share your sense of humor.

Visualize yourself in the exam. Every day take a moment to picture yourself thinking and typing, having your words flow. Every time you do a practice test, visualize doing it in that test setting. Picture yourself in that exam room, calm and confident. Breathe deeply and slowly. Believe you *can* pass. Positive thinking is critical! Tell yourself every day you *can* do it. Say it aloud several times each day.

SHOULD I POSTPONE TAKING THE BAR UNTIL THE NEXT ADMINISTRATION?

By the end of June (January), there are always students who question whether they should take the exam. They made a good-faith commitment to pass and started bar review with all the right intentions, but something interfered with total immersion. Sometimes the student or a close family member falls ill, or, because of job or personal responsibilities, the student was unable to give bar review his or her all. To determine whether it is best to defer taking the exam (which, in some circumstances, it may be), it is critical to distinguish whether this is just nerves or whether the student is grossly underprepared. (Discuss this with a trusted mentor or ASP faculty member who can help you see where you are.) I almost always have to talk people "off the ledge" around the beginning of July (February). Just about everyone feels overwhelmed, and that they will "never learn it all." *That is normal.* That is not a reason to defer. Other people genuinely are not where they need to be by the end of June (January), will not have time to catch up in July (February), and would be better served by waiting. (There is no magic formula to say where you need to be, but if, for instance, you have not listened to or understood a great deal of the bar review lecture material or if you have completed no (or only a very few) practice tests, you may well have fallen too far behind to catch up.) If you find yourself in this position, look honestly at July (February) and see if you can make up the time to master what you need to learn. If not, consider deferring and putting yourself on an extended study plan to slowly and surely get ready for the next administration. There is no shame in this decision, so long as it is well reasoned. Again, normal nerves hit everyone, but going into the exam knowing you have not prepared is a setup for failure.

Envision Success to Achieve Success

See success in your mind's eye. If you are a verbal person, write a short description of your goal(s). Write as specifically as possible. If you are a visual person, develop an image of yourself in the successful role you are working toward, perhaps a picture of yourself in your cap and gown.

Next, imagine yourself in the room of applicants, reading questions; finding issues; and writing solid, strong, logical analyses. You are calm, confident, and strong! You control the exam; the exam does not control you.

Now, picture yourself standing before a judge being sworn in—being asked to raise your hand and take that oath to uphold the laws of your jurisdiction. See your own smile and the pride of those who come to witness.

Then see yourself as a lawyer. Stand before the mirror and introduce yourself as a lawyer. Use the words, "Hello, nice to meet you. My name is _____ and I am an attorney here in [your jurisdiction]."

Eliminate Distractions and Focus Fully

When you started preparing for the bar exam, you worked to *reduce* distractions; when you are closing in on your goal, *eliminate* them. During this last month, shut virtually everything down. (Review earlier passages on combating distractions.) Until it's over, give this exam your single-minded, total focus.

That said, do not start the last laps too early. People who put in too much too early may peak and burn out before the exam. In plain English, if you spend fourteen-hour days studying in June (January) and are ready to take the exam on July 1 (February 1), you have peaked too early.

During the home stretch, you must cocoon. In those last weeks and days, it must be all bar exam, all the time. Learn to be "self-centered" in a good way, in a way that allows for success. If you want company or need a study break, do what it takes to ensure that these breaks are positive and uplifting. Avoid any negative thing or person, as much as possible. Reread Chapter 6 if you need help getting away from naysayers or people you love but don't have time for now.

For many of you, this part will be extremely difficult. Others will get in the way—intentionally or accidentally. Distractions and procrastination enticements will come in every shape and size. You may feel guilty spending so much time on yourself. Don't. This is what is necessary to achieve great things. You have worked too hard to lose the edge now. You must remain in high gear. This is your Super Bowl, your Mount Everest, the day you make your Broadway debut—whatever feels huge and awesome to you. And it's fast approaching.

ARE YOU AFRAID? GREAT! THAT MEANS YOU'RE HONEST AND REALISTIC

This is a huge challenge. It is not easy, but it is wholly doable. Do not feel weak because you are nervous. Fear can be a good thing! Especially if you redefine it and use it productively. Redefine fear? Yes. Try calling it "*R.E.S.P.E.C.T.*" (Do you hear Aretha?! If that's not power, I don't know what is.) It sounds different to say, "I have a healthy respect for this challenge," rather than "I'm afraid," right? With the first phrasing, you sound like an athlete facing a worthy opponent. Control the fear; don't let it control you. Let it not paralyze but propel you forward, toward the success you deserve! Use fears to boost productivity. When fear meets adrenaline, you can turn it into its productive counterpart: powerful energy. Remember my phrase: turn *panic* into *power* not *paralysis*.

"Courage is resistance to fear, mastery of fear—not absence of fear."

—MARK TWAIN—

Simulated Exams as the "Dress Rehearsal"

Make a simulated exam part of your plan. Taking a simulated bar exam can give you a much-needed reality check. You can identify weak areas to continue studying and see what times of day you have the most energy and when you are dragging. The real exam will seem less daunting after a trial run.

A simulated exam helps you plan logistics. You will see how long you can physically sit and write before you need to stand up and stretch. You can decide what you should eat for lunch for maximum efficiency. And you can plan some warm-up exercises before the exam begins, such as completing one practice question or going over your one page approaches. Simulating the exam helps you to practice your timing so you stay on target and finish.

DON'T LET YOUR SIMULATED EXAM FREAK YOU OUT

Simulated exams help you when they provide an opportunity to make necessary adjustments before the real thing. However, simulated exams do *not* necessarily indicate how you will perform on the actual bar. They are an opportunity to get lots of useful information and use the time left to improve. Consider the following:

- You don't have to take the real thing today. It's still some time away. (It may not feel like a lot of time—but think about how much you were able to learn in one day before certain finals! There is still a lot you can clarify.)

- Your simulated exam may have been harder than the real exam.
- The real thing is a pass/fail test; you don't have to get an A.
- The simulated exam can help you strategize ways to plan actual exam days to maximize energy and efficiency.

Reflection: Simulated Bar Exam and What You Can Learn from a "Dress Rehearsal"

After completing a simulated bar exam, ask the following questions:

Did you budget your time well? (Did you finish each question?) Note your thoughts and observations—points you want to remind yourself about timing:

____

____

____

Were you tired after lunch? What foods did you eat at lunch? How much did you eat? Perhaps you can eat a bit less and take some of that lunch hour to walk and burn off some stress or listen to motivating music. Or were you hungry during the afternoon sessions? Do you need to eat more or differently at lunch?

Note your thoughts on food and fatigue:

____

____

____

Did you "blank out" on any questions? If so, get a plan ready to work through a temporary "brain freeze" should one occur next week. (See more on test anxiety in Chapter 7.) Note your thoughts on dealing with writer's block and test anxiety:

____

____

____

Were there any subjects you hoped would not be on your exam? Look at those again now. Try not to go in with an exposed weakness. Note your thoughts on subjects you still want to review:

____

____

____

The Days Before the Exam: Getting Ready

- Review your condensed outlines—the "cheat sheets" we talked about earlier. Put the big outlines on the shelf (the virtual shelf if you are working entirely online). Use big outlines only to look up rules if you realize you still don't know or understand a concept after erring on practice questions. No more reading long outlines. No time left to do that.
- Memorize rules. You have been memorizing slowly and surely for months. Now is the time for your final push. Aim for instant recall of all key rules.
- Read numerous fact patterns and model answers. Read them aloud. Retype some of them. Tune your ear to success.
- If your exam is in person, visit the test site ahead of time, if possible. Even the day before, walk by and see if you can at least look in the room and get a feel for the surroundings. The "vibe" in the room will be stressful. There will be lots of nervous energy. People may be snippy, or downright rude. Don't let anything faze you. It's all about the exam and you. Keep your own head clear. Stay *calm, confident, and in control* (your "three Cs" on bar days.)
- Keep your daily routine. Drink your coffee, tea, hot water, or whatever you have when you wake up just like you do every day. Continue to exercise. Eat healthy meals at regular times.

- In the days before the exam, if you cannot focus on any sort of review or study, then exercise, eat well, and sleep. Or watch a movie! Do whatever will get your body and mind ready for peak performance.

NO ONE ELSE KNOWS WHAT'S RIGHT FOR YOU BEFORE THE EXAM

Some people will say, "You must keep studying even the day before the exam." Others will say, "Whatever you do, do not study the day before." It does not matter what others say. It's *your* exam. Do what works for *you*. Does reviewing additional practice questions and/or pacing while you read your "cheat sheets" out loud calm you or make you more nervous?

What have you done successfully to prepare for other big events or challenges in your life? (Think perhaps of the LSAT or SAT, a big game you played in, or theatrical production in which you starred.)

Do whatever works to get you focused for success. It's your exam. Run your own race.

Plan the Event: What You Will Do on Test Days and Nights

The more control you have over your environment, the more you will feel in control on the exam. (If you are taking the exam at an unfamiliar location, try to get there a day or two ahead of time to acclimate.)

Get in the zone. Do what you need to do to be in peak form. You are preparing for battle; your keyboard is your sword.

Determine well ahead of time what you can and cannot have with you for an online exam or bring in with you to an in-person exam. Have snacks or meals waiting for you so you can eat when you want to during breaks. (Hotel restaurants at some bar testing sites get very crowded.)

Sleep. Get as good a night's sleep as you can on nights before test days. You may be tempted to stay up all night studying just a bit more. There is always more to study! But now you are definitely at a place of diminishing returns. Stop. Sleep.

And rest if you cannot sleep. Why? Let's say you go in well rested, but another applicant stayed up all night and indeed learned or memorized some key rules of law that you don't know or remember. Is he better off? No. You are. Much of the bar exam is reading comprehension and analysis, skills you will perform more effectively if you are well-rested.

For some, it helps to think of the test not as a days' long ordeal but simply as a number of distinct and wholly doable sessions.

GUESS WHAT? THE BAR EXAM MAY BE THE HARDEST EXAM BUT MAY NOT BE THE HARDEST DAY OF YOUR LIFE

A secret for working students, students with families, or really any busy student with just a whole lot on your plate: A day where *all* you have to do is sit and think, uninterrupted, may feel like a break.

Compared with many of our day-to-day lives, the bar exam is much more straightforward. You have only one responsibility on the bar exam, unlike workdays where the juggling never seems to end: demands from bosses and clients, spouses or partners, parents, and children; not to mention leaky faucets, broken car parts, computer viruses, and bills to pay.

I am reminded of a cartoon that a friend expecting one baby sent a friend expecting twins. The cartoon showed five women, each phoning another mother. The woman with one baby phoned the woman with two babies, the woman with twins phoned the woman with triplets, and so on. Each one simply said, "How was your day?" It's truly all about perspective.

So, try, as you get ready for this exam, to put the exam in perspective. You can do this.

Getting Dressed on Exam Days

Be sure that you have read rules about what is and is not permitted attire. Secure permission for religious head coverings if you need them. Check your rules to see if there is a dress code.

Next, if you will be in a testing center, dress in layers. One day they may crank up the air conditioning in the exam room, but the next day it may feel like a furnace. (Someone might have complained the day prior or there may be a power failure and then the air conditioning breaks down.) The room may be cold on a February bar day. Expect the unexpected and remember your job is to be fully present and clear-headed and to read and answer every question to the best of your ability. It can throw you if you are too hot or too cold. Dressing in layers gives you a bit of control over your environment.

Next, dress for success. For many of you, that may mean dressing as comfortably as possible—for example sweats, jeans, maybe leggings. Other people feel more powerful dressing in business attire, as if going to work. One former student said she wore a suit; it made her feel like an attorney, and she wrote with confidence. Whatever you put on, make sure you feel good and strong, and, again, make sure you comply with any dress code or related rules.

DRESSING TO INTIMIDATE

Years ago, I met some former students to celebrate on the evening of the last day of their bar exam. They told great bar exam stories, among those describing a group who lunched next to them at a nearby table, wearing sweatshirts from a top tier law school and, seemingly, drinking beer. Despite the sweatshirts, they could have been from any school, and they might have been pretending to drink alcohol at lunch, but they were joking and laughing, saying how "easy" the morning had been so loudly that my students were certain they were trying to intimidate other bar takers in the restaurant. Unfortunately, that is not the only story I have heard of bar takers staging bravado to try to intimidate other exam takers. People often tell of leaving a morning session only to have another applicant ask something like, "Did you see the business organizations crossover issues on that contracts question?" knowing full well that it was a straight contracts question without any business organizations issues at all. As with many of life's greatest challenges, the bar exam may bring out the best in people, or their most competitive, nastiest side.

Finally, wear your lucky socks! OK, I'm joking a bit here, but not entirely. If you have some piece of clothing or tradition that makes you feel lucky, go with it. You are not alone. You are in good company with some of the nation's most successful lawyers.

Set out ahead of time what you plan to bring into the test site with you on exam days.

Determine what you need and are allowed to bring into the exam with you and get it all ready, so that you know you're not missing anything. Be sure you have your admission ticket, identification, and anything else you must bring in. Every jurisdiction has specific rules about what is not allowed in the testing site as does the NCBE. And, different rules may apply on different days of the same exam, so be sure to read the policies thoroughly.

Bar examiners are very strict about what you may bring in and what you may not. No fooling around. Many jurisdictions require you to bring everything in a clear plastic bag. No purses, backpacks, or briefcases. Can you imagine failing the bar because you inadvertently wore or brought in something that was prohibited. It has happened. Do not let it happen to you. Read all the rules carefully.

Reflection: Your Plan of Action (POA) for Test Days

I have read the bar rules. I am taking the exam at an in-person location and am allowed to bring in the following (perhaps include black ink pens, prescription medication):

I am **not** allowed to bring in (e.g., post-its, wallet, food):

I am taking my bar exam online. These are rules I want to remember:

Bathroom Breaks on the Bar Exam

Depending on the rules where you are taking the exam, you may be allowed to use the restroom during the exam, so long as a proctor permits you to. For online exams, you may only be able to use the restroom during an official break between questions. Study the rules. And, plan on using the bathroom during at least some of those breaks.

If you are permitted bathroom breaks on your exam, go; don't try to hold it and get distracted with discomfort. Do make the most of the break, though, by reading the next question before you go, then mentally outlining while you are gone. Return, thoughts organized, and get back to work.

Listen to Instructions and Pay Attention to What Proctors Say

You will get instructions on when to start (and they may make you wait a while). They will tell you when to stop, and they may rattle off a host of other details. Listen carefully. Be polite and attentive to proctors. They are in charge. (In an in-person location, a proctor may tell you that you must wait to go to the bathroom or leave the room. Do not get up and leave the room without permission.) Do what the proctors tell you. If there is an issue with a proctor during the exam, register a complaint when you are able to without interfering with your completion of the rest of the exam, for example after the session, day, or exam is completed.

Be Careful What You Eat Before and Between Each Testing Session

Remember, use practice test days and simulated exam days to figure out which foods for which meals make you most productive. Some people find the best bar exam breakfasts are small but healthy meals, with protein and carbohydrates but nothing too greasy, spicy, or unusual. (Do not eat anything that smells spoiled or in any way seems like it might not be fresh.) For bar lunches, don't eat foods that make you sleepy. (Many people avoid turkey sandwiches for this reason.) Some popular lunches are peanut butter sandwiches or salad with chicken or beef for protein. It can be wise to avoid big desserts and excessive caffeine on bar days, focusing instead on foods for lasting energy.

(For example, you do not want a sugar high at lunch that falls into a groggy low in the middle of the afternoon session.)

Be Careful Where and with Whom You Eat

If you are taking the exam online, have a lunch ready for the break. It may not be a long enough break to go out and get something.

Plan ahead if you are taking the exam in person. Restaurants at testing sites are often very crowded. (They may have to serve hundreds of people at once.) You can avoid the crowd and get the food you want without a long wait either by bringing a lunch with you, or from your hotel's room service (especially if you can order the lunch in the morning so that it's ready when you are allowed to leave for the break). Some law schools provide food for their students at the bar exam.

If you are staying in a hotel room that has a refrigerator, you might consider stocking it with healthy to-go options. This is a good choice if you have dietary restrictions. (One of my students who keeps kosher found it much easier to bring her own food than to have to worry about the food at or near the bar exam site. I have also heard that advice from students who were vegans or on gluten-free diets.) Another student who had heard my tips and packed her own lunch was particularly happy because she and a number of other applicants seated near her were kept in the exam room for a while after others were released for lunch because of some issue that had occurred during the morning session. Those seated next to her who did not have lunches simply did not get to eat at all during that break because there was no time left to order and wait for food at the restaurant.

Some people do well eating with friends who are also taking the bar, especially if you all agree ahead of time not to discuss the exam. Some people avoid other bar applicants completely until the exam is over. Will your classmates make you more nervous? If so, stay away from them. Stay away from anyone who does not make you feel great during exam days. (Remember Chapter 6, lose the naysayers—something even more important during actual bar days.)

Manage Your Stress and Don't Be Thrown by Curveballs

Listen when the proctors are giving instructions. During the exam, breathe and sit up tall. During breaks, listen to power music or close your eyes and rest.

Expect the unexpected: an earthquake or power outage during the exam, or the person next to you getting up and walking out, never to return. Strange and disconcerting things happen during exams. If something unplanned happens to you, adapt. Do what you need to do to continue as unfazed as possible. These will be *your* crazy bar horror stories; remember this book's introduction: we all have stories!

" 'Come to the edge,' He said. They said, 'We are afraid.' 'Come to the edge,' He said. They came. He pushed them . . . and they flew."

—GUILLAUME APOLLINAIRE—

The exam is your time to push off that edge and fly, to soar to success. Keep in mind not just the fears you may feel when you're poised to jump, but the excitement and empowerment that come with meeting the challenge. You are close to that edge now. You are ready to go. Sure, it's scary. It's supposed to be. But you are ready. This is your moment.

Some things to remember when you go in: If you love puzzles, think of the fact patterns that will be placed before you as puzzles. Every fact is there for you; you just have to connect the dots. Let it be interesting! If you are more of a people person than a puzzle person, think as you read the exam questions walking through the ultimate cocktail party, where clusters of people tell you their stories and problems. They may share concerns about contractual agreements entered into and broken, businesses or marriages fallen apart with assets left to be divided, or crimes of passion. In each situation, you have advice: good, solid, sound, and rationally reasoned answers!

Read your exam questions as if they were real people's stories. In your mind are the rules that help unravel how each of those stories can play out. If they might well go one way or another, say that. ("Defendant will argue; plaintiff will argue; and the likely conclusion will be . . ."). Feel the incredible power that comes with knowing you can do that unraveling. You can and will pick each fact pattern apart and put it back together in a logical way that answers the questions asked.

Have you ever thought about *the bar exam* as a cocktail party? I know there is an alcohol pun there; it's unintended. What is intended is something I have been reiterating from page one. You can view this experience as punishment if you so choose, or you can see it as a welcome challenge. You can grow and learn from every aspect of preparation and performance.

Take in and appreciate the feeling of richness that comes from having so many rules at your command. It's like being ready to run a marathon knowing that all your muscles are strong. The intellectual flab has melted away these past two months, through the long hours of mental work out. There are few if any times in your life when you will have so many rules in as many subjects memorized, at your fingertips, and ready to go. In daily work as a lawyer, one may almost always look up information. Here, all the rules you need will be packed into your memory in a usable place, ready to be called upon.

Appreciate how strong your wings are. When day one of your bar exam approaches, push off despite the fears. Push off with as much confidence as you can muster. You are ready.

A Walk Through Your Bar Days

The famous race car driver Bobby Unser once said, "Success is where preparation and opportunity meet." Your opportunity comes when you walk into that exam room and stays with you until the last "time" is called. When you start your engines, be ready to succeed!

Reflection: Notes to Yourself for Bar Days

Alright, let's say that it's Day 1 of your bar exam. What is your plan of action (POA) this morning? What do you want to eat at breakfast? At breakfast, do you want to outline one or two essays to warm up, so that the ones you see on the exam are not the first of the day, so your mind is limber? You have your timing down; you have your approaches and your systems for reading and answering the types of questions that will appear on this session. What else do you want to remember before the first segment of your exam? (What language will you use to talk yourself out of anxiety if nerves turn to panic? Remember, you will be nervous and that's OK. Just use it as energy to power through. *Turn panic to power, not paralysis.* You have trained for this, and you have a plan about what to do to combat nerves if they start dragging you down.)

What will lunch look like? With whom do you want to eat lunch? What will you eat?

What is your POA for the afternoon? What additional testing format(s) will you face? What would you want to look at or listen to at lunch to get you pumped up for the afternoon? Do you want to remind yourself?

Have a great dinner. Do not experiment with any foods that might make you ill. Do not drink excessively. And remember, no matter how you think you did, the first day is over. It's all about the future now. Do not look back. Do not second-guess yourself or allow in any doubts. I have seen far too many students fail because of a perceived "defeat" early on that they carried into later sessions. This also applies to individual questions. Let go of whatever is done and do your very best every minute that follows. The exam is not over until the last "time" is called. Success on this exam is *not* about perfection. It's a pass/fail test. This *is* your Olympics, but here, winning bronze is every bit as good as gold.

What will you do this evening?

Now Day 2. What do you want to do this morning? (How will you "warm up"?)

___

___

___

Day 2 Lunch?

___

___

___

Afternoon? (Not all exams will have a second afternoon, so this is only for those taking an exam with a full second day.)

___

___

___

After the bar, maybe head to a bar that actually serves drinks! Or go to a nice dinner? Or sleep? Or . . .

___

___

___

Handy Tips for Bar Days

Below are "Tip Lists" for selected types of testing. (Again, remember that testing formats are changing.)

GENERAL TIPS NO MATTER THE FORMAT:

Read carefully. Facts matter. Precision matters. Know what you are being asked and what is expected of you in a reply.

ESSAYS TIPS—Note: some of these tips apply to other written answer formats.

Finish the question.

A final heading with the word *conclusion* in it can signify to graders that you finished. You can also include the words "in conclusion" or "in sum" in the final paragraph of your answer.

Avoid abbreviations, slang, and humor.

Let your grader's focus be on seeing the main and important points you have made. Do not distract or confuse the grader. (Remember, you are on an "interview," so write in a lawyerly tone.) Avoid the first person. Focus on what the facts *prove* and why, not on what you think.

Avoid long canned speeches.

Graders do not want to see that you can spit back lengthy, memorized portions of your bar review outline. (Regurgitating law statements is something most people can do.) Graders want to see that you *understand* the law at issue here in this particular exam and how the facts in this fact pattern prove or disprove elements of applicable rules of law.

Avoid irrelevant discussions.

You will not impress a grader by discussing issues that do not bear on the problem at hand or are not raised by the facts given.

Give arguments for both sides, where appropriate.

Facts can cut both ways. (Stated otherwise, different inferences can be drawn from the same facts.) Keep in mind the phrase "Plaintiff will argue on the one hand . . . defendant will argue on the other hand . . .". Remember that proof and analysis are more important than conclusions. (Focus on the A in IRAC or the P in IRPC.) And, sometimes it is appropriate to conclude in a qualified manner, using language such as, "it appears for the reasons stated above that the plaintiff is likely to prevail," so long as you have in fact substantiated your reasons in the analysis or proof sections of your essay. (Note that some state's bar examiners prefer definitive answers, and some essay questions cry out for definite responses, so use your judgment on this technique. When in doubt, check with your bar review instructor or ASP faculty.)

Answer the question or questions asked!

If the question asks for the theories upon which Patty might recover, do not address the claims, however interesting they may be, of Paul.

The best advice here is to read the call of the question first. Read it again after reading the facts and read it periodically as you proceed through writing your answer to be sure you are being responsive.

Likewise, if a question asks about guilt or liability of two defendants, it is often wise not to lump them together; it is usually better to separate them and assess the differences and similarities. Note, though, where the exact same legal rule or standard applies in two different lawsuits or to two different defendants *within the same question*, you do not need to write the law out twice. You can say "see rule above."

Key into differences between "racehorse" questions (many issues) and "think-'em" questions (fewer issues).

Exams may have many issues that you need to discuss fairly quickly in order to analyze each one and still finish in time. Other exams have a smaller number of issues that require more in-depth analysis. Be able to distinguish between these types of exams so you can handle each effectively and still complete the exam.

Make your logic explicit.

Avoid writing in a conclusory manner. Make your reasoning complete and transparent. Proceed step by step, clearly stating each rule and explicitly showing how the facts satisfy or fail to satisfy each rule you have discussed. Do not assume the grader knows what is in your head.

Analyze all the discussable issues.

A discussable issue is a question raised by the facts. Note that what makes an issue relevant to discussion in a typical bar exam is not whether the moving party will prevail in a particular legal claim. Analyzing why a rule is not satisfied, given the facts present and facts lacking, may be just as important to your success on bar exams as showing how, in another cause of action, the moving party may prevail. Be sure to spot and discuss all of the significant questions the facts raise.

Write in an organized manner.

Make the grader's life easy. Let the grader see that you can take a set of facts and proceed through your analysis of them in a logical manner. Where legal rules break down into elements, or tests break down into components or factors, organize your reasoning using these as tools.

MULTIPLE-CHOICE TIPS

Don't leave questions blank: When you are close to the end of a session, guess on any questions you don't finish or don't know.

Read the question first: Try to reason through to the correct answer from reading the interrogatory and facts without first looking at the answer choices.

Use process of elimination: Look for and cross out answer choices that have internally incorrect or inconsistent statements.

Eliminate further: Look for and cross out answer choices that didn't answer the question asked. On most multiple-choice questions there will be a single *best* answer out of four choices. Note that on some newer bar exams, there may be two best answers out of a larger number of choices. One thing that makes an answer the best choice is that it focuses on the exact thread in the question. So, once again, read and reread the question.

Answer the correct question: Make sure you are completing the answer to the corresponding question.

Track questions you don't know: Cross out answer choices you know are wrong. Have a system to keep track of questions you guess on so that you can come back to them if you finish early and have extra time.

Watch the clock: Keep pace with timing.

Read answers carefully: Read the answer choices carefully. Read with your finger or stylus, your eyes, and your voice at the same time.)

Read facts carefully: Read the facts closely, using bar reading techniques.

Read the interrogatory carefully: Pay close attention to what exactly is being asked as you read.

PT TIPS

Finish: Complete the task or tasks requested in the task memo. Let the grader know you finished.

Write professionally: Avoid slang and humor. Spell out abbreviations the first time you use them. Do not distract or confuse the grader.

Use Library: Use every main case cited in the library.

Use File: Be aware of who your client is and what your client needs or wants. Look for this information in both the task memo (instructions) and the file.

Know your audience: Use the appropriate tone for your audience. Know to whom you are writing and why. (Adopt a more formal approach when writing to those outside of your office, especially the court, and, if appropriate, a more casual tone when writing to another lawyer on your team.)

Outline before writing: Find a logical way to organize. (Remember, there is often more than one effective way to organize, so do not spend time worrying that you haven't found *the* roadmap. Create your own. But know that organization is critical.)

Expect irrelevant information: Remember that much of what is in the file is irrelevant or redundant. Do not feel obligated to find a way to use every fact in the file.

Drafting more than one document: If you are asked to draft more than one document and the instructions make clear how much each is worth, respect those percentages and apportion your time accordingly.

Use headings: Even in a task that does not normally include headings, such as a letter or closing argument to the jury, use headings and subheadings so that the grader can easily see (and has guideposts to) your organization.

Review the task memo: Read the task memo carefully and read it several times. (Review this after the file, after the library, and again while you are drafting your outline and maybe even your answer.) If ever you feel stalled, reread the task memo. It is the most important document in an PT.

Chapter hashtags: #PasstheBar, #EssaysArePuzzles, #IAm Ready, #TurnPanictoPower, #CalmConfidentinControl, #Top TenTips, #BarExamSuccess

CHAPTER 10

CELEBRATE YOUR ACHIEVEMENT AND ACKNOWLEDGE AND THANK THOSE WHO HELPED YOU (THEN SET YOUR NEXT GOAL!)

- You Did It. You Completed Your Bar Exam! (Now, You Wait, and Wait, for Results)
- Just Before the Results Are Published
- You Did It. You Passed the Bar Exam! Congratulations! (Now, Set Your Next Goal!)
- What if You Pass, but a Close Friend or Classmate Didn't?
- Finding a Job (if You Don't Already Have One)
- Some Interviewing Strategies
- Volunteering
- Transferable Skills
- Bar Exam Success Takeaways: What Have You Learned That Will Help You in the Future?
- Keep Learning and Keep All Doors Open

"Feeling gratitude and not expressing it is like wrapping a present and not giving it."

—WILLIAM ARTHUR WARD—

This sounds silly; after all, you don't *know* yet that you passed. But it is really important to validate your hard work and acknowledge the support of those who helped you! Plan ahead so that a trip or some special celebration awaits after you finish the exam. It will keep your family or significant other on board (and willing to wait for you). It helps them stay on your side. It gives everyone something to look forward to and helps you see that light in the distance.

YOU DID IT. YOU COMPLETED YOUR BAR EXAM! (NOW, YOU WAIT, AND WAIT, FOR RESULTS)

Enjoy your after-bar celebration. Having a big reward to look forward to will help you get through June and July (January and February). Have something fun planned to celebrate *having done your best.*

You can live with whatever results arrive when you know you gave it your all. *You owe it to yourself to leave the exam able to honestly say, "I did my best."*

Just Before the Results Come Out

If the months before the exam are hard, the days before results are released are crazy nerve racking (*huge* understatement). But wait you must. At the appointed time, you will log onto your state bar's website with ID number in hand, and with a click you will know.

If you passed, which I very much hope you did (!), then you may be looking for a new job or possibly working hard at one already. If you did not pass this time, you will need to pull every ounce of confidence together to learn from this experience and train for success on the next administration. (Go right to Part II of this book if you find out you did not pass.)

Be especially kind to yourself just before the results come out. It's horribly stressful. Go see a funny movie. Take an afternoon off for a hike or walk. Have a bubble bath and champagne. Distract yourself with positives. You are smart and worthy, regardless of this one test result. Surround yourself with good and positive people who will love and support you no matter what.

If you are a friend or family member of someone awaiting results, be even more kind. Dredge up every ounce of respect and compassion you can find. Back off and wait to see what that person wants from you. Give them space. Provide comfort and laughter for when that is called. Be a positive distraction.

Realize that even if your loved one is not expressing it, he or she is consumed with getting on that site and finding out, one way or another.

YOU DID IT. YOU PASSED THE BAR EXAM! CONGRATULATIONS! (NOW, SET YOUR NEXT GOAL!)

Your swearing-in ceremony will mark this achievement. And throw yourself a party or let someone else throw you one! This is a big accomplishment. Be very proud. Whatever you do with it, as long as you remain ethical, this is a lifetime stamp of credibility.

Guard this license.

If you did not pass, skip to Part II of this book.

What If You Pass, but a Close Friend or Classmate Didn't?

As you prepare to look up your own results and get ready to hear news from friends and classmates, prepare for the possibility that someone you care about didn't make it.

In so many ways, this bar exam news mirrors the way all of life's news comes. One day it's a call from someone offering you or a loved one a promotion, the position you always dreamed of, a vote of confidence, a moment in the sunshine, an opportunity for change. Maybe it's a call to say a new, healthy baby was born. Then, another day, it's a call from a close friend your age, who has just been diagnosed with cancer and is facing surgery, chemotherapy, radiation, and the challenges of trying to rebuild a semblance of normalcy when the very core has been shaken.

Is it hyperbole or offensive to equate bar results with news of a life-threatening illness? It isn't meant offensively, so if it's taken that way, I apologize. What it's meant to acknowledge is how important this news is. Unless you have taken the bar exam, it's hard to convey just how big it feels. You work and dream of law school for a long time, then you work for three or four of the hardest years ever, then you study intensively, giving everything you have for another several months before taking a grueling, multi-day exam. After that, you wait even longer for results.

Many who are unfamiliar with law and law school think the bar exam is just another test. It is not. While it should not be, people will make it a referendum on your personal success. It's bigger than any test you have ever taken and likely ever will. Be as supportive as you can. Remember, many successful lawyers have failed the bar once, if not more than once. Stick around for your friends.

Finding a Job (if You Don't Already Have One)

Go to your law school career center. As an alumnus, you should have access to great resources through the career center at your own law school and possibly at other nearby law schools.

Tell people including former professors that you are looking for a job and ask them to keep their ears open.

FIND A CAREER MENTOR

A career mentor is someone who can help you strategize about finding job opportunities and whether to take a job opportunity that comes along.

WHAT HAVE YOU LEARNED THAT WILL HELP YOU IN THE FUTURE?

You have passed the bar exam. You have proved to yourself and the world that you can pull a ton of disparate material together *in your head* and write about it logically, reason, and think. This is important. You have shown yourself able to withstand significant pressure.

A former student—a recent law school graduate for whom law was a second career—once asked me to write a letter of recommendation. He sent the following documents: his résumé, the cover letter he had written to the person I was to write to, the job description, and some information he wrote directly to me about why he wanted the job and why he thought his background would help him thrive on the job. He joked that he was now giving *me* an assignment that looked a lot like a bar exam performance test! The more I thought about it, the more accurate he was.

What did we say is the most important piece of the PT? The task memo. The first thing I did was read the student's request several times, and then follow up confirming when he needed the letter and how (by mail or e-mail). I then had to figure out the appropriate tone for this audience. To whom was I writing? Who am I? Who do I represent? I had to sort through a bunch of documents that contained much information that was irrelevant to this job. His résumé alone was nearly five pages! I had to decide on my format. (I rewrote the letter numerous times after printing it to ensure that the format was clear and pleasing to the eye.) *I am a law professor, but my letter will be less credible if it is not formatted in an easy-to-read manner*, I reasoned. I had also decided that less was more. His own documentation gave all the facts and his qualifications; my piece was to give one unique angle: how I had come to know this student in class and why the skills he possessed would be an asset to this employer.

I thought further about the analogy of this letter to a performance test. There were also implicit ethical obligations and professionalism concerns. It was not in my contract with my employer to write letters of recommendation for students. I was not required to do it. But it is something I consider part of being a professional educator. (Recall that you might get points in a PT for identifying not only ethical obligations but good practice, such as returning calls promptly.) As a professional and a lawyer, I must make sure that what I write is accurate (I cannot lie), but to be effective, it must also be persuasively phrased to show that my former student is a fine candidate (or the best candidate, if that is my belief). If, for some reason, I felt I could not endorse the person for the position, I would politely decline the request as quickly as possible so that person could seek a letter from someone else.

My student was right. This "simple" task of writing a letter of recommendation was a lot like a performance test! Do not think for one minute that developing the skills you are working so hard to master to pass the bar exam is in any way, shape, or form a waste of your time. You will use these skills. They are important. And succeeding on the exam will make you stronger, more articulate, more efficient, and more powerful!

It is a gift—a treasured opportunity—to be able to challenge ourselves, to commit to success, and to work to achieve it.

Keep Learning and Keep All Doors Open

Read what is happening in the world and in the legal community at large. Don't get pigeonholed in one specialty.

Expanding your knowledge and awareness will bring new clients and may help you serve your existing clients more effectively. Additionally, you will be better prepared if you need, want, or are given an opportunity to change jobs.

Stay connected. Network. Stay in touch with people. Talk regularly with career mentors about planning your next steps.

Keep asking yourself what *you* want; try, to whatever extent possible, to be the master of your own professional destiny. Take what comes along when that makes the most sense, but do not shy away from opportunities to try something new. Trust yourself. You have climbed Mount Everest. You have achieved. You have the success strategies. You are a success story. Keep on writing your future, with confidence.

Chapter hashtags: #CelebrateSuccess, #WaitingisTheHardest Part, #AfterBarTrip, #NetworkSmart, #CareerMentor, #TransferableSkills, #PassedTheBar, #BarExamSuccess

PART II

REPEATING THE BAR EXAM: THIS WILL BE THE LAST TIME

INTRODUCTION TO PART II

This part is called "Repeating the Bar Exam," *not* "Failing the Bar Exam." Be careful with the words *failed, fail,* and *failure.* You may not *yet* have passed. But if you are committed to achieving the goal of passing and have not given up, *you have not "failed."* Giving up *would* be failure. This is just a temporary setback.

> **Note: All readers are urged to read the entire book.**
>
> The strategies and tools in the first part will help you achieve success on your next bar exam. First-timers: Force yourself to think in concrete terms about what failing the bar exam really entails. You will be more motivated to take the first time as seriously as possible and do everything in your power to pass.

I have helped thousands of repeating students. It is not an easy place to be, but it is common. You are not alone, and you are not stupid. Here are three steps or tools that can help you refocus:

1. **Accept, but do not absorb, the shock.** Do not let this be a referendum on what you believe about yourself or your ability to pass next time. Take the break you need to be angry, frustrated, scared, or whatever you feel. Then, as the expression goes, get back on the horse and ride on to success on the next exam.

2. **Analyze your scores.** (And, if you are able to get your exam answers back, analyze those.) Using all data available to you (including your own introspection, how you did on each part of the actual exam, for example, and how you did on practice exams), determine why you did not pass and what to correct for success next time. If you need help doing this analysis, ask an academic support faculty member at your law school or hire a reliable bar review expert to help you make that assessment.

3. **Get on an effective study plan.** Figure out which parts of your study schedule worked last time and which did not. Be honest. There is no point in doing otherwise.
4. **Work on the mental game.** Get back to (or get for the first time to) truly believing you will pass.

"Only those who dare to fail greatly, can ever achieve greatly."

—ROBERT F. KENNEDY—

Some Analysis of Past Performance Includes Asking these Questions:

- Did you put in so many hours that you were no longer effectively studying but daydreaming, falling asleep, or tuning out as you read? Were you otherwise distracted?
- Were there areas of law you didn't get and hoped would not be on the exam?
- Did you skip the practice writing, or skimp on it? (Did you outline but not write exams in full under timed conditions)?
- Did you complete all types of practice questions? Did you analyze the model and explanatory answers? If you did not study answers, you did not maximize the opportunity to perfect your skills from practice; you went through the motions but didn't realize the benefits.

Read through the remaining chapters in this part of the book, then go back and re-read Part I. Then, get to work. You've got this!

Chapter 11

Why Didn't I Pass the Bar Exam?

- Diagnosis and Treatment Plans
- What Did You Do That You Should Not Have, Last Exam?
- What Didn't You Do That You Now Realize You Should Have Done?
- Were You Healthy and Strong Enough to Focus for the Entire Exam?
- Did You Have a Mentor?
- Was Your Computer Working Properly?
- Use Your Scores to Help Determine Why You Did Not Pass

"There are no secrets to success. It is the result of preparation, hard work, and learning from failure."

—COLIN POWELL—

Diagnosis and Treatment Plans

Ask yourself if any of these fit your situation.

Ten Reasons People Fail the Bar

1. You were not worried enough.

You got by in law school—maybe not top of your class but you passed everything and graduated. You thought you would knock it out on the bar exam. You thought, *it can't be that tough.* But it was.

Solution:

If the bar exam was harder than you expected, you need to train more rigorously this time. This exam is a different ballgame from law school, physically and mentally. Bar exams last for days and are exhausting. In law school, each final exam covered one subject alone; the bar covers a host of subjects, all of which require you to memorize and quickly recall many rules. Bar applicants are more stressed-out than you may have anticipated; you may have been thrown by the psych-out factor. Get on a new study schedule now. Review all of Part I. If you can, take off time from work to study so you can give the months before your next bar your total concentration.

2. You were too worried.

You were filled with so much anxiety that you could not relax enough to learn the material. You couldn't absorb the rules because you were completely stressed.

Solution:

This time, plan to sleep more, take more breaks, and do more physical exercise. You cannot study effectively for twenty hours a day, and you don't need to in order to pass. Be diligent and disciplined, and give it a good seven-to-ten-hour day. (Remember: Any time estimate is just that. I cannot tell you how long it takes to learn something. Bottom line: Use every day as productively as possible. Slow and steady wins the race.)

3. You did not really learn the law.

You did not know enough law. You may even have memorized rules but didn't understand them and therefore did not know how to effectively apply them under the time pressure.

Solution:

Accept this and hit the books. You *will* learn the rules this time. If you don't understand the explanation of a certain concept in one source, try another. As a lawyer, if you did not understand the client's problem, would you wing it? No. You would find a way to learn what you need to know (or refer the case out if you must).

4. You learned law, but you did not train by doing hundreds of practice tests under timed conditions.

Solution:

Imagine an out-of-shape person wanting to be fit. He or she reads dozens of books on fitness, watches fitness videos, and reads fitness blogs, but does not exercise. That's what reading outlines without doing practice tests will get you: well-read but not ready to perform! Remember the Olympic metaphor: each testing format is a separate "event" in which you are competing. Train for each of them.

5. You were "The Dreamer."

You went beyond the scope of the fact patterns. You read into things. You assumed facts not in evidence.

Solution:

The graders want you to answer the questions asked and use the facts given. So, next time, read slowly and carefully. Stay away from "what ifs." Analyze the facts they give you. Use those facts and only those facts to prove your points. (Review Chapter 8 and master IRPC.)

6. You have weak reading comprehension skills.

You really don't understand what you are reading. Either you are nervous, trying to read too fast, or have not developed your reading skills thoroughly enough.

Solution:

The bar, like all standardized tests, is largely a test of reading comprehension. Reading is the success thread that runs through every form of testing. Your reading skills must be in top shape to pass. Work on reading and self-assessing. (Study Chapter 8.) Read aloud and touch each word as you read. Complete many practice tests and study the model answers so that you see where your reading is not careful or precise enough. (If you have time and want a good exercise, try reading and summarizing, in one to three sentences, all the articles in the opinion section of the newspaper or a news blog each day—this will develop your comprehension skills and keep you informed at the same time!)

Last, get help if your reading weakness is due to an English as a second language (ESL) issue.

7. You are a practicing attorney in another jurisdiction.

You are licensed to practice in another state. You may have been practicing for years. You took and passed at least one other bar exam but are having difficulties passing this one. First, acknowledge that you may be angry at having to take the exam in the first place. You are an attorney, after all. You are licensed. You have done your time. You shouldn't be asked to take another test. It's been a while since you were a student and you resent this imposition. (Note: This same challenge may be true if you are an accountant, physician, engineer, or any other professional who went to law school as a second or third career.) Next, you are knowledgeable in the real world. You might know too much. You think of too many practical issues.

Solution:

Try pretending you are back in school. Reread Chapter 8. (Try pretending you are back in math class, long before law school.) Be sure to spot the major issues and write a complete and logical analysis for every question. This is not shorthand to help you resolve a client's problem. This is longhand. Prove your skills for the grader. "Show the math." Also, lay off the jargon unless terms are used in the problem. Don't use flash to impress graders; it won't. Write in simple IRPC style (issue, rule, proof, conclusion)—in short, complete, plain English sentences.

8. Your answer was sloppy.

If the graders can't understand or read what you wrote, they won't. (See Chapter 8.) They will not assume you wrote the right things. They will not give you the benefit of the doubt. The burden is on you, not the grader.

Solution:

Use headings and subheadings, bold, underline, or otherwise make sure they stand out. (Make sure main headings and subheadings are consistent and clearly distinguishable.) Leave clear margins. Single space text but leave spaces between paragraphs and double spaces before and after headings and subheadings. Underline, bold, or italicize key terms sparingly.

Make your presentation easy to read! Be sure also to practice with exam software ahead of time.

9. You don't manage time well enough.

You didn't look at or couldn't see the clock during the exam. Either way, time ran away without you. You were caught with moments to go and unanswered or barely answered questions.

Solution:

Practice a lot, and under timed conditions, with a big, easy-to-read clock. (When you are in the exam room, find the clock and check it frequently.) Even one question left unanswered is enough to fail you.

10. You are not ready to or don't want to be a lawyer.

Maybe you went straight from college to law school and are still a little overwhelmed. Maybe you know too many lawyers who hate their jobs or maybe you are too focused on the difficulties in finding a law job.

Solution:

Quick fix: Put it all out of your mind. Pass the exam. Then decide what to do to earn a living. One step at a time. (See Chapter 2 for more thoughts on this challenge.)

> **Note: If none of those reasons fits your situation, maybe you were simply unlucky. Some people do just have a bad day or bad luck. If so, dust yourself off, and get back to work. Pass the next bar exam!**

WHAT DID YOU DO THAT YOU SHOULD NOT HAVE, LAST EXAM?

Your turn: If you are repeating the exam, why are you here and what steps will you take to ensure (not just *hope*) that this is your last exam? Did you get distracted with personal issues or social media? Did you worry too much? Did you hope it wouldn't matter that you didn't know the law in certain subjects as well as you should have?

Re-read Part I of this book, then complete the following self-assessment.

Reflection: A Look Back in Time

Take a moment now and jot down some things you did on your previous bar(s) that you now see hurt you.

What Didn't You Do That You Now Realize You Should Have Done?

Did you skip parts of bar review that would have given you the extra guidance or motivation on essay writing that you knew you needed? Did you skip or not do practice tests under timed conditions? Did you do practice tests but skip the crucial step of analyzing the sample answers?

Note several things you should have done last time, did not do, and are committed to doing next time:

Were You Healthy and Strong Enough to Focus for the Entire Exam?

Do you need to exercise regularly this time, and take better care of yourself?

Do you need to see a doctor about anything?

Would it help to talk confidentially to someone at your local LAP (lawyers assistance program)?

Did You Have a Mentor?

Did you have support from the people you love or with whom you live? Were there any detractors? Did you deal with any naysayers as well as you could have? (See Chapter 6.) Did you get "buy-in" from whomever affects your day-to-day life? Were you working and did your employer know you were taking the exam and support you in that effort? Did you have a credible, helpful mentor with whom you regularly talked or e-mailed?

Jot down any thoughts about lack of support you may have felt last time, and what you can do this time to bolster your support system.

Was Your Computer Working Properly?

Did you have any technical problems? Did you fear having such difficulties?

Was your laptop in good working order? Did you practice with the software you had to use during the exam?

Use Your Scores to Help Determine
Why You Did Not Pass

Were you weak on the law? All subjects or certain subjects? What must you do to learn what you need to between now and the next exam? Were you weak on particular types of questions? Was it your writing? Your analysis? Do you need to repeat your entire bar review or take a supplemental course? These are among the many questions you need to ask yourself, so you can move forward and create a bar exam success plan tailored for you to pass the next exam. Note: In some places, you just get back scores when you fail the exam, while other jurisdictions will allow you to review your actual exam. If you have an opportunity to look at your exam, take it. And if you do not see clearly what is wrong and how to improve, get help from a reliable expert reviewing your answers.

After reviewing your scores or answers (if you have access to them) on the last bar exam, what are your preliminary conclusions?

____

____

____

____

____

____

Now, if you have not yet read all of Part I of this book, go read each chapter. Then, look back at your answers to the questions in this chapter and see if you can add to your diagnosis of how to improve and make your next bar exam your last bar exam.

Chapter hashtags: #HowtoImprove, #NextTimeisTheLastTime, #Improvement, #ICanPass, #IWillPass, #BarExamSuccess

CHAPTER 12

I FEEL LIKE I WAS KICKED IN THE TEETH

- Get up and Dust Yourself Off
- Avoid Psyching Yourself Out
- Accept Where You Are and Refocus for Success *on the Next Bar Exam*
- Accept Responsibility; Do Not Try to Shift the Blame
- Put It in Perspective
- Dealing with Others Who Learn You Did Not Pass, Especially During the Holidays

---

"To bear failure with courage is the best proof of character that anyone can give . . . You will find that people forget the failures of others very quickly . . ."

—W. SOMERSET MAUGHAM—

One of the biggest barriers repeat takers face is moving past the hit to your confidence. Even for people who accurately diagnose what needs to be fixed, it may be rough to shake off bad feelings. Remember, *you* are not a failure. You never have been. You never will be. This is not a referendum on who you are or of what you are capable. It is information, like news; not good news, but news that you can learn from.

Learn from your past; don't let it define you. If you weren't frustrated, you would not be normal. How can someone invest so much and not be frustrated? You put in years of study—your time, your money, your sweat, and your pride. But you are not alone, and you can turn it around.

You did not pass this past bar exam, but you did not fail as a person. Once you get over the disappointment, you can turn this into a challenge and go into problem-solving mode. You can figure out how to pass next time.

If you think success means never failing, think again. Learn from this so-called "failure" and make it your step to success on the next bar exam. (And the powerful mindset of seeing setbacks as information to succeed forward may well be what sustains you when you lose a case, or get passed over for a promotion, or experience any number of disappointments that you will inevitably encounter right alongside your future successes.)

GET UP AND DUST YOURSELF OFF

What do you do when you trip and fall? Do you lie on the ground, give up, and say, *"I will never walk again"*? Do you lose confidence in your ability to walk? Of course not. Usually, you get up, brush yourself off, and are on your way. Even after a bad fall, even should you be hurt seriously and need medical care, what follows is healing. Except in unusual circumstances, as long as the will to succeed is there, anyone you talk to who tripped up on the last bar is a person who can move forward and pass the next exam.

You do not even get the opportunity to *take* the bar exam without a huge investment and many steps of proving yourself worthy. If you were a person who at the first stumble simply left the path and looked for a smoother trail, you would not have finished law school, let alone applied for and sat for an entire bar examination. The fact that you got far enough to even take the bar exam is itself evidence of your potential. Your job is to get up, get going, and realize that potential.

If you were the sort of person who gave up easily, it is doubtful that you'd have chosen law school. Learn from past experiences. Turn this into a strength!

Avoid Psyching Yourself Out

To pass the bar exam, *think* about passing. Believe you can pass, that you deserve to pass, and that you will pass. Don't let in the idea that you could fail again. I recently participated in a defensive driving class, led by professional race car drivers, and found an analogy to bar passage. The drivers reminded students that to drive safely and avoid crashes, you must keep your eyes focused on the road where you want to end up. Even if you swerve or your car loses control, keep looking where you want to go. Do not look at what you fear you may crash into. They led the students through one exercise, a slalom course with cones scattered on the pavement. We were supposed to drive fast, weaving in and out to avoid as many cones as possible without losing control of the vehicle. Their advice on how to do this was to focus on the open road in the distance, beyond the cones. We would see what we needed to avoid hitting the cones with peripheral vision. Stay focused on where we wanted to end up, they said, and we would get there. (If we looked at the cones, they warned, we would likely hit them.)

Don't look at the obstacles in your way. Look at the open road of the future ahead. It is common for people who failed a bar exam to believe they will fail again. Turn that belief around. Focus on success.

THINK FALL AND YOU WILL FALL; THINK FAIL AND YOU WILL FAIL

I went skiing for the first time in several years and was out for about an hour having fun and did not fall. Suddenly, I began thinking, *I haven't fallen yet. I wonder how many times I will fall today. Wouldn't it be great if I didn't fall at all. I hope I don't fall. What if I got hurt?* You can guess the rest. I soon thereafter went sprawling! When I hadn't been thinking about it, I was fine; but as soon as the thought of falling entered my mind, I fell.

Accept Where You Are and Refocus for Success *on the Next Bar Exam*

The first question many people ask is, should I take this very next bar or wait out an administration? Most often the answer is to take it again as soon as possible. If your scores were close and you can devote serious time to studying for the next exam, the answer is definitely yes. Momentum will help. Your memory will be fresher in relearning and reviewing the material now than it will be six to eight months from now if you delay until the next exam. If your scores were very far from passing, indicating a serious deficiency in all or a number of areas of law, or if you know that this upcoming bar you are otherwise occupied with commitments that cannot be postponed, then you may be better off delaying and putting yourself on an extended study plan. This decision—whether to retake the very next exam—is one you must make quickly, though, to avoid missing filing deadlines or paying late fees.

Take a few days to absorb the shock and to mourn, and then consider the advantages you now have, repeating the exam:

- The more you put in last time, the easier it will be for you to learn what you need and pass this next time. You may think you forgot everything you knew six months ago but you didn't. Depending on how far and where you fell short, you may be close, and with daily practice exams, you may get there fairly easily. (Many people fail but just a few points.) Or you may have to really work hard in one area, even though you are pretty strong in the others. The key is to learn where you are and where you need to be. Don't allow the frustration to take over. The bar exam is doable. Again, it may not even be as much work as it was the first time around. Do not decide that the bar exam is insurmountable. It is easier than law school. You can do this.
- You have data from which to create a smart, strategic plan to improve. Use that information!

Were you weak in a particular subject? If you were only weak in one or a small number of areas, you may not need to take another full bar review. You might just need to get some supplemental materials in that one area and get on a "maintenance" plan for the rest of the exam.

Were you weak in certain skills? Perhaps multiple-choice questions your Achilles heal? This indicates a need for deep knowledge of testable subjects and extensive training (with thousands of practice MCQs).

Or, maybe MCQs were easier for you but your scores on written portions were low. This may mean you know and understand the law, but do not articulate it well enough or have not trained sufficiently in using facts to prove or disprove rules of law, and your analysis is insufficient. You may benefit from a supplemental writing course while you continue to work on daily multiple-choice practice on your own.

Did you have a low score on a PT? Many people do not practice these (or do not practice sufficiently) because they mistakenly think PTs are the "easy part of the bar." Get reliable help to learn to write passing PT answers, including reading *Performance Test Success* and the many practice PTs that accompany this West Academic book.

Now remember, your review for February (July) must still cover every testable subject and training in every testing format. Avoid thoughts such as, *I only failed by a couple of questions, so I'll just focus on those, and I'll do fine.* No! You are taking the whole exam again, so your focus must include a comprehensive study approach that covers everything that is tested on your bar exam. You may and should give more attention to certain subjects than others, but you are studying everything carefully. You may need to train even more in certain testing formats, but be sure you are strong in every format that will appear on your exam.

Also consider exam day logistics: Did you get tired? When? In the afternoon? Both afternoons? Was day one more difficult or less difficult than day two?

You will likely not be as nervous as the first-time takers around you. You know what to expect. You have what I call the "*been there, done that* edge!"

Stay calm and focused this time. With your *slow-and-steady-wins-the-race* attitude, you will do it.

Accept Responsibility; Do Not Try to Shift the Blame

Get rid of any thoughts resembling this: "*Those stupid graders just must not have seen what I wrote. I know it was all there. I'm not even going to look at my old tests.*" Replace such thoughts with this: **I will look critically at what I did and what I did not do last time, and I will take the steps necessary to pass this time.**

Too many people spend precious time and energy blaming others for their failures. (*My professors in law school didn't cover that. My bar review didn't give me enough helpful critique on my writing. My ASP professor didn't warn us how hard it would be.*) All these thoughts are huge wastes of time. Don't engage with them.

You need to and have a right to get out the anger, sure. You need to move past the disappointment, of course. But take responsibility. This was your exam. The next one will be your exam as well. Decide what you will do differently. You make the changes.

SPENDING MORE MONEY

One of the toughest parts about retaking the exam is deciding what review courses to take and having to spend more money. Do not react impulsively. Do not just throw money at the problem without carefully thinking through where and what kind of help you really need. But, then, after you see what you need, do not skimp. If you need another course, take one. People will prey on your fears. Don't "jump" at everyone who promises that they can help you. But do take care of yourself.

Ask the ASP faculty in your law school or a trusted mentor or professor for advice.

Put It in Perspective

There are plenty of wise sayings. The adage "That which doesn't kill us makes us stronger" comes to mind. Or Babe Ruth's wonderfully inspiring "Every strike brings me closer to the next home run."

Wise sayings do not take away the pain, but they really can help if you let them. Seeing your name on the pass list was the home run you sought. But if last time was a strike, the key to future success will be to get closer to the home run. Reframe this from a "failure" to a "temporary setback." Turn things around. As soon as you can pull yourself out of the anger, frustration, and sadness, focus on success this coming February.

Dealing with Others Who Learn You Did Not Pass, Especially During the Holidays

The timing of bar results is such that those who do not pass the July bar will most often prepare to retake the exam the following February, which means they will be studying during the holiday season. The holidays (Thanksgiving through the New Year) are often a difficult time, even without bar results in the mix. It may be very hard this year to eat, drink, and be merry with family and friends. For those of you who are now formulating your game plan to turn things around in February, gala festivities can sometimes be devastating, either because of your own beating yourself up or because others make offensive or insensitive comments.

Try not to let bar results ruin your holidays. You are in control. Use these top ten suggestions to help you cope:

1. **Expect that these holidays will be particularly hard.** Knowing that this may be a stressful time will make it easier than if you are blindsided by the negativity you feel when confronted with cheer at a time you are not feeling cheery.
2. **Limit your time at holiday gatherings.** You should have a study schedule anyway, and you should have already canceled or be actively working on canceling or limiting as many things as you can to clear your path for studies in the next months. Accept those few invitations that will make you feel good (or better); turn down all the others. For events that you do attend, plan to go for an hour or two only. Leave on a high note—and get back to studying or go to sleep so that you can get an early start on studying the next morning.
3. **Unless cooking and entertaining inspire you, excuse yourself from hosting any holiday gatherings this year.** If it is a must that you host, make things as easy as possible. Take every shortcut you can. Buy prepared foods, let others bring dishes, and be sure you have help with setup and cleanup. (Excuse yourself while others clean up so that you can study, or sleep!)
4. **Surround yourself with positive people.** Avoid negative comments and negative vibes. This is a must! If there is anyone, anywhere or in any part of

your life, who is communicating to you directly or indirectly a lack of faith in your ability to pass the bar exam, get away from that person, minimize contact with that person, or put him or her off until March. It is a must to believe in yourself, to believe that you can and will pass the bar exam, and to surround yourself with like-minded people who will lift you higher. Avoid those who drag you down.

5. **If someone starts up a conversation, probing you on your results, end it quickly.** Ready yourself with responses to change the subject, and if necessary, politely excuse yourself. A direct response that can cut off probing may be something like, *Yes, I missed this past July. My focus is on the future now, so that's all there is to say about last time. Thank you for your concern.* Then launch right into a question about that person, to be certain the subject is changed.

COOKING THERAPY

Some people do find meal preparation cathartic. If this is you, cook away this holiday season. The methodical, repetitive action of chopping vegetables can be particularly soothing, and you can let out aggression without hurting anyone. If you peel or chop onions, you may end up crying. Once those tears begin, don't be surprised if you have a bar exam meltdown. (That may be great. No one looks "wimpy" because of onion tears! So let loose. If crying helps, jump up and volunteer to be the chief onion chopper.)

6. **You do not need to discuss the past.** If you want to—if it helps you to talk about it—go ahead. But if you do not want to talk about it, don't. That is your choice. You can always change the subject, or politely excuse yourself and walk away.

7. **You do not owe anyone any explanations.**

8. **Do not drink and drive.** Of course, that is advice for any occasion, but there are a couple of problems at holidays just after you learn bar results. First, well-meaning people might try to give you alcohol

to make you feel better, and second, you may drink more than usual to drown your own sorrows or escape. Be safe, and be careful.

9. **Exercise.** If nothing else, take walks. Schedule them. Don't skip them. Walk off the stress of it all.
10. **Sleep.** Do not neglect your sleep. Things tend to look gloomier when you are tired. To keep your spirits up and your study skills sharp, get lots of rest.

Armed with awareness and some solid strategies to avoid those parts of the holidays that might otherwise have gotten you down, you can move effectively through November and December, already on a powerfully positive study plan. You will begin the new year with the groundwork in place for the intensive, quality work you will do in January and February, in a diligent and disciplined manner, to pass the February bar exam.

Chapter hashtags: #RealizeYourPotential, #IDeservetoPass, #IwillPass, #FocusOnSuccess, #BeenThereDoneThatEdge, #TurnItAround, #I'veGotThis, #BarExamSuccess

CHAPTER 13

RETHINK "FAILURE" AND USE YOUR PREVIOUS EXPERIENCE AS PREPARATION FOR SUCCESS

- You Have the "Been There, Done That" Edge. Use It!
- Complete Your New Strategic Plan
- Change Your Approach

YOU HAVE THE "BEEN THERE, DONE THAT" EDGE. USE IT!

Whatever you did or did not do preparing for or on the last bar exam, now is the time to face up and make the necessary changes. Figure out what you need to do for success next time.

You can understand the major rules and theories. You got through law school, right? There may be weaker subjects but there is nothing tested on the bar exam that you are incapable of understanding.

- Maybe you need a different approach or a different professor or study guide to explain certain concepts. Perhaps you should try a new bar review this time.
- Maybe you were tired when bar review classes were held, or you were distracted by others in the classroom if you took a live class.
- Maybe you need substantive lectures (and even writing workshops) that are recorded or online, so you can listen again and review points you did not clearly understand the first time.
- Maybe you need to do some serious practice writing and submit your exam answers for real critique—not just a number grade at the top of the page, but

actual comments that tell you where and how to improve.

- Maybe you need your own tutor or bar coach—someone who will not just help you in a room of hundreds of other applicants but can guide you to the success you know is within your reach.

Whatever you decide, believe you *can* do it this next time. Reach out—make the effective changes that will take you to success next time. From pass rates alone, you know that many applicants did not pass. Probably some of your classmates and friends did not pass. Again, and always, keep at the forefront the knowledge that this is not a reflection on your ability to pass the next bar exam.

Complete Your New Strategic Plan

Read Part I of this book and create a smart, new strategic plan. Consider targeted improvement. You may not need a full-service bar review again. Or you may want a different full-service bar review course. (Do you get a free repeat course? If you do and you know that you just didn't do the work, that may be the way to go. On the other hand, changing courses may help. Talk with alumni who passed after more than one exam and see what they did differently and talk with your ASP faculty.)

Change Your Approach

The approach you will take to study for a second bar exam must differ from the first.

- If you did all the "right" things but not enough of them, do more this time.
- If you studied passively (reading outlines and listening to lectures) but didn't do many practice writing exercises under timed conditions, change that. Get cracking!
- If your focus was heavier in subject areas you were comfortable with, study the weak ones more thoroughly this time.

In addition to study changes, what other changes will you make? Consider a few life changes that might really help:

- Get more sleep.
- Minimize time spent on your phone and social media.
- Keep a more regular, disciplined study schedule that starts earlier in the day.
- Approach this exam differently; take it seriously enough to give it your all, but not so seriously that you freak yourself out with stress.
- Avoid all people other than those who believe you can pass and with whom you feel strong, smart, and capable.

Take a moment and write what you know needs to be in your strategic plan to pass this February (July).

____

____

____

Now go back and create your new bar exam success plan. Start fresh, adding in the points you made just above. Reread earlier chapters and replace the words *first time* with *this next bar exam*. Commit to success on the next bar exam. You can do it.

Chapter hashtags: #BeenThereDoneThatEdge, #I'veGotThis, #CommitToSuccess, #NewApproaches, #BarExamSuccess

CHAPTER 14

THE MENTAL GAME OF BAR SUCCESS

A thread that runs through this entire book involves the "mental game" of bar success. I want to take a moment here to reiterate and pull those thoughts together. Think of this as a motivational review.

There is no doubt that for bar success you need:

1) the skills (reading, writing, logical thinking),

2) the knowledge (fluency in every testable topic and substantive mastery in more heavily tested subjects, and starred subjects on NextGen bar), and

3) the training (with regular and extensive practice tests and study of sample answers in all testing formats).

On top of skills, knowledge, and training, you also need your "success mindset"—what in this chapter I am calling the "mental game."

There are many elements to the mental game, all of which we will discuss below, including these action items:

- Believe that you can and will pass
- See study as an opportunity rather than a chore (or worse still, hazing)
- Feed your success mindset
- Turn frustration into fascination
- Visualize success: see yourself passing
- Remain in the present moment

BELIEVE THAT YOU CAN PASS

A key component of your success mindset is to maintain an unwavering belief that you can pass. This belief must stand firm, from the time you begin preparation (really, day 1 of law school) until the last "time" is called on your exam. Don't ever doubt this. Deep down, own your future success fully and completely. This is the most fundamental component of the mental game. If you don't really believe you can pass, you are directing energy toward falling, and failing. You want your energy entirely focused passing.

A possible mantra: *I will pass.*

SEE STUDY AS AN OPPORTUNITY

A second critical component of your success mindset is to embrace this preparation process as an opportunity. "You *get to* study." You don't *have to* study. Remember that, especially when you feel discouraged. Studying, learning, becoming intellectually powerful is a gift. Don't begrudge time spent on bar prep. Lean in.

A possible mantra: *I get to study.* Or, *learning is a gift.*

People around you will be at the beach, shopping, making TikToks, going to parties—doing everything that looks fun. If you keep looking over your shoulder at what everyone else is doing while you are studying for the bar, it looks like you are suffering. But you are only suffering if you see yourself as suffering. If you see the work you are doing as a powerful investment in yourself, as high-intensity training in lawyering skills, you will feel very different about the process.

NOURISH THE SUCCESS MINDSET

Another component is the physical aspect of the mental game: Exercise, eating healthfully, and sleeping sufficiently. Movement, nourishment, and rest will help you feel good and strong; they support your success mindset. It is much easier to stay in the positive when you are feeling well. When doubt and difficulties creep in, one can easily fall prey to an overall loss of motivation. These become an attack on your success mindset. But, you are strong enough to fight back. Feed your brain healthy foods; let your body be as strong as it can be to house that mightily working analytical machine between your ears.

TURN FRUSTRATION INTO FASCINATION

A next component is accepting frustration as normal and turning it into fascination or curiosity. It's OK to be frustrated, especially when you get practice questions wrong or don't understand heavily tested rules of law. Take a breath and figure out whatever it is you aren't getting—be that a confusing rule or a tricky multiple-choice question that you don't quite see why the correct answer is the best answer.

Taking a breath is key. Slow down for a moment. When you don't see an answer instantly, it can be easy to lean into the frustration. But you can just as easily take yourself out of frustration. Frustration is in your mind. It's you bullying yourself with voices that say things like, "Why can't I figure that out? How come I don't know what this question is asking? Why don't I see the right answer?" All that is pressure—needless pressure. Take the pressure off.

When you read a question and are not sure of the answer, breathe. Re-read calmly. Try letting yourself into the facts—get really interested in what is happening and why: who is doing what (or failing to do what), who is injured or damaged or what interests are threatened if any? What is the question asking me to resolve?

Sometimes that's all that is needed, to flip the frustration into fascination, and you can see a path forward. (Remember, in written responses, you don't always have to have a definitive answer, just the issues and how to logically apply the law and analyze from the perspective of each side.)

VISUALIZE SUCCESS: SEE YOURSELF PASSING

Another key element of your success mindset is the power you derive from visualization. Visualize yourself passing. Your body doesn't know if you are actually in the testing room or in a simulation; your body is preparing either way—preparing to succeed.

Sit with a picture of the kinds of questions you will have practiced with all summer coming to you, and you reading and tackling them, one at a time. See yourself reading calmly, breathing. Even as you see questions that at first seem confusing, you picture yourself staying calm and thinking, re-reading when you need to, and plugging in knowledge that you have wired into your brain with months (and years) of study.

Imagine your fingers flying across the keyboard. Tap into that feeling of exhilaration when you know what you want to say and it soars out of your head into your hands—putting what is in your mind into full expression for full credit, racking up (exam) points as you make important (legal) points.

REMAIN IN THE PRESENT MOMENT

Be in the moment, in flow, in the zone—when you study and on the exam. Let yourself be fully immersed in the law when studying and in the law and facts when in questions or hypotheticals. Let your mind and body use the skills and knowledge you have been training to reason to logical conclusions.

When you are in the moment, you are not worrying about how much you studied yesterday or what you will study tomorrow. You are not thinking about whether you will pass, or who is counting on you to pass. You are simply and fully in this study flow. You are taking in learning the way a thirsty person drinks water. You are drinking in knowledge.

After you take the exam, you can take action on your career and other life matters that require attention. But during bar prep, give yourself the gift of being in the present moment, fully and completely. Our day-to-day lives are scattered with so many simultaneous demands that full focus on any one thing is often impossible. We're bombarded and pulled in dozens of different directions. But bar prep and exam days are times you can (and really must) be fully in the moment. Nothing else can matter. And, it can feel incredibly liberating to just do one thing.

YOU'VE GOT THIS!

There are many strategies throughout this book on the mental game of bar success. Go back and highlight anything you want to remember during bar prep and on the exam.

Think of yourself during bar prep as training for your Superbowl—or your Mt. Everest climb, your Broadway debut, your Supreme Court argument, your Top Chef final round, or whatever high stakes challenge resonates with you.

Reflection: What Is Your "Challenge" Metaphor?

I see the bar exam as my: ______________________________

____

____

What do you want to do during the big game? Be in flow—working at your best, remaining curious, alert, positive, and in the moment. You don't want to be worrying about the day before or the day after. You want to be all in.

Reflection: How I Act Affects How I Feel

What are my action items checklist during bar prep?

____

____

____

What are my action items checklist during the actual exam?

____

____

____

And, what do you want to feel? Adrenaline, strength, excitement. You know you'll also feel some (maybe a lot of) nervousness—so you welcome those nerves. Nerves will keep you awake and alert. And, as I always say, you will turn any "**p**anic into **p**ower not **p**aralysis."

Reflection: How I Feel Affects My Performance

When I am taking the exam, I want to feel:

____

____

____

When I am taking the exam, if I feel ______________________________ (nerves, for example), I will replace that feeling with:

____

____

Your Law License Is a Power Tool

Above all, remember, what you are doing by investing so much to become a lawyer is important—it's vital. It's worth everything that you are putting in. And studies show that taking action on behalf of others and doing things that are meaningful are the keys to not only a successful life but a happy and fulfilled life. So thank you!

Thank you for all your hard work and for your commitment to the profession, to your future clients, and to our world.

Conclusion

Hopefully, you now see the bar exam as something challenging but doable. Bar exam success will be yours when you are ready to do the work to realize your potential and achieve your goals.

When you pass and are equipped with a law license, a powerful and permanent stamp of credibility (so long as you guard it well), you *will* be able to work as an attorney. Or you may find your dream job outside of the law altogether, but in a setting where your legal education brings invaluable skills and credibility. Your J.D. degree and law license provide proof of your capability to read and think critically and perform under intense pressure.

Seeing your name on the pass list brings an incomparable high. In some ways it shows that you can accomplish whatever you set out to do. Making it across this "finish line," with credentials and license in hand, you will have lifelong opportunities and can take your place as a lawyer and leader.

Think of the exam as a very heavy door. It takes all the strength you can muster to open it. But once opened, you never have to open it again; you can simply keep climbing the steps on your pathway to ever-greater success, to those extraordinary places that lie on the other side of challenge.

Remember the strategies for success from this book whenever you embark on a new challenge. You will have many new challenges and opportunities ahead! Carry the positive mindset message of this book with you. The strategies you learned by reading the text and working through the reflection exercises will help you as you move forward; they will be with you, guiding you, on each step of your future path. And you will travel that path knowing that you are extraordinarily capable. You have what it takes. You *are* a success!

RESOURCES AND ATTRIBUTIONS

The notes below include resources referenced throughout the text; additional references are on file with the author.

Growth mindset. Recent empirical research establishes an important correlation between bar passage and mindset (and related concepts including belonging, fear of failure, confidence, financial concerns, and self-care) and confirms much of what was previously written in both editions of this book. See works of Professor Victor D. Quintanilla, Dr. Mary C. Murphy, Dr. Gregory M. Walton, and Dr. Sam T. Erman. *See also* C.S. Dweck, *Mindset: The New Psychology of Success* (Random House 2006) and extensive body of growth mindset and grit research.

Institute for the Advancement of the American Legal System (IAALS), *Foundations for Practice: The Whole Lawyer and the Character Quotient* (2016), https://iaals.du.edu/sites/default/files/reports/foundations_for_practice_whole_lawyer_character_quotient.pdf; *see also* K. Holmquist and M. Shultz, et al, *Measuring Merit: The Shultz-Zedeck Research on Law School Admissions*, 63 J. Legal Educ. 565 (2014).

Raising the Bar, dedicated to the exchange of evidence-based ideas about the bar exam, founded by the author and available at https://www.accesslex.org/raising-the-bar.

J. Howarth and J. Wegner, *Ringing Changes: Systems Thinking About Legal Licensing*, 13 FIU L. Rev. 383 (2019).

Michelle Obama, in her 2018 book *Becoming* (Random House), frankly discusses imposter syndrome and bar exam challenges.

Scott Turow, *One L: The Turbulent True Story of a First Year at Harvard Law School* (Penguin Group 2010) (1977).

Alexia Brunet Marks & Scott A. Moss, *What Predicts Law Student Success? A Longitudinal Study Correlating Law Student Applicant Data and Law School Outcomes*, 13 J.

Empirical Legal Stud. 205 (2016). A number of recent studies on file with the author confirm this.

W. Somerset Maugham, *The Mixture as Before, in* The Treasure (W. Heinemann Ltd. 1940).

G.R. Blair, *Goal Setting for Results: Success Strategies for You and Your Organization* (The Walk the Talk Company 2003).

A. Hamilton, J. Madison, and J. Jay, *The Federalist Papers* (originally published by J. and A. McLean in 1788 and reprinted recently by ABA Publishing in the ABA Classics series).

Yoda, fictional character in *The Empire Strikes Back* (1980), film created by George Lucas.

"A rising tide lifts all boats" is associated with economic growth and popularized in a 1963 speech by John F. Kennedy.

S. Berman, *Say It in Your Own Words: Translate and Reverse Engineer Legal Jargon to Read More Effectively,* The Learning Curve, Summer/Autumn 2017.

There is extensive stereotype threat literature. Among the first was by Steele and Aronson in the *Journal of Personality and Social Psychology* (1995).

The term *preventive law* was popularized by the late Louis M. Brown, Esq.

Financial literacy resources for law students include MAX by AccessLex, free and online at https://www.accesslex.org/maxonline.

J. Grisé, Critical Reading for Success in Law School and Beyond (West Academic Publishing, 2d ed. 2022).

ABA Mental Health Toolkit and other resources for law students https://www.americanbar.org/groups/lawyer_assistance/articles_and_info/law_student_resources/.

D. K. Rush, H. Matsuo, *Does Law School Curriculum Affect Bar Examination Passage? An Empirical Analysis of the Factors Which Were Related to Bar Examination Passage between 2001 and 2006 at a Midwestern Law School,* 57 J. Legal Ed. 224, 225 (2007).

D. DeBenedictis, *Bar Exam Insiders Debunk Myths about Test*, The New Lawyer Supplement to the Los Angeles and San Francisco Daily Journal (20 Nov. 2012); *see also* Bradley D. Bonner, *Removing the Veil of Secrecy from the Bar Exam*, 34 Wyoming Lawyer 18 (2011).

Bar Admission Guide at http://www.ncbex.org/publications/bar-admissions-guide/.

Information on UBE score portability at NCBEX.org

Information on the MPT at http://www.ncbex.org/exams/mpt/.

Information on the MBE at https://www.ncbex.org/exams/mbe/.

Information on the MPRE at https://www.ncbex.org/exams/mpre/.

Information on learning science includes P. Brown, H. Roediger, & M. McDaniel, *Make it Stick: The Science of Successful Learning* (Harvard University Press 2014) and Gabriel H. Teninbaum, *Spaced Repetition: A Method for Learning More Law in Less Time*, 17 J. High Tech. L. 273, 312 (2017).

John Quincy Adams, from 1802 speech commemorating the landing of the Pilgrims in Plymouth.

"I Fought the Law." Song written by Sonny Curtis, popularized first by the Bobby Fuller Four (1966) and then by The Clash (1979).

Anne Lamott, *Bird by Bird: Some Instructions on Writing and Life* (Pantheon Books 1994.)

D. Carnegie, *How to Stop Worrying and Start Living* (originally published by The Chaucer Press, Ltd. 1948).

C. Noreuil, *The Zen of Law School Success* (Carolina Academic Pres 2011).

John Quincy Adams, "Oration at Plymouth" (1802), available at: https://archive.org/details/orationdelivered00ada.

L. Schulze, Using Science to Build Better Learners: One School's Successful Efforts to Raise Its Bar Passage Rates in an era of decline, 68 J. Legal Educ. 2019.

D. Binder & P. Bergman, Fact Investigation: From Hypothesis to Proof (first published in 1984 by West Publishing) and P.

Bergman, Trial Advocacy in a Nutshell (West Academic Publishing 2016).

P. Bergman & S. Berman, *Represent Yourself in Court: How to Prepare and Try a Winning Case.*

S. Berman, *Integrating Performance Tests into Doctrinal Courses, Skills Courses, and Institutional Benchmark Testing: A Simple Way to Enhance Student Engagement While Furthering Assessment, Bar Passage, and Other ABA Accreditation Objectives,* 42 J. Legal Prof. 147 (2018).

Diane F. Bosse, *The MPT: Assessment Opportunities beyond the Traditional Essay,* 80 The Bar Examiner 17 (2011).

E. Zorn, *Without Failure, Jordan Would Be False Idol,* Chicago Tribune, May 19, 1997.

L. Pasteur, Lecture, U. Lille. (December 7, 1854).

M. Twain, Pudd'nhead Wilson at 115 (Harper 1894).

Virginia Board of Bar Examiners dress code, https://barexam.virginia.gov/bar/barmdc.html.

B. Weiser, *In a Field of Reason, Lawyers Woo Luck Too,* N.Y. Times, Feb. 17, 2011.

K. Jonson, *Being an Effective Mentor: How to Help Beginning Teachers Succeed,* at 167 (SAGE 2008).

Racing Legend Bobby Unser to Speak Nov. 8 at State, Indiana State University Newsroom.

L. H. Baucom, *Thrive Principles: 15 Strategies for Building Your Thriving Life,* at 97 (Morgan James Publishing 2016).

N. Hamilton, *Roadmap: The Law Student's Guide to Preparing and Implementing a Successful Plan for Meaningful Employment* (ABA Publishing 2016).

M. Shultz & S. Zedeck, *Final Report—Identification, Development and Validation of Predictors for Successful Lawyering* (2009).

R. Keyes, *The Quote Verifier: Who Said What, Where, and When,* at 122 (St. Martin's Press 2007).

H. Harper, *Letters to a Young Brother,* at 44 (Gotham Books 2006).

W. Safire and L. Safir, *Words of Wisdom,* at 135 (Simon & Schuster 1990).

APPENDICES

The Appendices below include sample exams of a variety of different formats including the MCQ, the Essay, the Integrated Question Sets, and the PT. Many practice exams are available on the websites of bar examiners in various jurisdictions and from your bar review course. As to practice PTs specifically, *Bar Exam PT Success: Strategies and Practice* (West Academic 2025) provides samples of five different types of PTs, (A PT 30, PT 60, PT 90, PT 120, and PT 180) including a 2-hour Nevada PT, robust 3-hour PTs, and mini-PTs for completion in 30 minutes.

APPENDIX A

SAMPLE NEXTGEN BAR EXAM MULTIPLE-CHOICE QUESTIONS[1]

About the Multiple-Choice Questions

Approximately 40% of the exam time will be devoted to stand-alone multiple-choice questions with between four and six answer options and one or more correct answers. Initially, many of these questions will closely resemble Multistate Bar Examination (MBE) questions; this will ensure stability between scores for the current and NextGen bar exams. In future administrations, the variety of multiple-choice question types will increase. This sample set of questions includes both new question types and questions in the current MBE format. Note that some multiple-choice questions may also appear in the integrated question sets and longer writing tasks.

Below are sample multiple-choice questions.

Multiple-Choice Question 1

You are a criminal defense lawyer representing a client who has been charged with fentanyl possession. The police found the fentanyl in the guest bedroom of the client's uncle's house when responding to a noise complaint at the house. Before entering the house, the officers knocked on the door. When the uncle answered the door, the officers asked if they could look inside the house, and the uncle agreed. The client did not live in the house and was not there at the time of the search. The client had stayed in the guest bedroom of the house two nights prior to the search. The uncle told the officers that the client was the last person to have slept in that room.

You are considering filing a motion to suppress the fentanyl under the Fourth Amendment.

---

[1] Reprinted with permission from the National Conference of Bar Examiners.

Which of the following legal topics are the most important for you to research to determine the likelihood of success on a motion to suppress?

Select two.

A. Consent search.

B. Exigent circumstances.

C. Hot pursuit.

D. Probable cause.

E. Reasonable suspicion.

F. Standing.

Multiple-Choice Question 2

Your client owns a carpet cleaning company. The company recently contracted with a customer to clean the carpets throughout the customer's ten-story building for $15,000, with payment due in 30 days. Before payment was due, the customer sent your client a check for $12,000 along with a note specifying that several of the carpets still had stains and included pictures of the stained carpets. The customer's note also said that if your client cashes the check, the remainder of the customer's debt will be discharged.

Your client now seeks your advice as to whether the company can cash the check without relinquishing its right to recover the remainder of the customer's debt.

Which of the following search term(s) would be the most likely to produce resources that will answer the client's question?

Select one.

A. Accord and satisfaction.

B. Consideration.

C. Novation.

D. Offer and acceptance.

Multiple-Choice Question 3

A defendant is being prosecuted for conspiracy to possess methamphetamine with intent to distribute. At trial, the government seeks to have its agent testify to a conversation that he overheard between the defendant and a coconspirator regarding the incoming shipment of a large quantity of methamphetamine. That conversation was also audiotaped, though critical portions of it are inaudible. The defendant objects to the testimony of the agent on the ground that it is not the best evidence of the conversation.

Is the testimony of the agent admissible?

Select one.

A. No, because the testimony of the agent is not the best evidence of the conversation.

B. No, because the testimony of the agent recounts hearsay not within any exception.

C. Yes, because the best evidence rule does not require proof of the conversation through the audiotape.

D. Yes, because the audiotape is partly inaudible.

Multiple-Choice Question 4

Your client, a bank, purchased a mortgage and promissory note from a credit union that had lent a borrower money to help finance the purchase of a home. The borrower has stopped making the payments on that obligation, and the client has initiated a foreclosure action. Another lender has now come forward, claiming that they have a prior mortgage on the same land and should be paid before your client from any money collected via foreclosure.

Which of the following legal topics is the most likely to affect whether the client can collect what is owed on its mortgage and promissory note before the other lender?

Select one.

A. Covenants of title.

B. Deficiency statutes.

C. Recording statutes.

D. Statute of frauds.

Multiple-Choice Question 5

A construction worker sued an insulation manufacturer in federal court, claiming that he had developed a chronic health condition as a result of 20 years of exposure to the manufacturer's insulation at his worksites. The manufacturer answered, denying all liability and stating that it had never supplied its insulation to the worker's employer.

The worker's attorney deposed the manufacturer's president, and the manufacturer's attorney deposed the worker. Immediately thereafter, the manufacturer moved for summary judgment on the ground that the worker had no evidence showing that the insulation had ever been used by the worker's employer.

What would be the worker's best response to the motion for summary judgment?

Select one.

A. Argue that more time is needed for additional discovery to show the manufacturer's liability, and attach a declaration describing the desired discovery.

B. Argue that the motion should be denied, because a central issue in the case will be the manufacturer's credibility on the question of its distribution of the insulation, and only a jury can decide questions of credibility.

C. Argue that the motion should be denied, because the manufacturer failed to attach any evidence to its motion to show that the insulation was not used by the worker's employer.

D. Make a cross-motion for summary judgment arguing that the manufacturer has introduced no evidence to show that its insulation did not harm the worker.

Multiple-Choice Question 6

You are representing a client in a dispute with a neighbor. The client owns a single-family home with several acres of surrounding land. Recently, the client noticed that his neighbor had built a fence that extends onto the client's land. The client is unsure when the fence was built because that part of the client's land is obscured by large trees. When the client contacted the neighbor about the fence, the neighbor claimed that she did not know the location of the property line. The client has shown you a recent survey of the property that confirms the encroachment and has asked you whether he has a claim against the neighbor.

Which of the following legal topics are the most important for you to research before advising the client?

Select two.

A. Adverse possession.

B. Conversion.

C. Implied easement.

D. License.

E. Negligence.

F. Trespass.

Multiple-Choice Question 7

Your client, a state college, hired a tennis coach at a salary of $60,000 per year. The parties orally agreed on a start date but did not discuss a contract duration. Seven months after the coach started, the client now wants to fire the coach without holding a hearing because of budget cuts to the college's athletic department. The client has asked for your advice about the potential legal repercussions of firing the coach.

Which of the following legal topics are the most important for you to research before advising the client?

Select two.

A. Employment at will.

B. Parol evidence.

C. Procedural due process.

D. Substantial performance.

E. Substantive due process.

F. Takings clause.

Multiple-Choice Question 8

A landlord and a tenant orally agreed to a commercial tenancy for a term of six months beginning on July 1. Rent was to be paid by the first day of each month, and the tenant paid the first month's rent at the time of the agreement.

When the tenant arrived at the leased premises on July 1, the tenant learned that the previous tenant had not vacated the premises at the end of her lease term on May 31 and did not intend to vacate. The tenant then successfully sued the previous tenant for possession. The tenant did not inform the landlord of the eviction action until after the tenant received possession.

The tenant then sued the landlord, claiming damages for that portion of the lease period during which the tenant was not in possession.

If the court finds for the landlord, what will be the most likely explanation?

Select one.

A. By suing the previous tenant for possession, the tenant elected that remedy in lieu of a suit against the landlord.

B. The landlord had delivered the legal right of possession to the tenant.

C. The tenant failed to timely vacate as required to sue for constructive eviction.

D. The tenant had not notified the landlord before bringing the eviction action.

APPENDIX B

SAMPLE NEXTGEN BAR EXAM PERFORMANCE TASK[1]

About Performance Tasks

Each performance task should take approximately 60 minutes to complete. Performance tasks pose a question or series of questions about a single client matter. The examinee will have two kinds of materials with which to work: a File and a Library. The specific task the examinee must complete will be described in a memorandum in the File. The File may also include interview transcripts, deposition transcripts, or other documents. Both relevant and irrelevant facts will be included, and facts may be ambiguous, incomplete, or even conflicting. Examinees are expected to recognize when facts are inconsistent or missing and to identify sources of additional facts when prompted to do so.

The Library may contain cases, statutes, or other rules, some of which may not be relevant to the assigned lawyering task. The examinee is expected to extract from the Library the legal principles necessary to analyze the problem and perform the task. Performance tasks do not assess memorized substantive law; the Library materials provide the substantive information needed to complete the task.

All performance tasks assess an examinee's skills in legal research and written legal analysis (Groups A, C, and D of the Foundational Skills), but some performance tasks emphasize some skills over others. Performance tasks that focus on legal research skills will consist of a series of multiple-choice and short-answer questions followed by one extended-response question. Performance tasks that focus on written legal-analysis skills will consist of one longer extended-response question.

---

1 Reprinted with permission from the National Conference of Bar Examiners.

Performance tasks may assess skills through subject areas that are partially or fully outside of the Foundational Concepts and Principles; however, when such an area is involved, the question will provide the resources the examinee needs to give a complete answer. For example, a performance task may include aspects of state family law when assessing research and writing skills, but the Library will provide all family law rules necessary to give a complete answer.

Below is a sample performance task that is a modified version of the *Butler v. Hill* MPT administered in February 2011.

PERFORMANCE TASK ASSIGNMENT

MEMORANDUM FROM SUPERVISING PARTNER

To: [You]

From: [Supervising partner]

Date: February 22, 2021

Re: Jennifer Butler v. Robert Hill

We represent Jennifer Butler in a suit against Robert Hill seeking a divorce and property distribution. Jennifer and Robert have two children; temporary custody and child support orders are in place that are not currently at issue. Robert has challenged the validity of the parties' underlying marriage. If there is no valid marriage, Jennifer cannot pursue a claim for divorce or a share of marital property.

I have attached the relevant material from Jennifer's file. I will meet with her later this week in anticipation of trial.

Please draft a short memo that I may use to prepare for my meeting with Jennifer. In the memo, explain whether Jennifer and Robert were legally married under Franklin Family Code § 301 et seq. Do not write a separate statement of facts, but be sure to incorporate the law and the relevant facts and reach a reasoned conclusion.

CLIENT INTERVIEW NOTES MEMORANDUM

To: Jennifer Butler File

From: [Supervising partner]

Re: Client Interview Notes

August 3, 2020

Today I met with client Jennifer Butler regarding a family law matter. Jennifer related her story to me as follows.

In 2013, Jennifer Butler was 17 years old and pregnant with her first child when Robert Hill, the child's father, convinced her to marry him against the wishes of her parents. Robert told her he was single. In fact, unbeknownst to Jennifer at the time, Robert, age 22, was already married and had not yet been legally divorced. Jennifer's parents would not consent to the marriage. Caught in a difficult situation, Jennifer married Robert in a civil ceremony with a forged parental consent form that Robert had signed, and then she moved in with him.

From the date of the marriage ceremony, September 2, 2013, Jennifer and Robert lived together in Franklin. The parties had two children: Christina Hill, born November 14, 2013, and William Hill, born February 22, 2017. Jennifer never changed her surname. Both Jennifer and Robert were employed and contributed financially to the household. Robert consistently earned about twice as much as Jennifer

In May 2020, Jennifer learned that Robert had been having an affair with a coworker and had lent the woman $10,000. Jennifer immediately decided to end the marriage. She and the children stayed in the home, and Robert moved to his mother's house one week later.

While Robert was moving out, Jennifer found in Robert's dresser drawer a copy of a divorce decree that granted Serena Hill a divorce from Robert. Jennifer had never heard of Serena before and had no knowledge that Robert had been previously married. When Jennifer confronted Robert, he claimed he had not bothered to tell her because he had thought he was divorced from Serena before he married Jennifer and only learned that he wasn't when he was served with the court papers.

EXCERPT OF INTERVIEW TRANSCRIPT

Excerpt of Transcript of Telephone Interview with Louisa Milligan

(January 28, 2021)

[Attorney]: Louisa, how well do you know Jennifer?

Milligan: We've been close friends for the past five years. I live just down the block from her. We have kids who are the same ages.

[Attorney]: Do you have reason to believe that Jennifer and Robert are married?

Milligan: Yes, we've been to many social gatherings together, including a celebration of their wedding anniversary.

[Attorney]: When was this?

Milligan: September of 2019. All of their family and friends came. We had a barbecue in their backyard.

[Attorney]: Did they specifically refer to themselves as husband and wife?

Milligan: Yes, always. And, in fact, at the anniversary party, Robert gave a toast saying that marrying Jennifer was the smartest thing he'd ever done.

[Attorney]: Did you ever have any reason to believe that they were not married?

Milligan: No, not until Jennifer called me recently and told me that Robert had apparently been married before and might not have been divorced when they married. She told me that she found a copy of a divorce order in Robert's dresser drawer when they separated last spring. She had not known that Robert was ever married before.

[Attorney]: Louisa, thank you very much for offering to testify to help Jennifer. We will be calling you again before the trial. Please call me if you have any questions or concerns.

CERTIFICATE OF MARRIAGE

Certificate of Marriage
State of Franklin

Ocean City Municipality

License Number 199330

I Hereby Certify that on the **2nd** day of **September 2013**, the following persons were by me united in marriage at the Ocean City Courthouse in accordance with the License of the Clerk of the Court in the jurisdiction shown above.

First Spouse's name: Robert Hill
Age: 22 **Birthplace:** Columbia

Residence: 6226 Berkeley Blvd., Ocean City
Marital Status: Single

Second Spouse's name: Jennifer Butler **Age:** 17
Birthplace: Franklin

Residence: 80 Octavia Street, Ocean City
Marital Status: Single

Relationship to First Spouse if any: None

Consent of Parent of Underage Party (if applicable):
Yes, signed consent form presented at time of application for license.

Monica St. George
Signature of Authorized Officer

District Court Judge
Title and Office

Ocean City Municipal Building
Address of Authorized Officer

August 30, 2013
License Date

JUDGMENT OF DIVORCE

STATE OF COLUMBIA
CIRCUIT COURT FOR BROOKFIELD COUNTY

[caption omitted]

JUDGMENT OF DIVORCE

The Complaint for Divorce was heard before the Magistrate on this 10th day of April, 2018, in the Circuit Court for Brookfield County, Columbia. It is hereby

ORDERED that the Plaintiff, SERENA HILL, is granted a Divorce from the Defendant, ROBERT HILL; and it is further

ORDERED that the Plaintiff is hereby restored to the use of her former name of SERENA JORDAN; and it is further

ORDERED that this judgment of divorce shall become final after 30 days.

Dated: 4/10/2018

Hon. Richard McBain

Hon. Richard McBain
Magistrate Judge

FRANKLIN FAMILY CODE

FRANKLIN FAMILY CODE

§ 301. Marriage of a Minor; Parental Consent; Pregnancy

Marriage of Individual 16 or 17 Years Old

(a) An individual 16 or 17 years old may not marry unless

(1) the individual has the consent of a parent or guardian and the parent or guardian swears that the individual is at least 16 years old; or

(2) if the individual does not have the consent of a parent or guardian, either party to be married gives the clerk a certificate from a licensed physician stating that the physician has examined the woman

to be married and has found that she is pregnant or has given birth to a child.

(b) A marriage by an underage person without valid consent as required by this section, though voidable at the time it is entered into, may be ratified and become completely valid and binding when the underage party reaches the age of consent. Validation of a marriage of an underage person by ratification is established by some unequivocal and voluntary act, statement, or course of conduct after reaching the age of consent. Ratification includes, but is not limited to, continued cohabitation as husband and wife after reaching the age of consent.

* * * *

§ 309. Common Law Marriage—Age Restrictions

(1) A common law marriage entered into on or after January 1, 1990, shall not be recognized as a valid marriage in this state unless, at the time the common law marriage is entered into,

(a) each party is 18 years of age or older, and

(b) the marriage is not prohibited as provided in § 310.

* * * *

§ 310. Prohibited Marriages

(1) The following marriages are prohibited:

(a) A marriage entered into prior to the dissolution of an earlier marriage of one of the parties;

(b) A marriage between an ancestor and a descendant, or between a brother and a sister, whether the relationship is by the half or whole blood;

(c) . . .

(2) Children born of a prohibited marriage are legitimate.

* * * *

Hager v. Hager, Franklin Court of Appeal (2006)

Hager v. Hager
Franklin Court of Appeal (2006)

This is an appeal from a decree of divorce. The trial court ruled that the parties' marriage was valid and granted a judgment of divorce to the Petitioner, Shirley Hager. Respondent Landon Hager has appealed, contending that the trial court erred in upholding the validity of the marriage. We agree and reverse.

In her petition, Shirley Hager alleged that she and Landon participated in a marriage ceremony on July 20, 1988. At that time, however, Landon had not secured a final decree of divorce from his first wife. He subsequently obtained that decree on March 2, 1989. Shirley's petition alleged that she was unaware that Landon was married to another woman at the time of their marriage and that Landon told her he was divorced. The dispositive issue on appeal is whether there was a valid ceremonial marriage.

Shirley argues that the marriage was valid. But a bigamous marriage is void *ab initio*. All marriages that are prohibited by law because one of the parties has a spouse then living are absolutely void. A void marriage is one that has no effect. Notwithstanding Franklin Fam. Code § 301, it cannot be ratified. Indeed, persons who engage in such a marriage may be subject to criminal prosecution.

As a result, the marriage ceremony on July 20, 1988, could confer no legal rights. It was as if no marriage had been performed. The parties' marriage is void and cannot support an action for divorce.

The trial court held that the parties' 1988 marriage was merely voidable and that, since Landon had presented himself as Shirley's husband in all respects, he had ratified the marriage. But, as we have said, the marriage was prohibited, therefore void *ab initio*, and thus not subject to ratification.

We conclude, therefore, that the trial court's ruling that the ceremonial marriage was valid was error and reverse the judgment.

Owen v. Watts, Franklin Court of Appeal (2013)

Owen v. Watts
Franklin Court of Appeal (2013)

Thomas Owen appeals from an order granting summary judgment in favor of Cora Watts, decedent Ruby McCall's surviving sister and personal representative, in her action for possession of McCall's home at 316 Forest Avenue. Owen refused to leave the home after McCall's death, claiming that he was McCall's common law husband and that he was therefore entitled to a possessory dower interest in the property. The trial court held that Owen and McCall had never entered into a common law marriage. The court further held that Owen could not claim an interest in the property. Owen appeals.

The record before the trial court on the motion for summary judgment reveals that Owen moved into McCall's home some time after her husband's death in 1991 but before his own divorce in 1996. Owen testified on deposition that following his divorce, he asked McCall to marry him, but that McCall refused because marriage would jeopardize her continued entitlement to a benefit check she was receiving as a result of her late husband's death. Owen testified that, over the years, he repeatedly asked McCall to marry him but that she refused these requests for the same reason. Owen claimed that McCall finally agreed in 2010 to marry him in 2011 but that she died before the marriage could take place. Cora Watts, McCall's sister, stated in an affidavit that McCall had told her that she had no intention of ever marrying Owen.

Owen represented that he and McCall cohabited and maintained joint bank accounts. He also produced affidavits from two members of the community who regarded him and McCall as husband and wife. Owen offered no evidence, however, that could persuade a rational and impartial trier of fact that, after his divorce, he and McCall had ever manifested an agreement that they were married, as opposed to a belief that they would become married at a later date.

Owen testified that, at the time he moved in with McCall, "she said, 'I want you to come and live with me. I want that we will be as husband and wife.' " He claimed that he "said okay" and moved in with her. He further related that he moved in "because she asked me to come and live with her and make our home together as long as we both shall live, until death do us part."

These words, however, were evidently spoken at a time when Owen was already married and not yet divorced, and therefore could not legally agree to marry McCall. Owen was not divorced until October 22, 1996.

Under Franklin law, a common law marriage requires agreement by parties legally capable of entering into a valid marriage that they have a marriage relationship. Cohabitation continued after the removal of a legal impediment cannot ripen into a common law marriage unless it was pursuant to a mutual consent or agreement to be married made after the removal of the barrier.

Owen and McCall conducted their business affairs as single persons rather than as a married couple. McCall referred to herself as single, or as a widow who had not remarried, in deeds and other documents relating to property transactions, as well as in her tax returns. Similarly, in her will, McCall referred to Owen as a "friend" and left him a bequest in that capacity.

The question before the trial court was whether any impartial trier of fact could reasonably find by a preponderance of the evidence that Owen was McCall's common law husband. We agree with the trial court that no reasonable judge or jury could so find.

Franklin has long recognized common law marriages, the elements of which are a manifestation of mutual agreement, by parties able to enter into a valid marriage, that they are presently married, followed by cohabitation of at least one year, including holding themselves out to the community as being husband and wife. *East v. East* (Fr. Ct. App. 1931).

Since ceremonial marriage is readily available and provides unequivocal proof that the parties are husband and wife, claims of common law marriage should be closely scrutinized, especially where one of the purported spouses is deceased and the survivor is asserting such a claim to promote his financial interest. The burden is on the proponent to prove, by a preponderance of the evidence, all of the essential elements of a common law marriage.

Owen's testimony established at most that he and McCall had, by the end of her life, agreed to be married at an unspecified future time. This is insufficient to establish the existence of a common law marriage under Franklin law.

For the foregoing reasons, the judgment of the trial court is hereby AFFIRMED.

APPENDIX C

SAMPLE NEXTGEN BAR EXAM INTEGRATED QUESTION SETS

About Integrated Question Sets

Just under a quarter of the exam time will be devoted to integrated question sets. Each of these sets is based on a common fact scenario and may include some legal resources (e.g., excerpts of statutes or judicial opinions) and/or supplemental documents (e.g., a police report or excerpt from a deposition) and include a mixture of multiple-choice and short-answer questions. In addition to testing doctrinal law, some integrated question sets will be focused on drafting or editing a legal document; other sets will be focused on counseling and/or dispute resolution.

Below are two integrated question sets.

Integrated Question Set 1[1]

Your law firm encourages you to take on pro bono cases. Recently, you agreed to take on a pro bono case through your local bar's volunteer lawyers program in which you represent a tenant whose apartment has flooded. The following is an excerpt from your notes from the initial interview with the client:

Notes from the Initial Interview

During a recent hurricane, a lot of water entered the client's apartment. The apartment has carpet throughout, which was completely soaked. The property manager refuses to do anything about the flooding and said that the lease the client signed makes this the client's responsibility. The property manager also claims that the client did not take proper precautions before the storm, which made the flooding worse. The client disagrees. After the storm, the property

[1] Integrated Question Set 1 Reprinted with permission from the National Conference of Bar Examiners. © 2023 National Conference of Bar Examiners.

manager recommended that the client buy a water pump and some fans to "dry things out." The client tried this, but it didn't fix the problem. The apartment is still wet and smells "unbearably bad." The client can't afford to try to fix it anymore. The client does not want to move but can't keep on living in these conditions.

The client is in a month-to-month lease. The lease identifies the landlord as "Rentals LLC." The lease was signed by both your client and the property manager, who signed as "the Managing and Sole Member of Rentals LLC." The lease includes the following provision:

Condition of the Premises

Landlord ("Rentals LLC") makes no covenants or warranties about the condition of the leased premises and disclaims all responsibility for the condition of the leased premises. Tenant agrees to be solely responsible for maintaining the condition of the leased premises. Tenant waives any and all rights to the contrary, including but not limited to a right to bring a claim related to the habitability of the leased premises.

The lease does not include any provision on what damages may be available in the event of breach. Your jurisdiction has a residential landlord-tenant statute that applies to the lease. The following is an excerpt from that statute:

6–20–5 Landlord's Duty to Maintain Premises; Prohibited Conduct

(a) Subject to subsections (b) and (c), a landlord has a nonwaivable duty to maintain the premises in a habitable condition, including making necessary repairs. The duty includes but is not limited to a requirement that the landlord ensure that the premises . . . have effective waterproofing and weather protection of the roof and exterior walls, including windows and doors. . . . Tenants have a cause of action for breach of this duty, with remedies as set forth in § 6–20–10 [Tenant Remedies]. This cause of action supplants any common-law claims for breach of the landlord's implied warranty of habitability.

(b) The landlord's duty in subsection (a) is relieved if the uninhabitable condition of the premises was caused by an unreasonable act or omission of the tenant, the tenant's immediate family member, or the tenant's guest.

(c) If the premises are substantially damaged by a fire, other casualty, or natural disaster and continued occupancy of the unit is unlawful or dangerous or requires repairs that can be made only if the tenant vacates the premises, the landlord may terminate the lease by giving the tenant reasonable written notice.

(d) Any provision in a lease that purports to waive the landlord's duty in subsection (a) is unenforceable. If the landlord seeks to enforce such a provision or accepts the tenant's voluntary compliance with such a provision, the tenant has a cause of action in the amount of three times the periodic rent. This cause of action accrues irrespective of any claim the tenant may have for breach of the duty described in subsection (a).

Integrated Question 1

Which of the following is an accurate application of Section 6–20–5 to the facts?

Select one.

A. The section allows the landlord to enforce the lease provision, making the client responsible for repairs, but the tenant may seek damages of three times the periodic rent.

B. The section makes the lease provision unenforceable but does not decide the issue of which party is responsible for which portion of the repairs.

C. The section makes the lease provision unenforceable and makes the landlord responsible for the full extent of the repairs.

D. The section does not decide the issue of the lease provision's enforceability but establishes the landlord's negligence per se.

Integrated Question 2

Section 6–20–5 of the statute does not define the term "habitable." A partner at your firm has asked a law clerk to determine the jurisdiction's meaning of the term for the purposes of potential litigation, and the law clerk has asked you for guidance.

Advise the law clerk on two specific legal sources that are the most likely to provide a controlling definition of the term "habitable."

Integrated Question 3

You receive an email from your client. In the email, the client asks you "whether it would be a good idea to sue." You begin your reply to the client by explaining that litigation will consume the client's personal time and will almost certainly take longer to resolve than reaching a settlement before litigation. You consider what other risks your client would face in litigation.

Considering your client's objectives and the applicable statute, describe two other potential risks of filing a claim or claims on the client's behalf.

Integrated Question 4

After discussing your research with the client and assisting the client in setting goals, you contact the property manager on the client's behalf and attempt to negotiate a settlement. The property manager agrees to replace the carpet but refuses to refund any of the client's past rent or to pay any of the client's costs. Eventually, negotiations break down, and you prepare to draft a complaint on behalf of the client.

Which of the following facts provide the most support to a cause of action under § 6–20–5(d)?

Select two.

A. The lease provides that the client "waives any . . . right to bring a claim related to the habitability of the leased premises."

B. The apartment has an unbearably bad smell.

C. The property manager claims that the client did not take proper precautions to prevent flood damage.

D. The client bought a water pump and fans at the property manager's recommendation.

E. The client cannot afford to make any other repairs.

F. The flooding was caused by a hurricane.

Integrated Question 5

Your legal research since the initial client interview supports a finding that the condition of the client's apartment after the storm fell below the standard of habitability in the jurisdiction. In addition, your factual investigation has established the following:

- There was nothing that Rentals LLC could reasonably have done to prevent the flooding from the hurricane.
- The client spent money on fans and a water pump.
- Since the client notified the property manager about the flood five months ago, the client has continued paying monthly rent in full.

List two claims you could bring on behalf of your client to seek the greatest possible damages for your client. For each claim, describe what remedy you will seek in the complaint. If the remedy is uncertain, describe the information you need to determine the appropriate remedy.

Integrated Question 6

Your firm has had some experience with Rentals LLC. The company does not always show up in court to defend small claims against it, and you are concerned that it might be difficult to collect a future judgment against the company.

List two factual issues you could investigate to help determine whether the LLC's veil can be pierced to collect a future judgment from the property manager personally. In your jurisdiction, the test for piercing the veil of an LLC is the same as the test for piercing the veil of a corporation.

For example, in a torts matter, a factual issue that might require investigation is "whether the plaintiff lost wages as a result of the accident."

Integrated Question Set 2[2]

You are an associate in a law firm. Your supervisor has asked you to work on a case for a new client, a landscaping company who recently completed a major project for a homeowner and is now in a dispute with the homeowner over payment.

Supervisor Email

The following is an excerpt from an email you received from your supervisor:

> We have been unable to negotiate a settlement with the homeowner, so we will file a complaint on behalf of the client against the homeowner. A law clerk created a first draft of the complaint. I need you to make sure that all the language in the draft is factually and legally supported and that it complies with Franklin Rule of Civil Procedure 10(b). I am attaching a transcript of my interview with the client for your reference.

> **Excerpt of Transcript**
>
> **The following is an excerpt from the transcript of the interview with the owner of the landscaping company:**
>
> **[Supervisor]:** Thank you for meeting with me today. My assistant told me that your company had a landscaping contract with a homeowner who is refusing to pay for the work. Did you bring the contract with you?

[2] Integrated Question Set 1 Reprinted with permission from the National Conference of Bar Examiners. © 2024 National Conference of Bar Examiners.

[Owner]: Actually, we had two contracts with this homeowner. I didn't bring them with me, but I can drop them off at your office tomorrow.

[Supervisor]: That's great. Let's start at the beginning. What is the problem you're having with the homeowner on the first contract?

[Owner]: This homeowner recently built a new house and wanted the backyard to be landscaped as a large entertainment space. There is a historic oak tree in the backyard, and she wanted it to be featured in the landscaping design. I visited the property and sketched a plan for the project that featured the oak tree, and then I drew up a contract and attached the landscaping plan as an exhibit. The homeowner signed the contract and paid $70,000 of the $140,000 contract price as a deposit before we started the work.

[Supervisor]: Did you complete the project as it was described in the plan?

[Owner]: Yes. I did everything the homeowner requested, but now she's refusing to pay the remaining $70,000 because she thinks we did something to damage the oak tree. She says the tree looks sick and that it might be dying. I guess the workers could have damaged its roots, but then again, it's a very old tree.

[Supervisor]: Okay, that gives me a good start on the issues concerning the first contract. Now tell me about the second contract.

[Owner]: After we started work on the project, the homeowner asked if we could add a large fishpond to the backyard. I said we could do it for $20,000. She agreed to that and I drew up another contract, which she signed. I billed her when we finished the work, but now she's refusing to pay the $20,000 for the fishpond until we do something about the oak tree.

Excerpt of Franklin Rule of Civil Procedure 10(b)

The following is an excerpt of your jurisdiction's rule regarding the form of pleadings:

Franklin Rule of Civil Procedure 10(b)

(b) Paragraphs; Separate Statements. A party must state its claims or defenses in numbered paragraphs, each limited as far as practicable to a single set of circumstances. A later paragraph may refer by number to an earlier paragraph in the same pleading. A later pleading may refer by number to a paragraph in an earlier pleading. If doing so would promote clarity, each claim founded on a separate transaction or occurrence—and each defense other than a denial—must be stated in a separate count or defense.

Excerpt of Draft Complaint

The following is an excerpt of the draft complaint created by the law clerk in your firm:

[caption omitted]

COMPLAINT AND JURY DEMAND

. . .

Facts

18. The initial contract signed by the homeowner included a landscaping plan.

19–29. [Properly pleaded facts related to the initial contract and work]

30. The scope of the work under the initial contract did not include construction of a fishpond.

31. While Plaintiff was completing work pursuant to the initial contract, Defendant requested that Plaintiff construct a fishpond; therefore, Plaintiff and Defendant entered into a second contract for the fishpond in the amount of $20,000.

32. Plaintiff completed construction of the requested fishpond on [date].

33. Defendant acknowledged that the fishpond was completed as requested.

34. When Plaintiff billed Defendant for the fishpond, Defendant stated that she would not pay for the fishpond.

35. Defendant has made no payment for this additional work.

Count 1: Breach of Contract (Initial Contract)

36–47. [Properly pleaded claim for breach of the initial contract]

Count 2: Breach of Contract (Fishpond)

48. Plaintiff incorporates by reference the allegations set forth above in paragraphs 30–35.

49. The parties formed a contract for Plaintiff to construct a fishpond and Defendant to pay $20,000.

50. Defendant breached the contract by failing to pay Plaintiff $90,000: $20,000 for the agreed-upon work on the fishpond in addition to the $70,000 still owed under the initial contract.

Demand for Jury Trial

51. Plaintiff demands a trial by jury of all triable issues pursuant to Franklin Rule of Civil Procedure 38.

Prayer for Relief

52. Plaintiff seeks an order of specific performance.

53. In the alternative, Plaintiff seeks an award of damages in the amount of: $90,000, and interest and costs.

Assignment

Following the instructions in the email from your supervisor, find five mistakes in the complaint. For each mistake, (1) identify the paragraph that includes the mistake, (2) describe the mistake, and (3) explain how you would correct the mistake.

A mistake can be a mistake of fact, a mistake of substantive law, or a violation of the provided procedural rule. Missing information is not a mistake. Assume that the following are correct: (1) all bracketed material and (2) all formatting and numbering.

APPENDIX D

CALIFORNIA BAR PERFORMANCE TEST[1]

Performance Test and Selected Answers

February 2018

Performance Test

INSTRUCTIONS AND FILE

MEANEY v. TRUSTEES OF THE UNIVERSITY OF COLUMBIA

INSTRUCTIONS

1. This performance test is designed to evaluate your ability to handle a select number of legal authorities in the context of a factual problem involving a client.
2. The problem is set in the fictional State of Columbia, one of the United States.
3. You will have two sets of materials with which to work: a File and a Library.
4. The File contains factual materials about your case. The first document is a memorandum containing the instructions for the tasks you are to complete.
5. The Library contains the legal authorities needed to complete the tasks. The case reports may be real, modified, or written solely for the purpose of this performance test. If the cases appear familiar to you, do not assume that they are precisely the same as you have read before. Read each thoroughly, as if it were new to you. You should assume that cases were decided in the jurisdictions and on the dates shown. In citing cases from the Library, you may use abbreviations and omit page citations.

---

1 This exam and selected answers were published on the website of the State Bar of California and are reproduced here with permission.

6. You should concentrate on the materials provided, but you should also bring to bear on the problem your general knowledge of the law. What you have learned in law school and elsewhere provides the general background for analyzing the problem; the File and Library provide the specific materials with which you must work.
7. This performance test is designed to be completed in 90 minutes. Although there are no parameters on how to apportion that 90 minutes, you should allow yourself sufficient time to thoroughly review the materials and organize your planned response. Since the time allotted for this session of the examination includes two (2) essay questions in addition to this performance test, time management is essential.
8. Your response will be graded on its compliance with instructions and on its content, thoroughness, and organization.

FOGEL & DAVIS, LLP

One Walton Avenue

Belleville, Columbia

MEMORANDUM

TO:	Applicant
FROM:	Melissa Saphir
DATE:	February 27, 2018
RE:	Meaney v. Trustees of the University of Columbia

We have been retained by the Trustees of the University of Columbia to defend them in a breach of contract action.

The late Edward Kemper (Edward) was a wealthy businessman and a generous donor to the University. Pursuant to an agreement, Edward transferred a garden to the Trustees, which the Trustees agreed to retain in perpetuity as the "Kemper Scottish Garden." Sometime later, Edward married Sarah Meaney (Sarah). Before her death two years ago, Sarah had grown quite fond of the Kemper Scottish Garden—so much so that it came to be known as "Sarah's Scottish Garden."

Notwithstanding the agreement, the Trustees recently made the difficult decision to sell the garden so as to use the proceeds for pressing educational purposes.

The plaintiff in the breach of contract action I referred to is Brendan Meaney. Meaney is the only child of Sarah by a prior marriage. By his action, Meaney is seeking to prevent the Trustees from selling the garden.

I believe that we may be able to persuade the court to dismiss Meaney's breach of contract action on the ground that Meaney lacks standing. To confirm my belief, I need to determine whether Edward transferred the garden to the Trustees by way of contract or gift and, if by way of gift, by way of what kind of gift.

To that end, please prepare an objective memorandum assessing whether Edward did indeed transfer the garden to the Trustees by way of contract or gift and, if by way of gift, by way of what kind of gift. Do not include a statement of facts, but use the facts in your analysis.

AGREEMENT

The Trustees of the University of Columbia (hereinafter "the Trustees") desire to obtain a garden parcel of real property now owned and occupied by Emily Gordon, located in Belleville, Columbia, commonly known as 625 Sierra Way.

Edward Kemper (hereinafter "Kemper") desires to facilitate such acquisition by acquiring the garden parcel and by transferring it to the Trustees, subject to certain restrictions as provided for herein.

Therefore, in consideration of the foregoing, the Trustees and Kemper do hereby agree as follows:

1. Kemper will acquire the garden parcel and transfer it to the Trustees.
2. The Trustees will cause the garden parcel to bear the name "Kemper Scottish Garden," use it for educational purposes, and retain it in perpetuity.

Kemper retains the right to modify the terms of this Agreement as necessary and appropriate to its purpose.

Dated: December 18, 1964.

Edward Kemper
Edward Kemper

Harold Williamson
Harold Williamson
Chairman of the Board of Trustees

Performance Test

LIBRARY

BEHRENS RESEARCH FOUNDATION v. FAIRVIEW MEMORIAL HOSPITAL

Columbia Court of Appeals (2008)

Behrens Research Foundation (Behrens), a non-profit public benefit corporation, gave Fairview Memorial Hospital (Fairview), a healthcare institution, a gift of $1 million. Fairview had a well-recognized Department of Cardiothoracic Surgery. Behrens had had a longstanding interest in advancing cardiothoracic surgery. Not long thereafter, as a result of various unforeseen changes, including departures of key staff, Fairview closed the department.

Behrens brought the underlying action in the District Court seeking an injunction directing Fairview either to reopen its Department of Cardiothoracic Surgery or to return Behrens' $1 million gift. Fairview moved to dismiss the action under Columbia Rule of Civil Procedure 12(b)(6), claiming that Behrens did not have standing to sue. The District Court granted the motion and entered a judgment of dismissal.

On appeal, Behrens contends that it did indeed have standing to sue.

We disagree.

It is well settled in Columbia that a donor is the master of his or her gift.

Because that is so, a donor can make a gift that is *absolute.* The donor can give property *unconditionally,* without (1) restricting use or disposition of the property, (2) retaining power to modify the gift, or (3) reserving a right to sue to enforce a restriction or to undo the gift in case of a restriction's breach by causing the property to revert to the donor him- or herself or to a third person. When a gift is absolute, the donor has relinquished, and the donee has assumed, full dominion over the property—i.e., the ability to use or dispose of the property at any time, in any manner, and for any purpose.

But a donor can also make a gift that is *not absolute.* The donor can give property *conditionally,* (1) restricting use or disposition, (2) retaining power of modification, and/or (3) reserving a right of enforcement or reversion. When a gift is not absolute, the donor has not relinquished, and the donee has not assumed, full dominion over the property; rather, both donor and donee share power over the property's use or disposition.

Although a donor is indeed master of his or her gift, the law presumes that a gift is *absolute* unless it clearly appears otherwise. In line with this presumption, the law further presumes that a donor has *not* restricted use or disposition, has *not* retained power of modification, and has *not* reserved a right of enforcement or reversion, unless it clearly appears otherwise.

These presumptions prove fatal to Behrens' position. The record on appeal contains the instrument by which Behrens made its $1 million gift to Fairview. In pertinent part, the instrument recites only that Behrens "hereby delivers" and Fairview "hereby accepts" the gift. Neither expressly, nor by implication, does the instrument evidence any reservation on Behrens' part of a right of enforcement. Behrens did not reserve any such right for itself. We cannot make up for its omission.

Affirmed.

COLLINS v. LINCOLN

Columbia Court of Appeals (2009)

Anita Collins brought an action for declaratory relief in the District Court against Stephen Lincoln, her adult son. In order to resolve various tax questions now pending before the State of Columbia Tax Board, Collins seeks a determination that the instrument by which she transferred certain property to Lincoln reflected a gift rather than a transfer by contract. Following a bench trial, the District Court entered judgment in Collins' favor, issuing the determination that she had sought. Lincoln appeals. We affirm.

The facts are undisputed: By deed dated June 26, 2002, Collins transferred to Lincoln a 260-acre vineyard in Parker County including a 20,000-square-foot Victorian main residence, guest house, pool, tennis courts, sports field, exercise studio, lake, olive orchard, and a stone winery with a tasting room and a permit to produce 5,500 cases of wine a year. The deed recited that Collins transferred the property to Lincoln "in consideration for his promise to use his best efforts to maintain the property in an ecologically sustainable manner." As of the date in question, the assessed value of the property was more than $35 million. Collins was then 65 years old, a widow, and the Chair of the Board of Directors of the Parker County Rural Conservancy, a locally-prominent environmental organization; Lincoln was 30 years old, unmarried, and the Rural Conservancy's Volunteer Coordinator; each was the other's sole living relative.

Property may be passed by gift. The elements of a gift consist of: (1) intent on the part of the donor to make a gift; (2) delivery, either actual or constructive, of property by the donor; (3) acceptance of the property by the donee; and (4) lack of consideration for the gift.

Property may also be passed by transfer by contract. The elements of a transfer by contract consist of: (1) an offer to buy or sell; (2) acceptance of the offer; and (3) consideration passing between the buyer and seller.

Gifts and transfers by contracts have two similar elements. First, a gift requires delivery by the donor and a transfer by contract requires offer by the buyer or seller. Second, a gift requires acceptance by the donee and a transfer by contract requires acceptance by the seller or buyer.

But one element is different. While a transfer by contract requires the *presence* of consideration, a gift requires the *absence* of consideration. In other words, without consideration, the passing of property is by gift, whereas with consideration, it is by transfer by contract.

Consideration has two requirements. The promisee must bargain with the promisor and must confer, or agree to confer, a benefit or must suffer, or agree to suffer, a burden.

The absence of consideration is clear when a gift is absolute. *See, Behrens Research Foundation v. Fairview Memorial Hospital* (Colum. Ct. App. 2008). In that instance, the donee does not bargain with the donor or confer, or agree to confer, any benefit. Neither does the donee bargain with the donor or suffer, or agree to suffer, any burden. Instead, the donor simply delivers the property and the donee simply accepts it.

But the absence of consideration is not clear when a gift is not absolute. *See, Behrens Research Foundation.* In that instance, the donee could be said to bargain with the donor, and could be said to confer, or agree to confer, a "benefit" on the donor or to suffer, or agree to suffer, a "burden." Consider the situation in which a university agrees to name a campus building in a donor's honor or to use the building for a specified purpose. The university could be said to "bargain" with the donor—negotiating the terms for the naming of the building or its use for the specified purpose—and to confer, or agree to confer, a benefit or to suffer, or agree to suffer, a burden—the naming of the building or its use for the specified purpose. Such a "bargain" and "benefit" and "burden" do not preclude a gift.

The presence or absence of consideration does not turn on the presence or absence of the term "consideration" in the instrument. For example, in *Salmon v. Wilson* (Colum. Supreme Ct. 1971), the Supreme Court held that a deed by which a father transferred 10 acres of land valued at $500,000 to his adult daughter effected a gift, even though the deed recited that he transferred the property to her "in consideration for $500." The Supreme Court reasoned that, in light of all of the circumstances, the $500 paid by the daughter to her father was "nominal and immaterial," and it was "clearly" the father's intent to "donate the land to his daughter and not to sell it to her."

Ultimately, what controls are the motives manifested by the parties. If the parties are motivated by a desire to buy and sell the property through a commercial transaction, there is a transfer by contract. But if the parties are motivated by a desire to deliver and accept the property through a non-commercial transaction, there is a gift.

Attacking the District Court's determination that the deed by which Collins transferred the property in question reflected a gift rather than a transfer by contract, Lincoln claims that the deed impliedly recited Collins' "offer" to transfer the property and his "acceptance" of the offer, and expressly recited the "consideration"—his "promise to use his best efforts to maintain the property in an ecologically sustainable manner." The "burden" of a promise to "use best efforts" is hard to quantify. But we have little doubt that it is adequate. Because that is so, such a promise could surely support a transfer by contract. But the fundamental question is whether there was in fact a transfer by contract rather than a gift. The answer is no. From all that appears, Collins and Lincoln were not motivated by a desire to buy and sell the property through a commercial transaction, but instead by a desire to deliver and accept the property through a non-commercial transaction. Collins was Lincoln's mother, and he was her son. Each was the other's only living relative, and each was an environmentalist. As the Supreme Court concluded in *Salmon*, so do we conclude here: In light of all of the circumstances, Lincoln's "promise" to Collins "to use his best efforts to maintain the property in an ecologically sustainable manner" was nominal and immaterial, and it was clearly Collins' intent to donate the property to him and not to sell it.

Affirmed.

HOLT v. JONES

Columbia Supreme Court (1994)

Almost one hundred years ago, Ralph Polk created the Polk Trust by giving the Trustees of the University of Columbia a parcel of 10 acres in Silveyville, as a campus for the then newly-founded College of Physicians and Surgeons, and a sum of $5 million for the upkeep of the grounds. The Trustees of the University of Columbia are ex officio trustees of the Polk Trust.

Plaintiffs are three trustees of the University of Columbia and the Polk Trust. Defendants are the seven remaining trustees and the Attorney General of the State of Columbia.

Plaintiffs filed a complaint in the District Court. They alleged that defendant trustees had wrongfully diverted assets of the Polk Trust and sought an injunction to prohibit further wrongful diversion.

The Attorney General filed an answer to the complaint, denying plaintiffs' allegation for want of information and belief. In her answer, the Attorney General stated: "The Attorney General has reviewed the management of the Polk Trust and has determined that suit is not warranted."

Defendant trustees moved to dismiss the action on the ground that plaintiffs did not have standing to sue. The District Court granted the motion and entered judgment accordingly. The Court of Appeals affirmed. We granted certiorari.

The sole issue—which is a question of first impression in Columbia—is whether plaintiffs, as minority trustees of the Polk Trust, have standing to sue.

In accordance with the common law, all jurisdictions recognize that the Attorney General has standing to sue to enforce provisions of non-private trusts. At the same time, a substantial majority of jurisdictions have adopted the position that the Attorney General's standing is not exclusive. These jurisdictions accord standing to any person with a special interest.

The common law recognizes the problem of providing adequate enforcement of provisions of non-private trusts.

The primary type of non-private trust is the so-called charitable trust. A charitable trust is created, as a matter of fact, whenever a settlor manifests an intent to give property, in trust, for a charitable purpose and actually gives the property, in trust, for such purpose. A charitable trust is also created, as a matter of law, whenever a person gives property to an educational, philanthropic, healthcare, or similar institution for an education, philanthropy, healthcare, or similar purpose.

Since there is usually no one who is willing to assume the burdens of suing to enforce the provisions of a non-private trust, the Attorney General has been accorded standing. But, in light of limited resources, the Attorney General cannot reasonably assume the burdens of suing to enforce the provisions of all non-private trusts.

The present case is representative. In her answer, the Attorney General stated that she had determined that suit was not warranted. But she also admitted that she had no information or belief as to plaintiffs' allegation that defendant trustees had wrongfully diverted property of the Polk Trust.

Although the Attorney General has primary responsibility for the enforcement of provisions of non-private trusts, the need for adequate enforcement is not wholly fulfilled by the authority given to him or her. There is no rule or policy against supplementing the Attorney General's standing by allowing standing to persons with a special interest, i.e., persons who are trustees or beneficiaries or would otherwise have an ownership interest in the property.

For this reason, we join the substantial majority of jurisdictions that have adopted the position that the Attorney General's standing is not exclusive. We hold that any person with a special interest has standing to sue to enforce provisions of the trust.

The trustees of a non-private trust, as trustees, have a special interest in the trust. The trustees are also in the best position to learn about breaches of trust and to bring the relevant facts to a court's attention.

Therefore, we conclude that plaintiffs, as trustees of the Polk Trust, have standing to sue to enforce its provisions.

Reversed and remanded.

PT: SELECTED ANSWER 1

PRIVILEGED & CONFIDENTIAL

CONTAINS ATTORNEY WORK PRODUCT

FOGEL & DAVIS LLP

One Walton Avenue

Belleville, Columbia

MEMORANDUM

TO:	Melissa Saphir
FROM:	Applicant
DATE:	February 27, 2018
RE:	Meaney v. Trustees of the University of Columbia

I. Questions Presented

This memorandum addresses two questions: (1) whether Edward Kemper ("Edward") transferred what is now known as the Kemper Scottish Garden or, to some, Sarah's Scottish Garden ("Garden") to the Trustees of the University of Columbia ("Trustees") by way of contract or gift; and, (2) if by way of gift, by way of what kind of gift. This memorandum does not intend to address the merits question of whether Plaintiff Brandon Meaney ("Meaney") has standing to sue the Trustees.

This memorandum concludes that: (1) Edward transferred the Garden to the Trustees by way of gift, not contract, even though the transfer contains the indicia of a contract; and that (2) Edward's transfer by gift likely constituted a conditional gift rather than an unconditional gift because of the express limitations placed on the Trustees, but that further research is required to determine whether Edward's conditional gift may also constitute a charitable trust.

II. Analysis

A. Whether Edward Transferred the Garden by Contract or Gift

Edward likely transferred the Garden by way of gift, even though many of the traditional hallmarks of transfer by contract are present in the 1964 Agreement signed by Edward and Harold Williamson ("Agreement"). Columbia law recognizes both gifts and contracts as legitimate mechanisms for the transfer of property. A property passes by gift when there exists: "(1) intent on the part of the donor to make a gift; (2) delivery, either actual or constructive, of property by the donor; (3) acceptance of the property by the donee; and (4) lack of consideration for the gift." *Collins v. Lincoln*, Library at 5 (Colum. Ct. App. 2009). Property passes by contract where there exists: "(1) an offer to buy or sell; (2) acceptance of the offer; and (3) consideration passing between the buyer and seller." *Id.* at 6.

1. Consideration Is Key, But Intent Is Often Dispositive

The key factor in determining whether a property passed by contract or gift, since both contracts and gifts share many elements, is the presence or absence of consideration. *See Collins*, Library at 6 ("While a transfer by contract requires the *presence* of consideration, a gift requires the *absence* of consideration. In other words, without consideration, the passing of property is by gift, whereas with consideration, it is by transfer of contract." (emphasis in original)). Consideration requires both a bargain between the promisee and the promisor and that the promisor confers, or agrees to confer, a benefit or suffers, or agrees to suffer, a burden. *Collins*, Library at 6.

The presence of buzzwords that signal consideration, including the word "consideration," do not suffice to render a transfer a contract. The Columbia Supreme Court has held that a $500 payment for land referred to as "consideration" in a contract did not convert a gift into a contract because, "in light of all the circumstances," the donor intended to "donate the land . . . and not sell it." *Salmon v. Wilson* (Colum. Supreme Ct. 1971), *quoted in Collins*, Library at 7. And in *Collins*, the Columbia Appeals Court held that a gift occurred, even though the transferring document contained the terms "offer," "acceptance," and "consideration," because the mother donor and son donee did not behave commensurate with a commercial transaction and the promise to use "best efforts" to maintain the property a certain way were "nominal and immaterial." Library at 7–8.

Even where indicia of a contract are present, whether a property transfer is a contract or gift ultimately depends on the "motives manifested by the parties." *Id.* at 7. For example, the parties' intent to transfer property by commercial transaction suggests a contract, while the parties' intent to transfer by a non-commercial transaction suggests a gift. *See id.*

2. The Agreement Contains Indicia of a Contract, But the Parties' Intent Suggests a Gift

The Agreement contains the markings and elements of a contract, but a court would likely find that the circumstances and parties' intent render it a gift. The Agreement contains the phrase "in consideration of the foregoing" and specifies that Edward incurred the burden of acquiring the Garden and transferring it to Trustees, while Trustees acquired the benefit of the Garden and the burdens of naming it "Kemper Scottish Garden," using it for educational purposes, and retaining it in perpetuity. *See* Agreement at 1. Because Edward appears to have acquired the Garden as part of the Agreement in an arm's length transaction with another, and because the Trustees agreed to name the Garden, use it for a particular purpose, and never sell it, there are certainly indicia of a bargain between Edward and the Trustees that created both burdens and benefits, as one would find in a contract. *See Collins*, Library at 6 (defining consideration as requiring a bargain and that the promisor confer a benefit or suffer a burden). And, unlike the transactions in *Salmon* and *Collins*, Edward and the Trustees have no familial relationship *id.* at 7. On the other hand, the Trustees did not make even a nominal payment for the land of the kind present in *Salmon*. *See id.* at 7 (quoting *Salmon*). And *Collins* reasoned that even, as here, a university "bargains" to grant naming rights to a donor and use property for a specific purpose, such a bargain does not "preclude a gift." *Id.* at 6–7 (citing *Behrens Research Foundation v. Fairview Memorial Hospital* (Colum. Ct. App. 2008)).

The Agreement here contains additional restrictions or "bargains" not contemplated by the *Collins, Behrens*, or *Salmon* courts: namely, the restriction that the Trustees agreement to "retain [the Garden] in perpetuity" and Edward's reserved right "to modify the terms of this Agreement as necessary and appropriate to its purpose." Agreement at 1. More research is required to determine whether Columbia courts have held these restrictions to suggest the presence of a contract or gift, but the totality of the circumstances appears to suggest that Edward gifted the Garden to the University. Edward paid what appears to be fair monetary consideration to another for the Garden and granted it immediately to the University for no monetary consideration in return. Edward specified in the Agreement use of the Garden for an educational purpose, which suggests the lack of a commercial transaction. And Edward's condition that the Trustees retain the Garden in perpetuity (note that this memorandum does not assess the legal propriety of a perpetual restriction on transfer by the Trustees) suggests that no further monetary value would be realized for the Garden.

Even though the Agreement contains many of the markings of a contract and contains arguably more "consideration" than was present in *Collins*, *Behrens*, or *Salmon*, the overall intent of the Agreement suggests that Edward gifted the Garden to the Trustees.

B. Whether Edward Conferred the Garden as an Absolute Gift or a Conditional Gift

Edward likely gifted the Garden as a conditional gift, and possibly also as a charitable trust. "It is well settled in Columbia that a donor is the master of his or her gift." *Behrens*, Library at 2 (Colum. Ct. App. 2008). Gifts can be "absolute" or "conditional." A donor can give property unconditionally without restricting its use or disposition, retaining power to modify the gift, or reserving a right to sue to enforce a restriction or cause reversion of the property. *See id.* "When a gift is absolute, the donor has relinquished, and the donee has assumed, full dominion over the property—i.e., the ability to use or dispose of the property at any time, in any manner, and for any purpose." *Id.* at 2–3. A donor can also give property conditionally by "(1) restricting use or disposition, (2) retaining power of modification, and/or (3) reserving a right of enforcement or reversion." *Behrens*, Library at 3. In the case of conditional gifts, donor and donee "share power over the property's use or disposition." *Id.*

1. Edward Likely Conferred a Conditional, Not an Absolute, Gift

Columbia law "presumes that a gift is *absolute* unless it clearly appears otherwise" and that "a donor has *not* restricted use or disposition, has *not* retained power of modification, and has *not* reserved a right of enforcement or reversion, unless it clearly appears otherwise." *Behrens*, Library at 3 (emphasis in original). In *Behrens*, the court found that a gift of $1 million without restrictive terms, which only said that donor "hereby delivers" and donee "hereby accepts" the gift, gave an unconditional gift and relinquished control over the donee's use of the gift. *See Behrens*, Library at 3. And an absolute gift evinces clear absence of consideration, such as where "the donor simply delivers the property and the donee simply accepts it." *Collins*, Library at 6 (citing *Behrens*).

The Agreement contains conditions that would prevent it from being adjudged an absolute gift. The gift at issue in *Behrens* contained no restrictions at all, and simply transferred money with the terms "hereby delivers" and "hereby receives." *Behrens*, Library at 3. The Agreement, by contrast, contains explicit restrictions on the Trustees' use of the Garden: it must be named "Kemper Scottish Garden," it must be used for educational purposes, and the Trustees may never dispose of it. *See* Agreement at 1. In the Agreement, Edward further reserves a right to modify the Agreement "as necessary and appropriate to its purpose." The Agreement thus presents all of the factors for a conditional gift envisioned by the *Behrens* court but not presented in the facts of that case: restricted use, restricted disposition, and reserved rights. *Compare id.* at 1, *with Behrens*, Library at 3. Nor is this a case where "the donor simply delivers the property and the donee simply accepts it." *Collins*, Library at 6 (internal citation omitted).

A court would almost certainly find that Edward did not confer the Garden as an unconditional gift, without regard to the enforceability of the Agreement's conditions. Edward's retention of rights to modify the Agreement and restrictions on the Garden's use and disposition suggest a conditional gift.

2. Edward May Have Created a Charitable Trust

Edward's gift may also constitute a charitable trust, although more research than this memorandum provides is necessary to determine the interplay between charitable trusts and conditional gifts. The Columbia Supreme Court has held that a gift can also take the form of a charitable trust in certain circumstances. *See generally Holt v. Jones*, Library at 10 (Colum. Supreme Ct. 1994). Even where a property grant is not placed in trust by the donor, a charitable trust can be created by operation of law "whenever a person gives property to an educational, philanthropic, healthcare, or similar institution for an education, philanthropy, healthcare, or similar purpose." *Id.*

The Agreement, to be sure, does not create a trust of any kind. But a court may find under *Holt* that Edward's restriction on use of the Garden "for educational purposes" and gift of the Garden to the University of Columbia, an educational institution, may satisfy the criteria for the creation of a charitable trust by operation of law. More research is required to determine whether other aspects of Columbia law, or decisions of Columbia courts, would suggest the lack of a charitable trust. And more research is needed to determine what effect, if any, the legal creation of a charitable trust would have on Edward's rights, the Trustees' rights, Plaintiff's rights in the instant lawsuit, or other claims that may arise.

IV. Conclusion

Edward more likely than not transferred the Garden to the Trustees by gift, rather than by contract, because the totality of the Agreement and the accompanying intent of the parties suggests a non-commercial transaction lacking proper consideration. If Edward's transfer of the Garden constitutes a gift, it is much more likely than not to be deemed a conditional gift than an absolute gift due to the Agreement's restrictions on use and disposition and Edward's retention of modification rights. Edward's transfer of the Garden may also constitute a charitable trust because the Agreement conveys property to an educational institution for an educational purpose, but more research is required to assess this possibility and its effects on the other issues discussed herein.

Please feel free to contact me with any questions regarding this memorandum, or if you would like additional research and analysis performed.

PRIVILEGED & CONFIDENTIAL

CONTAINS ATTORNEY WORK PRODUCT

PT: SELECTED ANSWER 2

FOGEL & DAVIS, LLP

One Walton Avenue

Belleville, Columbia

TO:	Melissa Saphir, Managing Attorney
FROM:	Applicant
DATE:	February 27, 2018
RE:	Meaney v. Trustees of the University of Columbia

I. Introduction

In order to persuade the court to dismiss Brendan Meaney's breach of contract action on the ground that he lacks standing, you have asked me prepare an objective memo first analyzing whether the Edward Kemper transferred the garden to the Trustees by way of contract or gift, and if the garden was transferred by gift, what kind of gift.

In short, a court will likely find that the transfer was by a not absolute gift in the form of a charitable trust.

II. Legal Analysis

Property may be passed by gift or by transfer by contract. *Collins v. Lincoln*, Columbia Court of Appeals (2009). The elements of a gift consist of: (1) intent on the part of the donor to make a gift; (2) actual or constructive delivery of property by the donor; (3) acceptance of the property by the donee; and (4) lack of consideration for the gift. *Id.* Alternatively, the elements of a transfer by contract consist of: (1) an offer to buy or sell; (2) acceptance of the offer; and (3) consideration passing between the buyer and seller. *Id.* Accordingly, gifts and transfers by contract have two similar elements. A gift requires delivery by the donor and a transfer by contract requires offer by the buyer or seller. Additionally, a gift requires acceptance by the donee and a transfer by contract requires acceptance by the seller or buyer. But one element is different. While a contract requires the presence of consideration, a gift requires the absence of consideration. *Id.* In other words, without consideration, the passing of property is by gift, whereas with consideration, it is by transfer by contract.

A. The relationship between Edward Kemper and the Trustees of University of Columbia manifested an intent that the transfer be by gift rather than by contract because the parties were motivated by a non-commercial transaction.

The element of consideration has two requirements: the promisee must bargain with the promisor and must confer, or agree to confer, a benefit or must suffer, or agree to suffer, a burden. *Id.* The absence of consideration is clear when a gift is absolute. See, *Behrens Research Foundation v. Fairview Memorial Hospital*, Columbia Court of Appeal (2008). This is plain when the donor simply delivers the property and the donee simply accepts it. But where the facts suggest a bargained for exchange, where the donee confers or agrees to confer a benefit to the donor, or where the donee suffers, or agrees to suffer, a burden, the type of transfer is not as plain.

In the situation where a university agrees to name a campus building in a donor's honor or to use a building for a specified purpose, the university can be said to have "bargained" with the donor. This is because there was a negotiation for the terms for the naming of the building or its use for the specified purpose, and to confer, or agree to confer, a benefit or to suffer, or agree to suffer, a burden. Here, it is arguable that the Trustees of the University of Columbia have "bargained" with Edward Kemper. Meaney will argue that because the garden parcel was to bear the name "Kemper Scottish Garden" and to be used for educational purposes in perpetuity in exchange for the parcel of property, that the exchange was bargained for. Additionally Meaney will argue that the Trustees of the University of Columbia negotiated the terms for the naming of the garden and agreed to suffer a burden, that is using the garden for educational purposes and retaining it in perpetuity. While this is likely, such a bargain and benefit and burden do not preclude a gift. *Id.*

The presence or absence of consideration does not turn on the presence or absence of the term "consideration" in the instrument. *Id.* For example, the Supreme Court held that a deed by which a father transferred 10 acres of land valued at $500,000 to his adult daughter effected a gift, even though the deed recited that he transferred the property to her in consideration for $500. *Salmon v. Wilson*, Supreme Court (1971). Rather than look at the terms of the deed objectively, the Supreme Court reasoned that, in light of the circumstances, the $500 paid by the daughter to her father was "nominal and immaterial," and it was "clearly" the father's intent to donate the land to his daughter and not to sell it to her. Here, we can show that Edward Kemper was a wealthy businessman and a generous donor to the University. To that end, he agreed to transfer a garden to the Trustees to use for educational purposes. Like in Salmon, we can argue that the naming of the garden was nominal and immaterial because the true purpose of the transfer was for educational purposes, not for the name of the garden to live on. To further show that the naming of the garden was a nominal and immaterial consideration, we can show that recently the garden came to be known as Sarah's Scottish Garden. Additionally, if naming of the garden was material, then Edward Kemper, having retained the right to modify the terms of the Agreement as necessary and appropriate to its purpose, would have taken actions to ensure that the name was not changed from Kemper Scottish Garden to Sarah's Scottish Garden. Additionally, in line with this argument, if the naming of the garden was material consideration for the transfer, Meaney would have brought suit earlier to enjoin the use of the name to require that the old name be used.

Ultimately, what controls are the motives manifested by the parties. *Collins.* If the parties are motivated by a desire to buy and sell property through a commercial transaction, there is a transfer by contract. *Id.* But if the parties are motivated by a desire to deliver and accept the property through a non-commercial transaction, there is a gift. *Id.* Here, we can argue that the transaction was a manifestation of the parties desire to deliver the property through a non-commercial transaction. To support our position, we will show that Edward Kemper was a wealthy businessman and a generous donor. He had no intent in benefiting financially from the transaction and he didn't need to. If he had intended to benefit from the transaction, then he would have sold the property rather than donate it, like he had often donated in the past.

To counter our position that the parties were not motivated by a commercial transaction, Meaney will likely argue that the agreement impliedly recited that the transfer was subject to the Trustee's acceptance of the terms and restrictions. He will argue that by signing the agreement, the Trustees are burdened with the promise to maintain the garden with the name Kemper Scottish Garden" for educational purposes in perpetuity. The Court in Collins stated, that the burden of a promise, although hard to quantify, is adequate, and could support a transfer by contract.

But the fundamental question is whether there was in fact a transfer by contract rather than a gift. The primary element in resolving this issue is determining whether the parties are motivated by a desire to buy and sell the property through a commercial transaction. Here, they most likely are not. The relationship of Edward Kemper to the University of Columbia is similar to the relationship of Collins to Lincoln. It was only natural, based on the parties' relationship and past donations, that Edward Kemper and the Trustees would intend for the transaction to be noncommercial in nature. Under the totality of the circumstances, it is most likely that the transfer was by gift rather than by contract.

B. What Kind of Gift

A gift can be absolute, not absolute, or by charitable trust.

i. Gift Absolute versus Gift Not Absolute

It is well settled in Columbia that a donor is the master of his or her gift. The donor can give property by a gift that is absolute or that is not absolute. A gift that is absolute is without (1) restricting use or disposition of the property; (2) retaining power to modify the gift; or (3) reserving a right to sue to enforce a restriction or to undo the gift in case of a restriction's breach by causing the property to revert to the donor him-or herself or to a third person. *Behrens Research Foundation v. Fairview Memorial Hospital*, Columbia Court of Appeals (2008). When a gift is absolute, the donor has relinquished, and the donee has assumed, full dominion over the property—the ability to use or dispose of the property at any time, in any manner, for any purpose. Alternatively, a donor can make a gift that is not absolute. The donor can give property conditionally, (1) restricting use or disposition; (2) retaining power of modification; and/or (3) reserving a right of enforcement or reversion. *Id.* When a gift is not absolute, the donor has not relinquished, and the donee has not assumed, full dominion over the property; rather, both donor and donee share power over the property. *Id.*

The law presumes that a gift is absolute unless it clearly appears otherwise. *Id.* Additionally, the law presumes that donor has not restricted use or disposition, has not retained power of modification, and has not reserved a right of enforcement or reversion, unless it clearly appears otherwise. Here, in the Agreement between Edward Kemper and the Trustees of the University, Kemper explicitly retained the right to modify the terms of the Agreement as necessary and appropriate to its purpose. Unlike in Behrens, Edward Kemper reserved a right of enforcement or reversion, and retained power of modification. Under this analysis, it is likely that a court will find the gift to be not absolute.

ii. Charitable Trust

We can argue, though, that the gift was a non-private charitable trust. The primary type of non-private trust is the charitable trust. A charitable trust is created, as a matter of fact, whenever a settlor manifests an intent to give property, in trust for a charitable purpose and actually gives the property, in trust, for such purpose. Holt v. Jones, Columbia Supreme Court (1994). A charitable trust is also created, as a matter of law, whenever a settlor manifests an intent to give property to an educational, philanthropic, healthcare, or similar institution for an education, philanthropy, healthcare, or similar purpose. *Id.*

Here, it is plain from the agreement that the property was transferred to the Trustees of University of Columbia to use it for educational purposes. Therefore, we can argue that it is both a charitable trust as a matter of law and as a matter of fact. It is a charitable trust as a matter of fact because Edward Kemper intended to give it in trust for a charitable purpose and actually gave the property in trust for such purpose. Additionally, we can argue that it is a charitable trust as a matter of law because the property was given to an educational institution for education. We can show that it was "given" to the educational institution because the terms of the agreement state that it is "transferred" to the Trustees and that it was to be acquired for the purpose of transferring it to Trustees.

If the gift, although likely not absolute, is found to be a non-private charitable trust, in accord with the majority of jurisdictions, only the attorney general and some persons with a special interest will have standing to sue. Persons with a special interest include those who are trustees or beneficiaries, or would otherwise have an ownership interest in the property. Here, it is unlikely that Meaney will be found to be a trustee or beneficiary, or to otherwise have an ownership interest in the property, and will likely not have standing to sue.

III. Conclusion

Because we will likely be able to show that the gift, although not absolute, is a non-private charitable trust, the Court will likely dismiss Meaney's suit for lack of standing.

This has been a challenging and interesting project. Please let me know if I can provide any additional research on this issue.

Signed,

Applicant

Fogel & Davis, LLP

One Walton Avenue

Belleville, Columbia

Appendix E

Sample One-Hour Essay[1]

Question

On Monday, Resi-Clean (RC) advertised its house cleaning services by hanging paper handbills on doorknobs in residential areas. The handbills listed the services available, gave RC's address and phone number, and contained a coupon that stated, "This coupon is worth $20 off the price if you call within 24 hours and order a top-to-bottom house-cleaning for $500."

Maria, a homeowner, responding to the handbill, phoned RC on the same day, spoke to a manager, and said she wanted a top-to-bottom house cleaning as described in the handbill. Maria said, "I assume that means $480 because of your $20-off coupon, right?" The RC manager said, "That's right. We can be at your house on Friday." Maria said, "Great! Just give me a call before your crew comes so I can be sure to have someone let you in."

Within minutes after the phone conversation ended, the RC manager deposited in the mail a "Confirmation of Order" form to Maria. The form stated, "We hereby confirm your top-to-bottom house cleaning for $500. Our crew will arrive at your house before noon on Friday. You agree to give at least 48 hours advance notice of any cancellation. If you fail to give 48 hours notice, you agree to pay the full contract price of $500."

About an hour later, Maria sent RC an e-mail, which RC received, stating, "I just want to explain that it's important that your cleaning crew do a good job because my house is up for sale and I want it to look exceptionally good."

On Thursday evening before RC's cleaning crew was to show up, Maria accepted an offer for the sale of her house. The next morning, Friday, at 10:00 a.m., Maria sent RC another e-mail stating, "No need to send your crew. I sold my house last night, and I no longer need your services." By that time, however, RC's crew was en route to Maria's house.

At 10:30 a.m. on Friday, Maria received RC's Confirmation of Order form in the mail. At 11:00 a.m., RC's crew arrived, prepared to clean Maria's house. Maria explained that she no longer needed to have the house cleaned and sent the crew away.

RC's loss of profit was $100, but RC billed Maria for $500.

Maria refused to pay.

---

1 This question was tested on the CA bar exam in July 2006.

Has Maria breached a contract with RC, and, if so, how much, if anything, does Maria owe RC? Discuss.

Be sure to complete this practice essay before reading the debrief below. Ask yourself both how your reading and thinking about the issues in the fact pattern can change, for example, can it be more detailed or more organized. Then, read the sample answers and ask yourself how your writing can be improved.

Debrief: Thinking Through This Essay

What follows here is essentially "thinking aloud," tracking one way of processing the information while reading and preparing to write an answer to an essay exam.

As with all essays, read the interrogatory or call of the question first! *Interrogatory: Has Maria breached a contract with RC, and, if so, how much, if anything, does Maria owe RC? Discuss.* What do you know from this interrogatory? The subject: contracts. You also know that there are two parties (M & RC). And there are two questions, one about breach and a second about damages. So, your outline of your answer will track a standard contract analysis: formation, performance, breach, and damages/remedies.

The first issue to discuss is which law applies: the common law, not the UCC. This is a services contract. Do not let the $500 number fool you.

Read and outline the facts. The re-read the facts and make a chronology on your scratch paper. Once you make a chronology, you will see that formation is the biggest issue. But, for maximum points, you want to use every fact and analyze every main issue. (Do not waste time looking for subtle issues or bonus points. There is nothing hidden here.)

The next discussable issue is contract formation. (Think of potential issues: mutual assent which includes offer, acceptance, communication; consideration; and possible defenses.) Looking at the communications in order, you see a handbill, phone conversation, a mailed confirming memo, and an email. Each of these raise discussable issues so look at these each in turn. (Note that we will separately analyze each part of the phone conversation.)

- *RC advertised services generally and $20 off top-to-bottom ($500) if call within 24 hours.* Is this an offer? Ads are generally invitations to offer, unless specific enough as to price, quantity, and identity for the offeree. Is this specific enough? Uncertain. What can be analyzed? Had M just called to inquire about what services RC had to offer, then it would be mere inquiry. But here it might be specific enough. The timing of service was not specified, but the type of service and price were, as was the method for accepting—*by phone w/in 24 HOURS.* Is that enough to identify an offeree—anyone who calls within 24 hours asking for this particular service? Maybe. But, as we will see in our analysis, and as we will write in our answer, if for some reason this ad does not suffice, then later communications were specific enough. . .

Next, *M responded by phone, saying she wanted service described "$480, right?"* Is this acceptance? She said she wanted what was described in the ad, and confirmed the price, so this might be deemed an acceptance. (She has capacity, it was unequivocal; thus, so far at least, she will be deemed to be accepting by return promise.) When she says she wants the service offered in the coupon, that is a mirror imagine of RC's offer (if it's an offer). Her clarification here is not a rejection and counter offer, but likely just a clarification.

Next, is there an offer? The facts state M phoned RC and "said she wanted a top-to-bottom house cleaning as described in the handbill. . ." If RC's ad is not an offer, then this is. This is now language that is creating in RC (a specific offeree) the ability to accept a contract to provide M a specific service for a particular price.

- In the same phone call, RC replied, "Right. Can be at house Friday." Again, this does not change the deal. It does specify the timing of performance, so it could be deemed a rejection and counteroffer. On the very odd chance both the ad and M's first words were not a valid offer, this certainly is—this is now language by RC creating in M (a specific offeree) a specific service on a particular day for a particular price.

Note that if the valid offer were found in M's previous statement saying she wanted the service, then this language on the part of RC would be a valid acceptance.

- Next issue. In the same call, M said, "Great. Just give me a call before crew so I can have someone let you in" Either this is M's re-confirming and clarifying RC's original offer, from the handbill ad that M already accepted. Or, this is now an acceptance of RC's counter offer (to do the requested cleaning on Friday). "Great" clearly indicates a willingness to be bound.
- Next issue. Is her "just give me a call first" a condition? Can it be read as, "Just give a call first" as a condition. Or, can it be read as "only if you call me first?" Or is this simply specifying how the agreed-upon performance will be facilitated. Likely the latter. It is likely not specific enough language to be deemed a condition. To be deemed a condition it would need to have language such as "only if" or "so long as." The "just give a call" sounds more like logistics. (Courts are not quick to interpret a provision as a condition because the failure to fulfill that condition will discharge the duty to perform entirely. That does not seem like what is intended here.)
- Next, consideration? Bargained for exchange. Here, this is satisfied: top-to-bottom cleaning in exchange for $480 & coupon. Remember as part of a mental checklist, while analyzing the fact pattern, ask yourself, if there is no consideration or possibly invalid consideration, was there a substitute for instance in promissory estoppel. Or, if no consideration but a benefit was conferred, is there an unjust enrichment argument?

- Next issue is defenses? There are no problems with capacity, public policy, or fraud. But, this contract is oral. The contract is not in writing, so it is appropriate to discuss the statute of frauds (SOF). Here, given the facts, you can quickly show why SOF is not an applicable defense. (This is a sale of services, not goods, so the dollar amount does not matter. Don't be fooled by the $500. It is not real property. It is certainly capable of being performance with a year—it's mean to be performed this coming Friday. No SOF problem.)

Next, let's look at performance. (Consider conditions, discharge, and breach.) Also, consider any post-formation issues, such as where a party is seeking to change the terms (a modification) or introduce evidence to explain a disputed term of the contract (raising a possible parol evidence discussion). Here, before we get to conditions, discharge and breach, we have two attempted modifications.

The first attempted modification: After the call, RC mailed Confirmation order, with new terms—$500 and 48 cancellation notice. This appears to be a unilateral attempt to modify. Common law requires additional consideration to modify so this is invalid.

Another possible issue is with respect to RC's Confirmation Order (discussed briefly in one of the released bar answers). This is an attempt to insert a liquidated damages clause. But this did not become part of K because the modification was not valid and not accepted by M. But even if it had been accepted by M, had RC given new consideration, etc., this would have been an invalid liquidated damages clause, unenforceable for a couple of reasons: 1) It's a penalty—the full price of the K for a cancellation? And, 2) damages for breach in this case are very clear; these damages are not at all uncertain or difficult to prove.

As to the second attempted modification, one hour later, M emailed to say house is for sale. They want cleaning that is exceptionally good. Again, so what if she wants great cleaning, a fantastic cleaning? The contract has already been formed. If this is another attempt to add a new term, a condition of satisfaction of sorts, it's invalid for lack of consideration. They agreed upon the regular top-to-bottom service, as described in the handbill.

M may try to use this communication of hers in a discharge argument, to show that RC knew she intended to sell the house at the time of formation. She will say that she communicated this "fairly contemporaneously," an hour later by email. But an hour later is not "at the time of formation" and her argument for frustration of purpose will still fail. (See below.)

Thursday: M accepted offer to sell house

Friday: 10am, M emailed RC saying "Sold house. No longer need services." The RC crew was already en route to M's.

Next issue? Anticipatory repudiation. The RC crew was already on way to M's house, so arguably performance had started. But, if the contract is still executory, then M is clearly by words indicating her unwillingness to perform. This would excuse RC's duty to clean M's house and allow them to sue for breach. But this is not a difference that is meaningful here because we are talking less than an hour's difference. When she emailed, they were already on route and arrived an hour after her email. So, whether they are entitled to sue at 10am or at 11am is not significant.

Note: <u>Timing</u> is important here because RC would have a <u>duty to mitigate</u>. There is no time here to arrange to clean another house; they are already en route. . . .

Next, M will try to argue discharge of duty. She will try impossibility, impracticability, and/or frustration of purpose. Here impossibility fails. It's not objectively impossible to clean the house. Impracticability also fails—It's not extremely risky or difficult to clean the house. Next frustration of purpose. While it is M's best argument, it still fails. M will argue that she only wanted the cleaning in order to sell her house. This will likely fail for two reasons: the first, that the purpose was not known at the time of formation. She told RC that she was selling her home one hour later in an email. And, second, so what that she accepted the sale offer. They probably still need to do a home inspection and go through escrow. And, it's a benefit to sell a clean house. Remember, frustration of purpose requires that the main contractual purpose be totally frustrated (the sole purpose of entering into this contract thwarted).

Next, excuse of a condition. M might also argue that her duty was discharged because RC did not call before coming. But, as noted above, that will likely not be deemed a condition.

Next, on Friday at 11am, the RC crew arrived to clean, and M sent them away. This is a present and material breach that is not excused; it is wrongful prevention.

Next, we think through and discuss remedies. The facts tell us that RC lost profit of $100. RC sued M for $500. What are damages? Had the contract been performed, RC would have cleaned a house and they would have earned $480. The facts state that "RC's loss of profit was $100." They did not perform so they would not get the full value of the contract, but only lost profit. (Giving them $500 or even $480 would unjustly enrich them since had they performed they would have had to spend money on the crew, supplies, etc. [A possible bonus issue is that of gas money to drive over to M'S house as "costs spent to date."]

Next, think about a remedies mental checklists: liquidated damages we discussed, incidental—no not UCC, consequential—no (see below); restitution—no she didn't give any deposit there is nothing to return; equitable remedies—no, not applicable here. (See the interrogatory.) No incidentals—only applicable in UCC contracts. And, presumably, "lost profits" included crew wages and supplies. There are also no consequential damages. There is nothing foreseeable known to both parties that would result from breach.

Specific performance is not applicable to the question which asked, "How much, if anything, does Maria owe RC?" (Be certain to answer the questions asked on the bar exam.) So the final discussable issue is mitigation, though you would likely conclude there is not mitigation opportunity here because of timing.

End of possible "thinking through" of this exam.
Now take a look at one sample answer below.

Sample Answer[2]

Applicable Law

The common law applies to all sales of service contracts and the UCC applies to sale of goods. Here, the contract is for cleaning services (a service) so that it clearly falls within the ambit of the common law. As such, none of the rules under the UCC will be applicable.

Valid Contract Formed

Before addressing whether Maria breached her contract with Resi-Clean ("RC"), it must first be determined whether she had a valid contract to begin with. A valid contract requires: (1) an offer; (2) an acceptance of the aforementioned offer; (3) consideration from each party; and (4) no defenses to formation. Each will be discussed below.

Offer

For an offer to be valid there must be an intent to be bound, communicated to the offeree, with sufficient and definite material terms. Here, there are several points at which the parties may argue an offer was made. Whether or not a valid offer is made (i.e. whether above factors are met) is determined by looking at whether a reasonable person receiving the communication would feel that their acceptance of the offer would create a binding obligation.

First, it may be argued that the handbills placed on the doorknobs of the houses created an offer from RC to all of the houses. However, this argument is likely to fail. An advertisement that merely states the cost of services, a phone number, and possible coupons would not be construed by a reasonable person to evidence the intent of advertising to be bound to a contract upon acceptance.

Thus, this would not likely be construed as a valid offer. However, a court may accept an argument by Maria that the coupon attached that specified that the party would get $20 off if they called within 24 hours and ordered a top-to-bottom cleaning was a valid offer because it was specific with the terms of how it could be accepted, when it had to be accepted by, and a reasonable person would feel that the party giving the coupon would be bound by the offer. The effect of the binding effect of the coupon will be discussed further with respec[t] to the damages that Maria receives below.

A second possibility for the offer could be the phone call that Maria made to RC to order to the top-to-bottom cleaning service. She requested that they come and clean her house, as described on the handbill, and specified the $480 price ($500 less the $20 coupon). This would be construed by a reasonable person in RC's shoes to be [an] offer than [sic] they could accept

[2] This is one answer to the July 2006 CA bar exam question, reproduced here as published on the examiners' website.

to form a binding contract so that it likely would be deemed to be an offer. Moreover, even if this offer was deemed rejected by RC's manager indicating that "they would be there Friday" because this was an additional term, that statement would be an [sic] counteroffer to Maria on the same terms but including the Friday cleaning provision.

If, for some reason, the court determines that the above was not an offer, then the confirmation order may also be deemed to be an offer to Maria. Thus, Maria would be free to accept that order at any point after receiving it. This is very unlikely to be the case, however, as Maria's phone call would almost certainly be construed to be the offer in this case.

Acceptance

A valid acceptance requires that a party who is able to accept the contract unequivocally accepts the offer and communicates that acceptance to the offeror. Of course, if and when a valid acceptance occurred would depend on when the offer occurred. Because the advertisement described above was not an offer (except to the extent of the coupon which was incorporated into Maria's offer) it will not be discussed here with respect to acceptance.

Assuming that Maria's phone call is deemed to be the offer then RC likely accepted the offer when its manager stated "[t]hat's right. We can be at your house on Friday." While Maria may argue that the statement "we can be at your house on Friday" was an additional term that did not create a valid contract but, rather, was a rejection and counteroffer, this argument would have little effect given that Maria promptly said "Great[,]" thereby accepting the counteroffer with the additional Friday term. Maria may also argue that by telling them to call her before they come [sic] so that someone is there to let them in she did not unequivocally accept their offer. However, this statement was not intended to modify the terms of the contract but, rather, just told [sic] them that they should call in advance to ensure someone would be home. Whether or not this amounted to a condition precedent will be discussed below. Thus, Maria's offer was accepted by RC (or Maria accepted RC's counteroffer on the same terms with the Friday provision) upon their phone call and a binding contract was completed at the time.

If the phone call was not deemed to be a valid offer so that the offer was the confirmatory memo, then Maria did not accept it and there would be no valid contract. Maria only received the memo on Friday morning and from that point on tried to send RC away. Thus, there would be no acceptance. However, this argument would be unlikely given that they almost certainly formed a valid contract during the phone call as described above.

Consideration

Here, Maria agreed to pay RC $480 and they agreed to clean her house from top-to-bottom. This exchange of promises provides the required bargained[-] for exchange and legal detriment to each party for there to be valid consideration.

Thus, this element is met.

Defenses

Statute of Frauds

The Statue of Frauds does not apply to services contracts that will be completed in less than one year. Here, the contract was to be completed in its entirety by Friday so that the statute of frauds was inapplicable.

As no other defenses are applicable, a valid contract was likely formed at the time of the phone conversation between Maria and the manager of RC.

Terms of the Contract Formed

Once it is determined that a valid contract was formed between the parties, the next step is determin[in]g the terms of that contract. In this case, Maria called RC and stated that she wanted a "top-to-bottom" house cleaning "as described in the handbill." Moreover, she indicated (and the manager of RC agreed) that the price would be $480 once the coupon from the handbill was taken into consideration. The contract likely also contains the provision that RC will complete the work on Friday as that was agreed upon by the parties during the course of the phone conversation. Thus, the contract will certainly be for a top-to-bottom house cleaning at Maria's house on Friday for $480.

A question exists as to whether Maria's statement that they had to call her before their crew comes in order to be sure that someone was there to let them in. It is unlikely that this would become part of the contract given that the parties had already agreed on the contract before Maria made that statement. Moreover, the statement does not affect the performance of the obligation but was merely intended to ensure that the contract would move forward with no hassles. Thus, this is not likely to be considered part of the contract.

The provision in the "Confirmation of Order" memo sent by RC also does not likely become part of the contract. The contract was completed over the telephone and RC may not unilaterally make modifications to that contract (i.e. the 48 hour notice provision) without additional consideration provided by the other party. Here, RC gave no additional consideration to Maria for requiring the 48 hour notice provision). This does not mean, however, that Maria was free to cancel the contract at will[;] because the contract became enforceable over the phone, she is bound by the contract unless she has some excuse or defense to its enforcement or unless she is for some reason relieved of her duties under the contract.

Finally, for the same reasons as the 48-hour provision above, Maria's subsequent e-mail regarding the "exceptionally good job" would not become part of the contract. There was no additional consideration for the this [sic] provision and to require RC to do an "exceptionally good job" would deprive them of the benefit of the bargain their [sic] received when they negotiated for the $480 price. Thus, this would not become part of the bargain and RC would be required to do a reasonable job in good faith.

Thus, the contract was for a full house cleaning on Friday for $480 and it did not include the 48-hour notification provision or the "exception[al] job" provision.

Did Maria Breach or Does She Have Any Excuses/Defenses For Her Breach?

Because a valid and enforceable contract existed, Maria is liable to RC if she breached the contracted [sic] as [she] is not excused from performance.

Maria's Breach

Under the terms of the contract, Maria was required to pay RC $480 and allow them into her house in order to complete the cleaning to which she agreed. Here, rather than allowing RC to come and clean her house, she sent them an e-mail at 10 a.m. on the morning of performance indicating that she was repudiating the contract and, when they showed up to perform, she turned their workers away. Thus, Maria anticipatorily repudiated the contract which would allow RC to: (1) treat it as an offer to rescind the contract and rescind; (2) treat the contract as materially breached and sue for damages immediately; (3) suspend their performance and sue once the contract becomes due; or (4) do nothing and encourage performance.

Here, Maria breached the contract the morning of performance so that suspending their performance or encouraging Maria's performance would be infeasible. Moreover, RC would not want to rescind the contract because that is exactly what Maria wanted to do and it would cost them $100 in lost profits. Thus, RC would treat the contract as materially breached and Maria would be liable for damages unless she had a valid excuse for her breach.

Possible Defense/Excuses of Performance

Condition Precedent Not Met

Maria may argue that she had a valid excuse for not performing because in the course of their telephone call she indicated that the crew should call her before they come so that someone may be there. However, this argument would fail for a few reasons. First, as I indicated above, the provision that they call on Friday before they come was not likely part of the contract because they had already agreed on the terms of the agreement at that point and Maria's statement was only intended to make sure she could make arrangement to let them into her house. Second, the purpose of the covenant was not breached because they showed up to clean her house when she was there (because she turned them away). Third, she repudiated the contract before they could make the phone call by sending them her repudiating e-mail that morning so that they could treat the contract as breached immediately without adhering to the condition precedent. Thus, this argument would fail to excuse Maria's material breach.

House sold (Impossibility, Impracticability, Frustration of Purpose)

Maria may also a[r]gue that the fact that she no longer owned the house at the time the contract came due excused her performance by way of: (1) impossibility; (2) impracticability; or (3) frustration of purpose. As will be shown below, all of these arguments would fail.

Impossibility—For performance to be excused by way of impossibility an unforeseeable and supervening event must render performance impossible for any person to perform. Here, Maria's sale of her house was not unforeseeable because she knew that [she] was trying to sell her house and it was not a supervening outside factor because it was entirely within Maria's control. Moreover, it was still possible for RC to complete performance—it just would not be as valuable to Maria now that she no longer owned the home that she contracted with them to clean. Thus, this argument would fail.

Impracticability—For performance to be excused by way of impracticability an unforeseeable and supervening event must render performance by one party inordinately difficult so as to create an injustice if the contract was enforced. Here, as noted immediately above, Maria controlled the event and it was foreseeable so this did not excuse her performance. Morever, paying $480 to have a house that you have just sold cleaned does not seem unduly difficult on Maria. Thus, this defense would fail as well.

Frustration of Purpose—For performance to be excused by way of frustration of purpose an unforeseeable and supervening event must intervene to render the entire purpose of the contract—known by both parties to the contract at the time the contract was formed—a nullity. Like the two arguments above, this would fail because the supervening event was in Maria's control and was entirely foreseeable so that Maria assumed the risk that her house would be sold by Friday. Moreover, at the time the contract was formed RC had no idea that she was selling her house so that the purpose was to fix the house up for its sale. Thus, the fact that this purpose was frustrated would not excuse Maria's performance because RC had no idea of that purpose at the time the the [sic] contract was formed.

Potential Damages that Maria Owes RC For Her Breach

In a contracts case where one party materially breaches the other party is entitled to damages to compensate them for their expectancy under the contract. They may also receive consequential and incidental damages as appropriate. However punitive damages are typically unavailable in contract actions.

Expectancy Damages

For expectancy damages to be provided to a party they must be causal, foreseeable, certain, and unavoidable. In this case, providing RC with the full $500 for Maria's breach as is claimed in their bill to Maria would unjustly enrich them given that they only lost $100 in profit as a result of her breach. Their expectancy under the contract was to make $100 in profit so they should be entitled to the $100 from Maria. Note, however, that the "loss of profit" provided in the facts does not indicate whether this includes the $20 coupon or not[;] it it[sic] does not then [sic] they should only get $80 because their expectancy was only $80 profit but if it does then they should get the full $100. This $100 is causal because they lost the money as a result of her breach, certain because they clean places like this all the time and can likely show what they typically make, and foreseeable because Maria knew that by breaching they would not be able to find another customer right away. So long as RC made reasonable efforts to find another house to clean to make up for the lost profits so as to mitigate their damages the damages would also be unavoidable. Thus, RC would be able to recover their $100 (or $80) of expectancy damages.

Consequential Damages

Consequential damages are those damages that are causal, foreseeable, certain, and unavoidable but that do not stem directly from the breach. There is no evidence of such damages in this question.

Incidental Damages

In the course of finding a new customer to mitigate their damages if RC was forced to expend resources, they would be entitled to those reasonable costs as incidental damages. There is no evidence of such damages here.

Specific Performance

Here, because the $100 (or $80) lost profit damages are adequate to compensate RC for its losses, specific performance (i.e. by forcing Maria to allow them to complete the contract) would be unavailable.

Thus, RC would be entitled to $100 (or $80 if the $100 lost profit does not take the coupon into account because the coupon was enforceable as described above) for their lost profits as a result of the contract so long as they took adequate reasonable steps to mitigate their losses.

INDEX

References are to Pages